Maria Marcia Fanny Trench

The Life Of Saint Teresa

Maria Marcia Fanny Trench

The Life Of Saint Teresa

ISBN/EAN: 9783741113673

Manufactured in Europe, USA, Canada, Australia, Japa

Cover: Foto ©Lupo / pixelio.de

Manufactured and distributed by brebook publishing software (www.brebook.com)

Maria Marcia Fanny Trench

The Life Of Saint Teresa

THE LIFE

OF

SAINT TERESA

BY THE AUTHOR OF
'DEVOTIONS BEFORE AND AFTER
HOLY COMMUNION'

> '*Yet she's to me but such a light*
> *As are the stars to those that know*
> *We can at most but guess their heights,*
> *And hope they help us here below*'

London
MACMILLAN AND CO.
1875

PREFACE.

THE most complete and full information concerning St. Teresa is to be found in the volume of the Bollandist series which contains her 'Acta,' and the greater part of the materials for the following Life have been gathered from its pages. Amongst other books which have been consulted are Helyot's 'Histoire des Ordres Monastiques;' the 'Compendium Vitæ B. V. Teresiæ a Jesu,' written, in 1608, by Johannes a Jesu Maria, a Carmelite; and thirteen 'Orationes in Natali S. Teresiæ,' by the same author, delivered by him before the Cardinals at S. Maria della Scala, between 1602 and 1614, the year of her beatification by Paul V. They are interesting as showing the estimation in which she was held by one who must have been her contemporary, and in the years immediately after her death.

Two later notices of St. Teresa which have been used must be mentioned: 'Les Mystiques Espagnols,'[1] by Paul Rousselot; and 'Ein Beitrag zur

[1] Paris, 1867.

Geschichte der mönchischen Contrareformation in Spanien im 16ten Jahrhundert,'[1] by Professor Zöckler: the latter is of course written from a Lutheran point of view, but is the more interesting on that account, since it is full of sympathy and admiration for St. Teresa and her school.

Probably no saint has ever left so full a record of both inner and outward life as St. Teresa has given us in her Autobiography and 'Book of Foundations.' Almost the whole of them are contained in the 'Acta Sanctorum,' translated into Latin, and also the whole of her 'Life,' by Francisco Ribera, S. J., her friend and confessor. F. Vandermoere, her Bollandist biographer, says he has carefully compared the latter (a translation made in 1620) with the first edition of the original, published at Salamanca in 1590, 'La Vida de la Madre Teresa de Jesus,' and that it had been not without cause preferred by his predecessor Bueo (the fruit of whose labours in collecting materials he had reaped) to the Lives of the saint by Yepez, Johannes a Jesu Maria, and others. 'He wrote before the rest, and was a man of excellent abilities, acute judgment, and tenacious memory.'[2] He has left Commentaries on St. John's Gospel, the Epistle to the Hebrews, the Apocalypse, and the Minor Prophets, and was a 'not

---

[1] In *Zeitschrift für Lutherische Theologie.*
[2] *Acta Sanct. De S. Teresia Virgine,* § i. 4.

less diligent than pious and learned writer, eminent for sanctity, assisting and consecrating study by prayer, and in any special difficulty seeking light from God with fasting and self-denial.' He was, besides, remarkable for accuracy and truthful candour in all that he wrote; and on account of these qualities, as well as his intimacy with St. Teresa, F. Vandermoere gives him the first place amongst authorities concerning her. The second he gives to Diego Yepez, Bishop of Tarrazona, in Aragon, who in the dedication to Paul V., prefixed to his Life of the saint, says that he wrote of such things as he had seen and known himself.[1] 'For more than fourteen years,' he adds, 'I was her confessor; and she entrusted to me the direction of her soul, both within and without the sacred tribunal. The spiritual treasures which God had bestowed on her soul she disclosed to me, hoping that I also might profit by them.' He pronounced a panegyric on St. Teresa in 1585, three years after her death, in the convent of Discalced Carmelites at Madrid, newly erected by Philip II., to whom he was confessor, and wrote a long letter concerning her to Luis de Leon, who had undertaken to be her biographer. Yepez died in 1613, and was buried, as he had wished,

---

[1] The edition quoted in the *Acta Sanctorum* is *Vida, Virtudes, y Milagros de la B. Virgen Teresa de Jesus.* Madrid 1776, 2 vols. in 4to.

in the convent of Discalced nuns which he had founded in his own episcopal city.

The third great authority mentioned by Vandermoere is the Venerable F. Joannes a Jesu Maria, General of the Discalced Carmelites, who wrote 'an excellent Compendium of the Life of St. Teresa, and presented it to Paul V. in 1609, with the object of promoting her beatification.' The Pope read the whole of it. The author is said by Vandermoere to have been well acquainted with all of which he wrote, and so learned that Cardinal Bellarmine took much pleasure in his works; Bossuet also calls him 'a great theologian and great mystic;' and St. Francis de Sales speaks of him with praise in the preface to his treatise of the 'Love of God.' Jerome Gratian, the closest friend of Teresa's later years, in a letter to Cardinal Bentivoglio, says that he has read almost the whole of the Compendium, and testifies to its 'most pure truth and fidelity.'

Other authorities mentioned by Vandermoere, besides the saint's own works (including her letters[1]), are the Acts of her canonization; the 'Reforma de los Descalzos de Nuestra Señora del Carmen,' written by Fr. Francisco de S. Maria, a kinsman of Teresa; and a few other lesser notices, chiefly by Discalced Carmelites. He also notices Padre Federigo di S. An-

---

[1] Published in four 4to vols., with notes by Bishop Palafox.

tonio's 'Life of St. Teresa,'[1] in Italian, compiled from the narratives of Ribera and Yepez; and two French Lives of the saint by Villefore[2] and by Boucher;[3] besides Eméry's 'L'Esprit de Ste Thérèse.'[4]

Her Life is by far the longest in the sixty Bollandist volumes published from 1643 to 1867,[5] occupy-

[1] Four vols. in 8vo. Rome, 1837.
[2] Two vols. in 12mo. Paris, 1756.
[3] Two vols. in 12mo. Paris, 1810 and 1828.
[4] London, 1799. In 8vo.
[5] 'The most remarkable book which has ever been produced, whether it be regarded as to its subject-matter, the period of time which has been required for its production, or the indefatigable industry, great learning, and untiring research of the authors. In giving the acts and achievements of saints, it unfolds the history of Europe, during the middle ages, on a more extensive and minuter scale than is done in any other production, including at the same time much of Eastern history, and containing innumerable important documents and interesting historical dissertations. . . . Its production has already occupied above 200 years, and it is still going on to its completion. Two interruptions have occurred during that period: first, when the Jesuits were suppressed in 1773, after which the work was resumed in 1779; and the second, when the French troops entered Belgium, in 1794. It was again resumed in 1837, and a volume published in 1845. As one of the great efforts of the Jesuits, that body has always been able to furnish the men most qualified to continue the gigantic work as one after another has deceased. The honour of commencing the undertaking is due to F. Heribert Rossweide, of Utrecht, born 1569. He made great collections towards it, but died in 1629, before any part was published. He was succeeded in his labours by John Bollandus (born 1596, died 1665), from whose name the authors who have been engaged in the work are now called Bollandists. Having found his labours accumulate, he associated others with him, one of whom, Daniel Papebroch, continued his labours for fifty years, and brought into contribution an ample private fortune.'—*Cyclopædia Bibliographica*, by James Darling, A.-H. p. 13.

ing, as it does, the whole of the seventh October volume, a folio of 790 pages, with the exception of the first 108 pages; while all the preceding saints for the year, up to October 15, her feast-day, are contained in fifty-three volumes; the number of saints, and therefore of separate biographies for each day, being sometimes very large.[1] While St. Teresa's 'Acta' occupy 682 pages in this great work, only 258 are given to St. Augustine, although the nine first books of his 'Confessions' are appended to his Life; 290 to St. Jerome, and 267 to St. Bernard. This may partly be accounted for by the fact that the folio containing her life was the first published (in 1845), after the fifty-one years' interruption caused by the French Revolution; so that her biographers possessed all the assistance which they might derive from modern research: still this cannot be the chief cause of the immense proportion of room given to her in the series, since the six other folios, published from 1845 to 1867, ending with October 29, contain the lives of four hundred and seventy-five saints.

'One thing I regret,' F. Vandermoere writes, 'that in this work it is not permitted to me to quote Teresa in the original language in which she wrote; for, in-

---

[1] For January 1, there are forty-three lives of saints, besides an article on the Circumcision; and yet all the saints for the first fifteen days of January are contained in a volume of 1,122 pages, the index of names alone occupying sixteen folio pages.

deed, our saint wrote with so much elegance, that she has attained to the true perfection of her language.' A similar regret must be felt by all unacquainted with Spanish, 'the stateliest of the daughters of the Latin,'[1] and who can, therefore, only know her works through the veil of English, although the admirable translations made lately by Mr. David Lewis of her 'Vida' and 'Fondaciones'[2] seem to have done all that it is possible to accomplish for English readers. Only one other translation of her 'Life' into English has been made (by Canon Dalton) since that by Abraham Woodhead, which appeared in 1671; and although the former was published so lately as 1851, it is said by Mr. Lewis to be almost as scarce as its predecessors.[3] A copy which the writer was kindly allowed to use has been examined, but there could be no doubt of the great superiority of Mr. Lewis' work, to which are given all the references for quotations from the 'Life' and 'Foundations' in the following pages. Other references have been given, with some care: if any words, once heard, and like music taking possession of the mind, and becoming its own, have unconsciously or almost involuntarily been used, this must be forgiven.

The Frontispiece (engraved by Mr. Jeens) is from

[1] See 'Essay on Calderon,' by Archbishop of Dublin, p. 52.
[2] Burns, Oates & Co., 1870 and 1871.
[3] Two translations had been published at Antwerp, in 1611 and 1642, both by English Jesuits, but copies of either are very scarce.

an engraving in the 'Acta Sanctorum,' of Boada's copy, made for that work, of the original portrait of St. Teresa, painted, at Gratian's desire, by Fra Juan de la Miseria, and now preserved at Avila: her signature is from the fac-simile of the document mentioned at p. 247, which faces p. 617 in the folio. Fra Juan was but a poor artist; Boada's copy is probably a far better drawing than the original. Teresa is said to have exclaimed, on seeing the latter, 'So after all, father, you have made me blear-eyed and ugly.' She lived too late to be glorified by art: there was no one to create such a portrait of her as Raphael has left to us of Pope Julius II., and Bernini's statue is but an example of the extreme injustice which has been done to her by all who have attempted to represent her. 'Qu'on ne la décore pas du bonnet de docteur, comme en certains de ses portraits,' M. Rousselot writes, 'je ne demande pas mieux, mais qu'on lui fasse plus d'honneur que ne lui en a fait le Bernin, qu'on ne la rapetisse pas à des proportions inintelligentes. La Sainte Thérèse de l'histoire, celle que ses contemporains ont vue à l'œuvre, celle qui ressort de ses propres écrits, cette haute intelligence, ce grand cœur, cette femme héroïque supportant le froid, la pauvreté, la fatigue, la maladie, travaillant de ses mains, je ne la reconnais pas dans le marbre plus profane que chrétien de l'église della Vittoria. Cette patricienne romaine du 17ᵉ siècle, à la pose affaissée, aux traits alanguis . . . palpitant, presque évanouie, sous la voluptueuse angoisse de l'extase, est peut-être une élève de Molinos ; elle n'est pas la personification du mysticisme héroïque de l'Espagne.'

So many descriptions, however, of her personal appearance exist, written by contemporaries, that we can form a nearer notion of her as she really was than we can of many saints who have been idealised by art. 'She was of middle stature, elegant and of fair proportions, plump and perfectly well-formed, possessing a kind of beauty which advancing age did not, as it is wont, impair ; her complexion was bright, the white and red distinct and clear ; her hair was black and curly, the forehead broad and smooth ; the nose small, the mouth slightly open, with white and even teeth, short upper lip, the under lip rather full. Her eyes, "beautiful with gazing upon God," were very dark and bright, sparkling and shining when she spoke or smiled. Her hands were small, the fingers slight and tapering ; her whole appearance forming a striking combination of dignity and beauty.'[1]

Yepez speaks also of 'a certain loveliest glow which, when she was pouring out prayers to God,

---

[1] The above description is taken from those given by Yepez and Johannes a Jesu Maria. *Acta Sanct.* § liii. 1027. *Orat. in Nat. S. Teresiæ*, v. p. 499.

rendered her countenance sweeter and more splendid,' and of the light which, in discourse with others, seemed at times to shine over her face, causing her whole aspect to be so grateful and pleasant to others as to beget love alike and reverence in those who beheld her. She seems to have possessed in a very remarkable degree 'that nameless grace which hangs about some, and opens their way before them as by a royal letter;' also her humility and gracious deference to others must have greatly added to the influence she quickly gained over the hearts of men. 'I will put this as the finishing stroke of prudence,' Johannes writes ... 'namely, that Teresa, however much knowledge she might have, never relied much on herself, but with incredible anxiety sought out men most celebrated both for learning and for sanctity, by whom a trial might be made concerning her divine affections; of whom I would promptly recount a most choice array, were not my discourse hastening to an end.... In which matter certainly this is quite wonderful, that she softened most easily the minds of most eminent men when opposed to her, and persuaded them, as it were with the touch of a magnet, to change their opinion and disposition.'[1]

She lived at a time of bitterest national antipathy, both political and religious, between England and

[1] *Orat. in Nat. S. Teresiæ*, vii. p. 512.

Spain: this may partly account for the fact that she is less generally known and cared for amongst us than many others far less eminent in genius as well as sanctity. Perhaps also some of the virtues which shone brightest in her are not those for which we have been as a nation distinguished. *Laborare est orare* is a favourite saying with Englishmen; perhaps we forget that the reverse is also true, and that especial regard is due to those who, knit together with us in one communion and fellowship have set a shining example of graces in which we may be deficient.

Nor should her influence, directly and indirectly, on two of our great poets be forgotten in England, or the debt which at least in part we owe to her for the lovely poem of 'Christabel.' 'Crashaw seems in his poems,' S. T. Coleridge writes, ' to have given the first ebullience of his imagination, unshapen into form, or much of, what we now term, sweetness. In the poem "Hope," by way of question and answer, his superiority to Cowley is self-evident; in that " On the Name of Jesus" especially so: but his lines on St. Teresa are the finest. Where he does combine richness of thought and diction nothing can excel, as in the lines you so much admire :—

> ' " Since 'tis not to be had at home,
> She'l travail to a martyrdom.
> No home for hers confesses she,
> But where she may a martyr be.

She'l to the Moores ; and trade with them
For this unvalued diadem :
She'l offer them her dearest breath,
With Christ's name in't, in change for death :
She'l bargain with them ; and will give
Them God ; teach them how to live
In Him : or, if they this deny,
For Him she'l teach them how to dy :
So shall she leave amongst them sown
Her Lord's blood ; or at least her own.
Farewell, then, all the World ! adieu !
Teresa is no more for you.
Farewell, all pleasures, sports, and joys
(Never till now esteemèd toyes) :
Farewell, whatever dear may be,
Mother's arms, or father's knee :
Farewell, house, and farewell, home—
She's for the Moores, and martyrdom."[1]

'These verses were ever present to my mind whilst writing the second part of " Christabel ;" if indeed, by some subtle process of mind, they did not suggest the first thought of the whole poem.'[2]

[1] From *A Hymn to the Name and Honor of the Admirable Sainte Teresa*, 1646, by Richard Crashawe.

[2] *Letters, Conversation, and Recollections of S. T. Coleridge*, vol. i. pp. 194-196. Brought up in Puritanism, Crashawe's natural tastes and his studies at Cambridge alike led him in another direction. He was Fellow at Peterhouse when the 'Ejection' of 1644 came; he 'found no resting-place in England,' seeing her Church, as he thought, finally shattered, and so passed over to the Roman Communion, one chief influence being his study of St. Teresa's writings. He went to Italy, became secretary to Cardinal Palotta, but got into trouble by his 'plain speech' concerning immorality among priests at Rome, and retired to Loretto, where his friend the Cardinal procured him a shelter, and where he died in 1654. See Grosart's *Complete Works of Richard Crashawe*.

Crashawe, on reading St. Teresa's works, composed and took for his motto—

> 'Live, Jesus, live, and let it be
> My life to die for love of Thee.'

He wrote afterwards 'An Apologie for the foregoing Hymn, as having been writt when the Author was yet among the Protestants,' in which he mentions the reading of her books as having inspired it :—

> 'Oh pardon, if I dare to say
> Thine own dear books are guilty.'

His 'Apologie' ends with these noble lines :—

> 'O thou undaunted daughter of desires !
> By all thy dower of lights and fires ;
> By all the eagle in thee, all the dove ;
> By all thy lives and deaths of love ;
> By thy large draughts of intellectual day,
> And by thy thirsts of love more large than they ;
> By all thy brimfill'd bowls of fierce desire ;
> By thy last morning's draught of liquid fire ;
> By the full kingdom of that final kiss,
> That seiz'd thy parting soul, and sealed thee His ;
> By all the Heav'n thou hast in Him
> (Fair sister of the Seraphim !) ;
> By all of Him we have in thee—
> Leave nothing of myself in me.
> Let me so read thy life, that I
> Unto all life of mine may die.'

December 31, 1874.

CONTENTS.

CHAPTER I.

Autobiography of St. Teresa—Her Birth and Lineage—Her Childhood—Books of Chivalry—Childish Faults—Education in the Augustinian Convent 1

CHAPTER II.

Disinclination of Teresa to become a Nun—Her Illness—She visits her Uncle—Mental Conflict—Determines to take the Veil—Is received at the Convent of the Incarnation—Makes her Profession—Severe Illness—Is taken to Bezedas—Begins to use Mental Prayer—Conversion of a Priest—Teresa's increased Sufferings—Returns to the Convent—Her Patience and Charity—Restoration to Health 16

CHAPTER III.

Unprofitable Conversations—Teresa gives up Mental Prayer—Perils of a Monastic Life—Her Father's Illness and Death—She resumes Mental Prayer—Hindrances and Struggles—Spiritual Suffering—Entire Conversion 35

CHAPTER IV.

St. Teresa's Inner Life—Beginning of Mental Prayer—She attempts to describe it—Comparison of the Garden—Four Ways of Watering it—Four Degrees of Prayer—Description of the First Degree of Mental Prayer—Advice and Warnings concerning it 52

CHAPTER V.

The 'Prayer of Quiet'—The 'Prayer of Union'—Fourth Degree of Prayer, Trance or Rapture 72

CHAPTER VI.

Characteristics of St. Teresa's Spiritual Relations—Her Humility and Simplicity 93

CHAPTER VII.

The Jesuits—Teresa consults Francisco de Salcedo and Gaspar Daza—Her Perplexity at their Advice—She has Recourse to a Jesuit—He encourages her to persevere—She consults St. Francis Borgia—Doña Guiomar de Ulloa—Balthasar Alvarez becomes Teresa's Confessor—Her first Trance—Divine 'Locutions'—Doubts of Teresa's Friends—Her Distress—She is comforted and strengthened 103

CHAPTER VIII.

Outward Trials from Friends—Vision of the Seraph—Teresa's Vow—Peter of Alcantara—His Friendship for Teresa—Restlessness and Desire for Work—Vision of Hell . . . 121

CHAPTER IX.

Maria de Ocampo—Project to found a Reformed Convent—Teresa is encouraged by St. Peter of Alcantara and St. Luis Bertrand—Opposition raised in the City and in the Convent—Gaspar de Salazar comes to Avila, and assists her—Teresa is sent to Toledo—Meets Maria de Jesus—Returns to Avila—Foundation of St. Joseph's—Anger of her Superiors, and Disturbance in the City—Brief from Rome—Teresa retires to St. Joseph's 142

CHAPTER X.

Spain in the Sixteenth Century—Her Political and Literary Eminence—Religious Character of Spaniards—Their Chivalry—The Inquisition—Mysticism in Spain—Malon de Chaide—St. Teresa's Influence on Mystical Theology—Her Position among the Mystics—Juan D'Avilla—Luis de Granada—Luis de Leon—His Imprisonment by the Inquisition—John of the Cross 166

CHAPTER XI.

The Convent of St. Joseph—Teresa finishes her 'Life'—Her other Writings—The 'Interior Castle'—Increasing Peace and interior Joy—Longings to benefit others—Visit and Sermon of Alonso Maldonado 187

CHAPTER XII.

The Carmelite Order—Introduction into Europe—Attempts at Reform previous to St. Teresa—Controversy between the Carmelites and Bollandists—Rule of St. Teresa—Influence of her

Reform on the Spanish Church—The General gives her Leave to found two Convents of Friars—Foundation of Medina del Campo—Antonio de Heredia and John of the Cross . . 204

CHAPTER XIII.

Journey to Alcala—Foundations at Malagon and at Valladolid—Story of Casilda de Padilla—Beatrix Oñez—Early History of John of the Cross—First Convent of Reformed Friars founded at Durvelo—Removed to Mancera 220

CHAPTER XIV.

Foundation at Toledo—Letters of St. Teresa—She goes to Toledo—Princess of Eboli sends for her to Pastrana—Fra Mariano—Two Convents of Men and Women founded at Pastrana—Troubles caused by the Princess—Visitation of the Carmelite Order by Hernandez—Foundation of Reformed Friars at Alcala—Teresa goes to Salamanca—Founds a Convent of Nuns—Teresa Layz—Foundation at Alva—St. Teresa returns to Avila—Hernandez visits her, and makes her Prioress of the Incarnation—Opposition of the Nuns—Her Government of the Convent—Letter to Maria de Mendoza—She is sent to Salamanca 234

CHAPTER XV.

Foundation at Segovia—Teresa returns to Avila—Goes to Veas to found a Convent—Fra Jerome Gratian—Reformed Friars in Andalusia—Difficulties with the Mitigated Friars—Reform encouraged by the Nuncio Ormaneto—Gratian's Influence upon it—He is made Visitor of the Carmelites—Desires Teresa to found a Convent at Seville--Her Difficulties—Foundation at Caravaca—Exhortations to her Sisters—Her Niece Teresita . . . 257

CHAPTER XVI.

General Chapter of the Carmelite Order at Piacenza—Decrees against the Reform, and against Teresa—Her Letters to the General, and to the King—Disturbances at Seville—Teresa's Writings examined by the Inquisition—Chapter at Moraleja—Chapter of Discalced Friars at Almodovar—Teresa's Letter to Gratian—Her Cares and Difficulties—Death of the Nuncio . 273

CHAPTER XVII.

Enmity of the new Nuncio, Sega, to Teresa's Reform—She is elected Prioress of the Incarnation at Avila—Scene at the Election—Imprisonment and Sufferings of John of the Cross—Philip II. favours the Reform—Submission of Gratian to the Nuncio—Continued Troubles—Letters of St. Teresa—Second Chapter of Discalced at Almodovar—Anger of the Nuncio—Teresa's Confidence and Courage—Letter to Fra Juan—Nicholas Doria—Death of Rossi—Troubles at the Convent of Seville—Letter to the Nuns—The King interferes—Sega withdraws his Opposition to Teresa—Severance of the Reform from the Mitigated Order—Chapter at Alcala—Teresa's Letters to Gratian 287

CHAPTER XVIII.

Story of Catalina de Cardona—Foundation of Friars at La Roda; and of Nuns, by St. Teresa—She founds a Convent at Palencia, and at Soria—Velasquez, Bishop of Osma—Teresa returns to St. Joseph's—Foundation at Granada—Letter to Anna de Jesus—Teresa leaves Avila for the last Time—Founds a Convent at Burgos 307

CHAPTER XIX.

St. Teresa's last 'Relation'—Sufferings and Peril at Burgos —She sets out for Avila—Fra Antonio brings her to Alva— Last Illness and Death—Her Burial—Canonized by Paul V. —Rapid Spread of her Order 324

LIFE OF SAINT TERESA.

Chapter the First.

1515—1531.

Scarce has she learnt to lisp the name
Of martyr; yet she thinks it shame
Life should so long play with that breath
Which spent can bring so brave a death.
She never undertook to know
What Death with Love should have to do;
Nor has she e'er yet understood
Why to show love she should shed blood;
Yet, though she cannot tell you why,
She can love and she can die. CRASHAW.

'THINK that Carlyle expresses himself too broadly' (they are the words of Sara Coleridge) 'when he says " that the degree of vision that dwells in a man is the correct measure of the man," and illustrates his meaning by a reference to Shakespeare. Was Shakespeare as much better than other men as he was deeper and clearer sighted? The truth is that *vision* considered in the concrete, as found in this or that individual, is always specific. The saints and servants of God have a vision of their own. But here let me pause,

B

for I am at the mouth of a labyrinth.' Yet it is at the mouth of this labyrinth that any who would become acquainted, however slightly, with St. Teresa must begin their journey. There is no history so interesting as that of a human soul, but there is also none of which we possess so few that are of surpassing interest; and indeed the only marvel would be if it were otherwise, since such a history must always be an autobiography, and, if it is to become the inheritance of generations, must be the biography of both a genius and a saint. For how many there are whose history, as regards their intellectual life or outward work, would be of richest interest, while poor indeed if the story of their *soul* were told. There would be scarcely anything to say about it. Many a lamp which might have burned brightest at the Bride-Feast has wholly gone out, and others have been only just not entirely extinguished—no vivid flame ascending heavenwards has shone before men. Precious gifts of the spiritual nature, bestowed by the Father of spirits, have been spent upon idols of this lower air, and the story of genius, imagination, intellectual power, is too rarely the story also of a saint.

On the other hand, many whose want of education might make their spiritual history only the more interesting have had no power to speak or write about themselves. They could ascend the heights of spiritual contemplation, drinking of the springs which run among the hills, but could declare little to others of what they had seen and known in those serener regions. And then, amongst those possessing both genius and sanctity—the great men whose great natural gifts were devoted to greatest ends—how few have told us much or anything of their own innermost spiritual life; far less have they given us a continuous relation of it.

Perhaps there are only two such histories which can really be reckoned amongst the great books of Christendom, the ' Confessions of St. Augustine,' and the 'Life of St. Teresa;' and it is remarkable that one of them should have been the work of a woman. It is indeed possible that her wonderful autobiography would never have been written had it not been preceded by the still greater ' Confessions;' not that there is the least imitation or want of originality in her 'Life,' but it would have been impossible that she should not have been influenced by such a book as St. Augustine's in relating, at the command of her spiritual superiors, her own experiences. She tells us herself of the impression it made upon her while still far from the rest and peace afterwards vouchsafed to her. 'At this time the "Confessions of St. Augustine" were given me. Our Lord seems to have so ordained it, for I did not seek them myself, nor had I ever seen them before. When I began to read them, I thought I saw myself there described. . . . When I came to his conversion, and read how he heard that voice in the garden, it seemed to me nothing less than that our Lord had uttered it for me: I felt it so in my heart.'

There were indeed many points of resemblance between these two great souls, and the spiritual history of both might be summed up in the well-known words of St. Augustine, ' Fecisti nos propter Te, et inquietum est cor nostrum donec requiescat in Te.' For both were endowed with a depth and ardour of soul which could never be satisfied with earth, and with a perseverance and nobility which could not permit them to rest unsatisfied. Both had the desire for sympathy, for communication with other souls, and the power of expression which is always united to deep feeling in the richest and most beautiful natures. Both, after they had found rest for their souls, led lives of active work; moulding, in large measure, the religious life of their own and of succeeding times. St. Teresa is probably the only woman who ever exercised an important influence on any school of theology; that school of 'mystical theology' which had so deep an influence upon Fénélon, St. Francis de Sales, the Arnaulds, &c., and also upon many separated from the Catholic Church.

But perhaps the most remarkable parallel between St. Augustine and St. Teresa is that nothing in the business and important *work* of their lives equals in interest the stories which they have left of their inner life. The breath of Life, by which man first became a living soul, was from God; and it is the living soul which speaks to us in these books, telling us of all its struggles, sufferings, and blessedness in its upward striving after Him from whom the soul proceeds.

In both cases we are permitted to become acquainted with souls rare indeed in natural nobility and truthfulness. The great Bishop's 'Confessions' are so well known that all will at once acknowledge him as the prince of spiritual biographers; but St. Teresa holds only second rank to him as such; and the following pages are not so much an account of her outward life, as an attempt to gather, if it may be, from her own words a true view of the character and inner history of a great and noble woman.

She was born in Avila,[1] a city of Old Castile, on March 28, 1515, and was baptized the same day at the parish

[1] 'Abula Santos y Cantos' ('saints and stones at Avila') was a Spanish proverb before her time. It had also been called 'the City of Knights,' from the bravery of its inhabitants in their long wars with the Infidels. See Note A, p. 341.

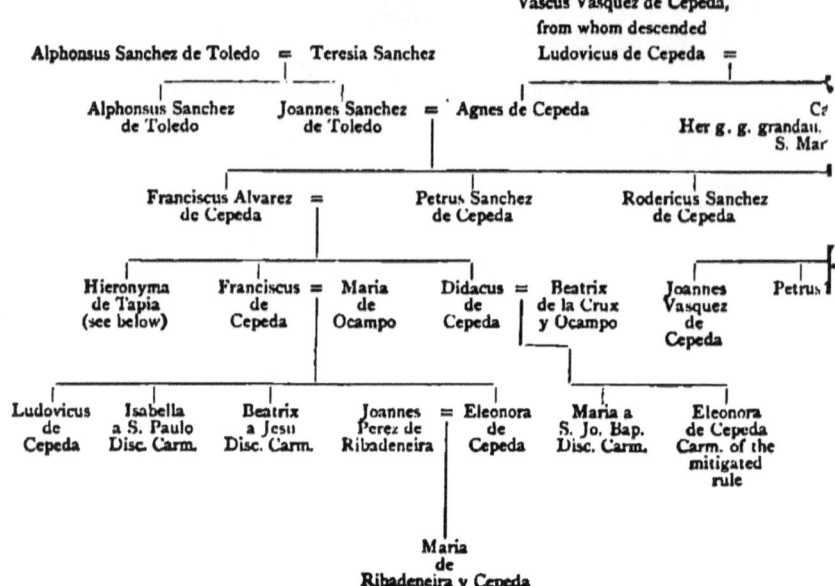

church of St John. She was styled in the world, and also for long after she became a nun of the mitigated Carmelite Rule, Doña Teresa Sanchez Cepeda Davila[1] y Ahumada, the last two being her mother's family names, which she assumed, as was usual at that time.

Her father, who was twice married, had three children, two sons and a daughter, by his first wife, and nine by his second marriage with Beatrix de Ahumada, seven sons and two daughters. Teresa was the elder daughter and third child of the second family.[2] The genealogical table is copied from that given by the Bollandists, and is interesting as showing how many amongst her kinsfolk joined her Reformed Order. Her family was noble and of ancient lineage. It is recorded of her niece, the daughter of her youngest sister, Juaña, that when she was five years old, being called playfully 'Ahumadita' by one of the nuns of the Benedictine convent at Alva, where she was brought up, she answered, 'I am called the Lady Beatrix de Ahumada;' taking, as was usual, her mother's maiden name.[3]

The mother of Teresa was of no less illustrious descent than her father. Her ancestors are said to have derived their name[4] from the incident of their escape, under cover of the smoke, from a castle to which the Moors had set fire.[5]

---

[1] The name of Davila is borne now by some of the grandees of Castile, who greatly pride themselves on their relationship to Teresa.

[2] In the table St. Teresa is marked as the fourth child of the second marriage, but in the text of the Bollandists, which gives a full account of all her brothers and sisters, she is said to have been the third, born after Roderigo, her playfellow in childhood. Lorenzo, who is placed before her in the table, was her next brother, and four years younger.

[3] *Acta Sanct.* Oct. t. vii. § iii. 51.

[4] A Humada, or Fumada.

[5] The crest over the shield of the family is a castle on fire surmounted

She was singularly happy in her parents, brothers, and sisters. She says herself, in the very beginning of her celebrated history: 'I had a father and mother who were devout and feared God. My father was very much given to the reading of good books; and so he had them in Spanish, that his children might read them. These books, with my mother's carefulness to make us say our prayers .... began to make me think seriously when I was, I believe, six or seven years old. It helped me, too, that I never saw my father and mother respect anything but goodness. My father ... was a man of great truthfulness; nobody ever heard him swear or speak ill of anyone; his life was most pure. My mother also was a woman of great goodness, and her life was spent in great infirmities. She was singularly pure in all her ways. She was very calm, and had great sense. The sufferings she went through during her life were grievous, her death most Christian.'[1]

Teresa's childish expedition, at seven years old, with her brother of eleven, to find out the country of the Moors, and there obtain martyrdom, is well known; but, perhaps, the deep impression made on her at so early an age by reading that bliss and pain are everlasting was still more remarkable. 'We happened,' she says, 'very often to talk about this; and we had a pleasure in repeating frequently, "For ever, ever, ever." Through the constant uttering of these words, our Lord was pleased that I should receive an abiding impression of the way of truth when I was yet a child.' Finding her attempts at martyrdom hindered—for the chil-

by a cross. This shield, containing four quarterings, was carved over the doors of Teresa's home, and is now placed on the façade of the church attached to the Carmelite convent built on the site of her father's house.

[1] *Vida*, c. i. 1.

dren were met outside Avila by an uncle and brought back
to their mother—she tried with the same brother, Rodrigo,
to build hermitages in an orchard, for even then she felt the
longing for solitude with God. 'We contrived,' she wrote,
'as well as we could, to build hermitages, by piling up
small stones one on the other, which fell down immediately;
and so it came to pass that we found no means of accomplishing our wish. Even now I have a feeling of devotion,
when I consider how God gave me in my early youth what
I lost by my own fault.'

Teresa was thirteen when her mother, Doña Beatrix,
died, at the age of thirty-three. Of Maria de Cepeda, her
half-sister, who took charge of her, she writes: 'I had a
sister much older than myself, from whose modesty and
goodness, which were great, I learned nothing, and learned
every evil from a relative who was often in the house. She
was so light and frivolous that my mother took great pains
to keep her out of the house, as if she foresaw the evil I
should learn from her; but she could not succeed, there
being many reasons for her coming. Until I knew her—I
mean, until she became friendly with me, and communicated to me her own affairs,—I was then about fourteen
years old; a little more, I think,—I do not believe that I
turned away from God in mortal sin, or lost the fear of Him,
though I had a greater fear of disgrace. When I would
complain of my parents I cannot do it, for I saw nothing in
them but all good and carefulness for my welfare. Then,
growing up, I began to discover the natural gifts which our
Lord had given me—they were said to be many; and when
I should have given Him thanks for them, I made use of
every one of them, as I shall now explain, to offend Him.'

[1] *Vida*, c. ii. 4; i. 8.

She says, however, that her mother's excessive fondness for books of chivalry was harmful to her children; though 'it did not hurt her so much as it hurt me, because she never wasted her time on them. Only we, her children, were left at liberty to read them . . . It annoyed my father so much that we had to be careful he never saw us. I contracted a habit of reading these books; and this little fault which I observed in my mother was the beginning of lukewarmness in my good desires . . . I thought there was no harm in it when I wasted many hours night and day in so vain an occupation, even when I kept it a secret from my father. So completely was I mastered by this passion, that I thought I could never be happy without a new book.'[1]

Teresa and her mother did but share in the passion for fictions of chivalry which, 'overbearing every other in the Peninsula, was now busily at work producing romances, both original and translated, that astonish us alike by their number, their length, and their absurdities.'[2] Spanish literature seems to have been singularly devoid of such forms of fiction until the end of the fifteenth century, the imagination of the people being sufficiently fed by the history and tradition of their national heroes. But the romances of France had by this time plainly exercised an influence in Spain; and, at first translated, they were soon imitated, giving rise to 'the extraordinary family of romances, whose descendants, as Cervantes says, were innumerable,—the family of which "Amadis de Gaula" is the poetical head and type.' Written by a Portuguese gentleman, Vasco de Lobeira, who died in 1403, its great fame arose in Spain; an edition of a Spanish translation being cited as having been printed at

---

[1] *Vida*, c. ii. 1.
[2] Ticknor's *History of Spanish Literature*, 1863, vol. i. p. 216.

Salamanca in 1510, six years before Teresa's birth. The earliest edition now accessible to us dates from 1519, and 'twelve more followed in the course of half a century; so that the 'Amadis' succeeded at once in placing the fortunes of its family on the sure foundations of popular favour in Spain.' It was imitated in a multitude of other romances: 'The History of Esplandian, son of Amadis,' of 'Florisando his nephew,' of 'Lisuarte of Greece, son of Esplandian,' &c.; all infinitely inferior to the 'Amadis,' its graceful and often tender extravagances changing into monstrous absurdities in these later fictions.

Many, however, took the romances to be true histories. We are told gravely by Castillo, a chronicler writing in 1587, that Philip the Second, when he married Mary of England, 'promised that if King Arthur should return to claim his throne, he would peaceably yield to that prince all his rights.'

'But whatever we may think of this belief in the romances of chivalry,' says Mr. Ticknor, 'there is no question that in Spain, during the sixteenth century, there prevailed a passion for them such as was never known elsewhere.' It was so strong, 'and seemed so dangerous, that, in 1553, they were prohibited from being printed, sold, or read in the American colonies; and in 1555 the Cortes earnestly asked that the same prohibition might be extended to Spain itself, and that all extant copies of romances of chivalry might be publicly burned. And, finally, half a century later, the happiest work of the greatest genius Spain has produced bears witness on every page to the prevalence of an absolute fanaticism for books of chivalry, and becomes at once the seal of their vast popularity, and the monument of their fate.'[1]

[1] Ticknor's *History of Spanish Literature*, 1863, vol. i. p. 227. An

Teresa's reading must have been amongst the best of such fictions, since most of the nearly worthless imitations of 'Amadis' were published long after she had given up such reading. It is not wonderful that she should have been fascinated by a fiction to whose merits Cervantes[1] himself was not insensible; and which had, probably, at one time fascinated him also, if we may judge by his intimate acquaintance with it. He notices in 'Don Quixote' that the *name* of Galaor's esquire, Gasabal, is mentioned but once in the 'Amadis.'

The noble and tender romance of 'Amadis' is, however, generally felt to possess far more literary merit than Mr. Ticknor concedes to it, and it is hard to imagine Teresa

attempt was made to counteract these effects by religious romances; and *The Celestial Chivalry*, published in 1554, contained nearly all the striking stories of the Bible under the form of a chivalrous allegory—the Temptation, for instance, being related as a combat between the Knight of the Serpent and the Knight of the Lion, wearing the shield of the Lion of the tribe of Judah, and riding the steed of Penitence given to him by Adam. The author declares it to be his object to drive out of the world the profane books of chivalry; the mischief of which he illustrates by a reference to Dante's account of Francesca da Rimini.

[1] The first book that, as he tells us, was taken from the shelves of Don Quixote, when the curate, the barber, and the housekeeper began the expurgation of his library, was the *Amadis de Gaula*. 'There is something mysterious about this matter,' said the curate, 'for, as I have heard, this was the first book of knight-errantry that was printed in Spain, and all the others have had their origin and source here; so that, as the arch-heretic of so mischievous a sect, I think he should, without a hearing, be condemned to the fire.' 'No, sir,' said the barber, 'for I too have heard that it is the best of all the books of its kind that have been written, and, therefore, for its singularity, it ought to be forgiven.' 'That is the truth,' answered the curate; 'and so let us spare it for the present.'—*Hist. of Spanish Lit.* vol. i. p. 206.

deeply fascinated by a book of little worth.[1] Perhaps she would have felt less self-reproach in after years if the 'pure imaginative power' which she possessed in such large measure had been discreetly fed, and if there had been no temptation to clandestine reading. We shall see, however, that the fault of her childhood pursued her into the cloister, though in another form, and that the food which her imagination and intellect craved caused her to spend much time in conversations which she considered profitless and harmful. Such a mind as hers could never have found occupation or interest in the then usual life of a Carmelite convent ; it must either have risen, as hers did, to the cónverse of angels—of more than angels—or, sinking to an earthly level, have sought distraction and companionship outside, which, in the condition of the Order, and under the mitigated rule, was easily done.

It is not difficult to imagine the effect which must have been produced by constant and inordinate romance-reading on the mind of the ardent and enthusiastic Spanish girl. Her first dreams were doubtless of such a life and such love as were pictured in her books, and hers was a nature too rich in love and womanliness not to respond to the beauty and pathos which abounded in those old romances, however unfit they may have been to form the chief reading of a girl of fourteen. She doubtless felt that deep, true human love is the most beautiful *earthly* gift of God—beautiful because it comes from Him ; and she who could rise to such heights of heavenly love must have felt instinctively that she could

[1] The best of the original Spanish romances which succeeded *Amadis*, *Palmerin de Oliva*, was written by a carpenter's daughter at Burgos, and was first printed at Salamanca in 1511. It was probably one of Teresa's 'new books.'

attain to whatever was noblest and greatest in earthly love. She speaks with compunction of her womanly desire at this time to please others by her appearance: 'I took pains with my hands and my hair, used perfumes and all vanities within my reach—and they were many, for I was much given to them. I had no evil intention, because I never wished anyone to offend God for me.'[1]

But the really perilous time for Teresa was after her mother's death. Her father appears to have had the same notion as regarded both society and books of imagination,— that entire separation from them was the only method of shielding his motherless child from their dangers. And as this course had been a failure in the matter of books, so it proved as to worldly conversation, although no men except relatives were allowed intercourse with his daughter. Of them she writes, 'These cousins were nearly of mine own age—a little older perhaps. We were always together; and they had a great affection for me. In everything that gave them pleasure I kept the conversation alive, listened to the stories of their affections and childish follies, good for nothing; and what was still worse, my soul began to give itself up to that which was the cause of all its disorders. If I were to give advice, I would say to parents that they ought to be very careful whom they allow to mix with their children when young.'[2]

There is nothing which strikes us more in reading St. Teresa's autobiography than her deep and truthful humility and contrition, a humility which enabled her to walk calmly and steadily beneath the perilous weight of grace and glory laid upon her; and without doubt this clear-sightedness caused her to make a very different estimate of

[1] *Vida*, c. ii. 2.   [2] Ibid. 3.

her childish follies from what would commonly be made, even by good people. Enough, however, was apparent to cause anxiety to her father and sister, the more so as the latter was on the eve of marriage with Don Martin de Guzman y Barrientos. Especially, Teresa tells us, her friendship with the female relative before mentioned distressed them exceedingly. 'They often blamed me for it, but, as they could not hinder that person from coming into the house, all their efforts were in vain. . . . Now and then I am amazed at the evil one bad companion can do; nor could I believe it if I did not know it by experience,—especially when we are young: then it is that the evil must be greatest. Oh that parents would take warning by me, and look carefully to this! So it was; the conversation of this person so changed me that . . . I became a reflection of her and of another who was given to the same kind of amusements. I know from this the great advantage of good companions; and I am certain that if at that tender age I had been thrown among good people I should have persevered in virtue; for if at that time I had found anyone to teach me the fear of God, my soul would have grown strong enough not to fall away.'[1]

Perhaps none have ever possessed strong influence over others who were not themselves sensitive to influences; certainly, however much she may have been acted upon by outward circumstances, all with whom she had to do, even in her girlhood, appear to have been impressed and acted upon by her. As she says herself, 'I kept the conversation alive;' and this, joined to her beauty and affectionateness, must, with not very wise companions, have continually led to conversations and incidents which she would afterwards feel to be matters for self-reproach. 'Still,' she writes, 'I was never

[1] *Vida*, c. ii. 5, 6.

inclined to much evil, for I hated naturally anything dishonourable, but only to the amusement of a pleasant conversation. The occasion of sin, however, being present, danger was at hand, and I exposed it to my father and brothers.' It does not appear certain whether at this time she had not been led into a secret engagement of marriage. She says herself, 'Were it not for my many faults there was some excuse for me, I think, in this: that the conversation I shared in was with one who, I thought, would do well in the estate of matrimony; and I was told by my confessors, and others also, whom in many points I consulted, used to say that I was not offending God.'[1] But for these words, the deep contrition with which she writes of her faults at his period might lead us to imagine that they were far more serious than the reality; still, any concealment from those to whom she owed duty and confidence must, of course, have been a heavy burden on her conscience; the more, because her natural openness and truthful nobility keenly perceived and abhorred the evil, even while she yielded to it. The thought of being in disgrace with her father, or with others, was anguish to her; but she had not yet learned to live in the light of that Countenance whose smiles were soon to be all in all to her. 'I never considered,' she says, ' that I could conceal nothing from Him who seeth all things. O my God, what evil is done in the world by disregarding this, and thinking that anything can be kept secret that is done against Thee! I am quite certain that great evils would be avoided if we clearly understood that what we have to do is not to be on our guard against men, but on our guard against displeasing Thee.'[2]

Her father, however, evidently knew enough to make

[1] *Vida*, c. ii. 12. [2] Ibid. c. ii. 9.

him desire further protection for her, though she says he
'waited for an opportunity which would make the change
seem nothing out of the way; for, as my sister was married,
it was not fitting I should remain alone, without a mother,
in the house.' He therefore placed her under the care of
the Augustinian nuns of the monastery of Our Lady of
Grace in Avila, 'in which,' she says, 'children like myself
were brought up.' It had been founded in 1509 by the
Venerable Fra Juan of Seville, Vicar-General of the Order,
and St. Thomas of Villanova had been director and confessor of the community. The Bollandists notice that in a
sermon on the Eucharist he spoke of this house with praise.

Chapter the Second.

1531—1539.

*In her youth
There is a prone and speechless dialect,
Such as moves men: besides, she hath prosperous art
When she will play with reason and discourse,
And well she can persuade.*
                      'MEASURE FOR MEASURE.'

THE removal to a convent must doubtless have been a keen trial to the talented and high-spirited girl, who could be in no society without becoming a centre of attraction. Even here, she writes, 'all the nuns were pleased with me; for our Lord had given me the grace to please everyone, wherever I might be.' But she felt no kind of propensity for a cloister-life, and says, 'for the first eight days I suffered much; but more from the suspicion that my vanity was known than from being in the monastery. . . . I was very uncomfortable; but within eight days—I think sooner—I was much more contented than I had been in my father's house. Though at this time I hated to be a nun, yet I was delighted at the sight of nuns so good; for they were very good in that house—very prudent, observant of the rule, and recollected.'[1]

[1] *Vida*, c. ii. 10.

She was not, however, forgotten by those who had cared for her outside, and who, she says, 'sought means to trouble my rest with messages and presents. As this could not be allowed, it was soon over, and my soul began to return to the good habits of my former years, and I recognized the great mercy of God to those whom He places among good people. It seems as if His Majesty had sought and sought again how to convert me to Himself.'[1]

One of the nuns, Doña Maria Brizeno, mistress of the children who were educated in the convent, was especially of use to her young pupil. She writes that she 'began gradually to like the good and holy conversation of this nun. How well she used to speak of God! for she was a person of great discretion and sanctity. I listened to her with delight. I think there never was a time when I was not glad to listen to her. . . . She would speak of the reward which our Lord gives to those who forsake all things for His sake. This good companionship began to root out the habits which bad companionship had formed, and to bring my thoughts back to the desire of eternal things, as well as to banish in some measure the great dislike I had to be a nun, which had been very great.'[2] She mentions as a proof of the hardness of her heart at this time, ' I could not shed a tear, even if I read the Passion through. This was a grief to me.' Alas! alas! for the coldness to which such hardness is not even a grief!

She remained in the monastery a year and a half, 'and was very much the better for it.' She used to ask the nuns to pray for her, that God would place her in that state wherein she was to serve Him; but still she says, ' I wished *not* to be a nun, and that God would not be pleased I should

---

[1] *Vida,* c. ii. 11.   [2] Ibid. c. iii. 1.

be one, though at the same time I was afraid of marriage.' At the end of her stay in the convent these inclinations became somewhat stronger, but having a great friend, Juaña Suarez, in the monastery of the Incarnation, she resolved, if ever she became a nun, 'not to be one in any other house than where she was;' she adds, 'These good thoughts of being a nun came to me from time to time. They left me very soon; and I could not persuade myself to be one.'

She was taken back to her father's house on account of a serious illness, and on her recovery went to visit her now married sister Maria in the country village, Castellanos de la Cañada, where she lived. Teresa speaks of her brother-in-law's affection for her, saying, 'At least he showed me all kindness. This too I owe rather to our Lord, for I have received kindness everywhere.'

On the road to her sister's, at Hortijosa, four leagues from Avila, lived her uncle, Don Pedro Sanchez de Cepeda, and with him she abode for some days. He was, she says, 'a prudent and most excellent man, then a widower His practice was to read good books in Spanish; and his ordinary conversation was about God and the vanity of the world. These books he made me read to him, and though I did not much like them, I appeared as if I did; for in giving pleasure to others I have been most particular, though it might be painful to myself—so much so, that what in others might have been a virtue was in me a great fault, because I was often extremely indiscreet. O my God, in how many ways did His Majesty prepare me for the state wherein it was His will I should serve Him!—how against my own will He constrained me to do violence to myself!'[1]

Ex forti dulcedo. There is no real sweetness without

[1] *Vida,* c. iii. 5.

strength; and she on whose sweet nature such sweetnesses
of grace were to be poured cannot attain to them without
violence. 'The violent take it by force.' She must assay
the Siege Perilous before she can gaze on the Holy Grail.

But these few days with her uncle (who afterwards 'left
all his possessions and became a religious') decided her
vocation; though even then she says, 'I could not bend my
will to be a nun.' 'Aut pati aut mori' might have been
her motto now as in later years, for through no happy longings after a life separate from the world did she enter upon
the narrow and thorny though Heaven-lit path she was
henceforward to tread, until her weary feet stood within the
gates of Jerusalem. 'I resolved,' she writes, 'to force myself into it. The struggle lasted three months. . . . I was
more influenced by servile fear, I think, than by love. . . .
The devil put before me that I could not endure the trials
of the religious life, because of my delicate nurture. I
defended myself against him by alleging the trials which
Christ endured, and that it was not much for me to suffer
something for His sake; besides, He would help me to bear
it. I must have thought so, but I do not remember the
last consideration. I endured many temptations during
these days. I was subject to fainting-fits, attended with
fever, for my health was always weak.'[1]

At this time she found a great source of strength in that
which had formerly been a snare to her,—in reading. 'I had
become by this time fond of good books, and that gave me
life.' Her entire reading seems to have been henceforward
among the 'great masters.' 'She despised books of inferior
note,' the Bollandists say, 'and read whatever is best of
its kind, perusing the treatises, congenial to her, of such

[1] *Vida*, c. iii. 7, 8.

doctors as SS. Jerome, Gregory the Great, and Augustine.'[1] Having tasted the old wine, she had no desire for the new; and at a time when we are overwhelmed with second-rate books of piety and devotion, her example may not be without profit;[2] for only in great writers are found enthusiasm without sentimentality, intensity without exaggeration. The Epistles of St. Jerome especially turned her aspirations into definite purpose;

> The blood was hers
> That at the trumpet's summons stirs,

and she resolved to tell her father of her purpose, which, she

---

[1] *A. SS.* t. vii. Oct. § v. 74.

[2] ' Quels livres faut-il choisir ? Comment! est ce que tous les livres spirituels ne sont pas bons ? Assurément non, mesdames, et l'Église est bien loin d'endosser la responsabilité de tous ces petits livres qui circulent partout, et qui n'ont quelque fois ni science, ni jugement, ni sens pratique. Écoutons Mgr. d'Orléans: " Defiez-vous même," dit-il à son clergé, "de certains livres de piété. La librairie, la meilleure librairie, hélas, trop peu surveillée aujourd'hui sous ce rapport, jette chaque année dans le monde, dans les maisons religieuses, dans les bibliothèques paroissiales, dans les distributions de prix, des milliers de petits livres de piété sans valeur, sans doctrine, sans solidité, pleins d'une quantité d'idées inexactes, d'exagérations ridicules, et de sentiments faux, qui altèrent et abaissent la religion, dénaturent la dévotion, rebutent les hommes sérieux, scandalisent les chrétiens éclairés, et sont comme une sorte de corruption subtile pour les âmes. Bannissez ces livres, messieurs, et préférez toujours les bons livres connus, les livres dont la réputation est faite, à ceux qui n'ont souvent pour eux d'autre attrait que celui de la nouveauté et de l'inconnu." (*Lettre de Mgr. d'Orléans à son Clergé*, 8 Mai, 1863.) Je ne vois rien à retrancher à ces sévères expressions. Fénélon disait, "Il n'y a rien de plus noble que la religion : rien n'est plus bas ni plus méprisable que l'idée qu'en ont communément tous ceux qu'on appelle dévots." (*Essai sur le Gouvern.* c. x.) J'ajouterai, rien n'est plus bas ni plus méprisable que l'idée qu'en donnent communément tous ces ouvrages.'—*Conférences aux Dames du Monde* par Mgr. Landriot, 20ᵐᵉ Conf. pp. 275, 276.

says, 'was almost like taking the habit; for I was so jealous of my word, that I would never, for any consideration, recede from a promise when once my word had been given.'

She failed, however, in obtaining her father's consent, either through her own persuasions or those of others. She says, 'The utmost I could get from him was that I might do as I pleased after his death. I now began to be afraid of myself and of my own weakness, for I might go back.'

She therefore turned the powers of persuasion, which with her seldom failed, upon her brother Antonio, and so wrought upon him that she prevailed upon him to be a friar, and to help her in the very questionable step of leaving her father's house secretly. 'We agreed,' she writes, 'to set out one day very early in the morning for the monastery where that friend of mine lived for whom I had so great an affection: though I would have gone to any other monastery if I thought I should serve God better in it, or to any one my father liked, so strong was my resolution now to become a nun—for I thought more of the salvation of my soul now, and made no account whatever of mine own ease. I remember perfectly well, and it is quite true, that the pain I felt when I left my father's house was so great that I do not believe the pain of dying will be greater, for it seemed to me as if every bone in my body were wrenched asunder; for as I had no love of God to destroy my love of father and of kindred, this latter love came upon me with a violence so great that, if our Lord had not been my keeper, my own resolution to go on would have failed me. But He gave me courage to fight against myself, so that I executed my purpose.'[1]

The Carmelite convent of the Incarnation was just

[1] *Vida*, c. iv. 1.

outside the town of Avila, on the southern side. It was founded in 1513, and 'grew in course of time into a very noble fabric, an excellent church, a singularly large cloister, a spacious garden and shrubbery, with offices such and so many that about the year 1550 it could contain 190 nuns.'[1] St. Teresa speaks of 180 in her time; in 1840 the number had dwindled to twelve. The Holy Eucharist had been celebrated within its walls for the first time on the day of Teresa's baptism.

There are two interesting engravings of the exterior edifice and of the interior cloister in the Bollandist volume containing St. Teresa's *Acta*, from accurate drawings made for the work by D. Valentine Carderera, Associate of the Royal Academy of History, who obtained for this purpose special faculty of entry into the cloisters from the Bishop of Avila. The first engraving represents a plain and unattractive-looking building, of the type with which we are familiar in many Roman churches. It is apparently just outside one of the gates of Avila. The second engraving gives a garden surrounded, as it seems, by a quadrangle of building with a low-pitched roof of tiles, an open gallery with wide round arches, separated by columns, running round the upper storey, the parapet of the gallery apparently pierced by sculpture. The court or garden contains trees, flowers, and a fountain; and close to the latter there is a nut-tree, spreading its branches over the fountain, which is held in especial reverence, as it is said to have been planted by Teresa: the fruit of it is sought for with much devotion by Carmelite convents. There is also a small octagon building in the garden, said to be on the spot where

---

[1] Lezana, *Annalium Carmelitarum*, quoted by Bollandists, tom. vii. Oct. § v. 76.

St. John of the Cross lived while director of the convent. The wood of which this building is constructed is left unpainted, as it is supposed to be the same of which his house was built.

To this house St. Teresa was drawn through her affection for her friend, although it was then in a far lower condition as to fervour and obedience to rule than the Augustinian convent where she had spent a year and a half. The buildings have been altered, so that Teresa's cell is now a sumptuous chapel in the north transept of the church, which has been restored within recent times, but which (with the exception of this chapel) does not boast of much richness or beauty of any kind. Various inscriptions on tablets, over the 'grate of the Communion,' the grate of the locutory, &c., record events in the life of the Saint which occurred in those places. She lived in this convent for thirty-two years, twenty-nine as a nun, three as prioress; and it is said that she always 'loved that house as her mother,' resting there for short seasons of refreshment during the continual toil and journeyings of her later years—taking a tender and almost playful repose within its walls. How little could the nuns have foreseen that the runaway girl who, on November 2, 1533, asked for admittance at their gate was not only to reform that house, but to breathe new life into their whole constitution! How little could they have imagined the grace to be bestowed upon her who, through whatever imperfections, was faithful to God's leadings, and, responding with a generous self-surrender to every 'energising of grace,' to every 'tightening of the cord of love,' pressed onwards and onwards toward the mark for the prize of her high calling of God in Christ Jesus!

The nuns at the monastery of the Incarnation sent to

tell her father of Teresa's arrival at their house. He came there, and, we are told, 'offered up his Isaac upon Mount Carmel.' She was his favourite child, but he no longer opposed himself to so decided a vocation. She made her profession Nov. 3, 1534, a year and a day after entering the convent, in her twentieth year; and the early morning of that inward life which for eighteen years was overclouded by trial and aridity, glowed with the sunshine which at length dispersed every cloud, filling her soul with light and love. 'When I took the habit,' she writes, 'our Lord at once made me understand how He helps those who do violence to themselves in order to serve Him. No one observed this violence in me; they saw nothing but the greatest good-will. At that moment, because I was entering on that state, I was filled with a joy so great that it has never failed me to this day; and God converted the aridity of my soul into the greatest tenderness. Everything in religion was a delight unto me; and it is true that I used now and then to sweep the house during those hours of the day which I had formerly spent on my amusements and my dress; and calling to mind that I was delivered from such follies, I was filled with a new joy that surprised me, nor could I understand whence it came.'[1]

The words which follow are too striking an instance to be omitted of that spiritual and supernatural insight mingled with clear common-sense which was one of St. Teresa's most marked characteristics: 'Whenever I remember this, there is nothing in the world, however hard it may be, that, if it were proposed to me, I would not undertake without any hesitation whatever; for I know now, by experience in many things, that if from the first I resolutely persevere in

[1] *Vida*, c. iv. 2.

my purpose, even in this life His Majesty rewards it in a way which he only understands who has tried it. When the act is done for God only, it is His will before we begin it that the soul .... should be afraid; and the greater the fear, if we do but succeed, the greater the reward and the sweetness thence afterwards resulting. I know this by experience, as I have just said, in many serious affairs; and so, if I were a person who had to advise anybody, I would never counsel anyone, to whom good inspirations from time to time may come, to resist them through fear of the difficulty of carrying them into effect; for if a person lives detached for the love of God only, that is no reason for being afraid of failure, for He is omnipotent. May He be blessed for ever! Amen.'[1]

She was not to be left long, however, without the discipline of suffering, and trials, of which she was to have abundance spiritually, began with the body. Her health, always fragile, suffered from the change in her life, and she says: 'Though my happiness was great, that was not enough. The fainting-fits began to be more frequent; and my heart was so seriously affected that everyone who saw it was alarmed; and I had also many other ailments. And thus it was I spent the first year, having very bad health, though I do not think I offended God much in it.'[2] There was no vow of enclosure in the convent at this time, and her father removed her from it to her sister's house at Castellanos de la Cañada, her friend, Juaña de Suarez, accompanying her. This was in the autumn of 1535; and she remained there 'nearly a year, for three months of it suffering most cruel tortures—effects of the violent remedies which they applied.' In April 1536 she was taken by her father and sister to Bezedas, to be

[1] *Vida*, c. iv. 3.   [2] Ibid. 6.

under the care of a woman famous for certain cures which she effected; and on the way they stayed with Don Pedro de Cepeda. He gave her a book called 'Tercer Abecedario,' 'which treats of the prayer of recollection.' She says: 'Though in the first year I had read good books,—for I would read no others, because I understood now the harm they had done me,—I did not know how to make my prayer, nor how to recollect myself. I was therefore much pleased with the book, and resolved to follow the way of prayer it described with all my might.'[1]

This was the beginning of that wonderful vocation to the interior life of mental prayer, to which, through sharpest trials, she was, with short interruption, faithful; and of which she became one of the most eminent examples and teachers. Her account of her progress in it must be related separately.

She tells us that in the place to which she had gone for her cure 'there lived a priest of good understanding and birth, with some learning, but not much. I went to confession to him, for I was always fond of learned men, although confessors indifferently learned did my soul much harm.' Up to this time there is no mention of her having received the slightest assistance in her spiritual life from her confessors—'there was no man to care for her soul,' and she seems only to have perplexed and tormented them, being herself in turn perplexed by them. 'I know by experience,' she continues, 'that it is better, if the confessors are good men and of holy lives, that they should have no learning at all than a little; for such confessors never trust themselves without consulting those who are learned—nor would I trust them myself: and a really learned confessor never deceived me. Neither did

[1] *Vida*, c. iv. 8.

the others willingly deceive me, only they knew no better.
I thought they were learned, and that I was not under any
other obligation than that of believing them, as their instructions to me were lax, and left me more at liberty—for
if they had been strict with me, I am so wicked I should
have sought for others.'[1] This last assertion we may be permitted to doubt, for her inability to rest satisfied with com-
mon-place and unspiritual teaching, and her instant seizing
and using earnestly the best guidance that came in her way,
were remarkable throughout her life.

She had certainly no fit guide in the priest above mentioned, who 'took an extreme liking' to her, since for seven
years he had led an evil life. She says, 'There was no harm
in the liking he had for me, but it ceased to be good because
it was in excess. . . . Our conferences were many. But at
that time, through the knowledge and fear of God which filled
my soul, what gave me most pleasure in all my conversations
with others was to speak of God; and as I was so young,
this made him ashamed; and then out of that great good-
will he bore me he began to tell me of his wretched state.'[2]
What the general tone of religion and morals must have been
which could make such a communication possible is too
shocking to imagine; that a girl, carefully and religiously
brought up, should even know of the existence of such evil
seems strange, but that a priest, and her spiritual guide,
should discuss his own misery with her is almost incon-
ceivable. Nor does Teresa's whole nature seem to have
been outraged, as we should have expected, by such a pro-
ceeding, though she blames herself for thinking more of
her friendship for him than of his sin. 'I was extremely
sorry for him, because I liked him much. I was then so

[1] *Vida*, c. v. 6.   [2] Ibid. 9.

imprudent and so blind as to think it a virtue to be grateful and loyal to one who liked me.' She immediately applied herself to try and effect his conversion, and—strange task for a girl scarce twenty-one—'procured further information about the matter from members of his household.' 'I spoke to him most frequently of God; and this must have done him good, though I believe that what touched him most was his great affection for me.' Her influence, as almost always happened, prevailed through God's grace. 'He began to consider all that he had done in those years,' 'like a man roused from deep sleep,' and breaking off his sin he 'was never weary of giving God thanks for the light He had given him.' He died at the end of a year from the day of his first meeting with St. Teresa,—the first of the multitude who through her burning love for souls were to be turned from sin to grace. 'I believe,' she writes, 'that all men must have a greater affection for those women whom they see disposed to be good; and even for the attainment of earthly ends, women must have more power over men because they are good, as I shall show hereafter.' She tells us that the priest in question 'died most piously, and completely withdrawn from that occasion of sin. It seems that it was the will of our Lord that he should be saved by these means.'

She remained for three months in that place, nothing bettered by severe medical treatment, but the contrary. 'The severity of the pain in my heart, for the cure of which I was there,' she writes, 'was much more keen: it seemed to me, now and then, as if it had been seized by sharp teeth. So great was the torment, that it was feared it might end in madness. There was a great loss of strength, for I could eat nothing whatever, only drink. . . . The pains I had were unendurable, and I was overwhelmed in a most deep sadness, so that I had no rest either night or day.'[1] Her father took her back to her home, but her ailments only increased. 'I was in pain from my head down to my feet.'

For three months she bore, with what even she calls patience, almost unendurable sufferings. ' It was a great help to me to be patient that I had read the story of Job in the "Morals" of St. Gregory (our Lord seems to have prepared me thereby), and that I had begun the practice of prayer, so that I might bear it all, conforming my will to the will of God. All my conversation was with God. I had continually these words of Job in my thoughts and in my mouth : " If we have received good things of the hand of our Lord, why should we not receive evil things?"'[2]

She was very anxious at this time[3] to go to confession, but her father, thinking that she wished it through fear of death, would not permit it, 'in order to quiet me!' That very night her illness increased so acutely that for four days she was insensible. Extreme unction was administered, and a grave was prepared for her in the monastery, for there was no expectation that she would ever return except as a corpse to the house which was to become world-famous through her. But she revived, and desired at once to confess, communicating afterwards 'with many tears;' her father having previously lamented his having before prevented it through mistaken tenderness. She speaks of herself as in much blindness of heart at this time, 'partly because my confessors were so unlearned, and partly because I was so very wicked.' Yet she says at this very time, 'This grace, among others, did His Majesty bestow on me, that ever since my first Communion never in confession have I failed to confess anything I thought to be a sin.'

[1] *Vida*, c. v. 14.   [2] Ibid. 6.   [3] August 1536.

She only returned to life to endure still greater pains, and says, 'My tongue was bitten to pieces; there was a choking in my throat because I had eaten nothing, and because of my weakness, so that I could not swallow even a drop of water; all my bones seemed to be out of joint; and the disorder of my head was extreme. I was bent together like a coil of ropes, for to this was I brought by the torture of those days, unable to move either arm, or foot, or hand, or head any more than if I had been dead, unless others moved me: I could move however, I think, one finger of my right hand. Then as to touching me, that was impossible, for I was so bruised that I could not endure it. They used to move me in a sheet, one holding one end, and another the other. This lasted till Palm Sunday.'[1]

She now became extremely anxious to return to her convent; and about Palm Sunday 1537 she was removed there, and the nuns received alive her whose grave they had prepared. More could not be said, for her pains continued to be extreme, and she 'was nothing but bones.' She speaks of praising God when she began to crawl on her hands and her knees. She must have made herself beloved during the year of her novitiate, though some of her edifying behaviour was owing to the keen desire for approbation which she says partly kept her from evil in the world. So in the convent she writes that before her illness she 'delighted in being thought well of by others;' and suffered much from being found fault with when she was blameless. The nuns thought that her tears of contrition and desire for solitude proceeded from discontent, and laughed at little acts of kindness which she performed; such as folding up the nuns' cloaks after they had left the choir.

[1] *Vida*, c. vi. 1.

Even then she tells us 'all religious observances had an attraction for me, but I could not endure any which seemed to make me contemptible.'

She had shown great charity to a nun previously ill from painful ulcers, of which she died, and while the other sisters 'were afraid of her malady' the eyes of the future Saint rested on the beauty of her soul. She says she envied her patience, praying to God for the like. And now that she herself was laid low her prayer was granted. She speaks of herself continually at this time as 'very wicked,' giving way to temptation, under delusions, far from the light. Yet great must have been her faithfulness to whatever light she possessed, for her virtues were such as are rarely seen save after long exercise in saintliness. She writes: 'I was resigned to the will of God, even if He left me in this state for ever. My anxiety about the recovery of my health seemed to be founded on my desire to pray in solitude, as I had been taught; for there were no means of doing so in the infirmary.... All marvelled at the patience which our Lord gave me—for if it had not come from the hand of His Majesty, it seemed impossible to endure so great an affliction with so great a joy.... I never spoke ill in the slightest degree whatever of anyone, and my ordinary practice was to avoid all detraction; for I used to keep most carefully in mind that I ought not to assent to, nor say of another, anything I should not like to have said of myself.'[1] Thus it came to be understood that where she was, 'absent persons were safe;' as they also were with her friends and kinsfolk, and with those whom she instructed. It would be hard to exaggerate the power of influence for good which the confidence she had thus won must have given her. 'Absent

[1] *Vida*, c. vi. 3, 4.

persons were safe' with her. Her nobility felt the treachery which always lies in detraction; the kind of advantage taken, as it were, of the unprotectedness of the absent.

'O my God!' she exclaims, 'I wished for health that I might serve Thee better.... I thought I might serve God much better if I were well. This is our delusion: we do not resign ourselves absolutely to the disposition of our Lord, Who knows best what is for our good.'[1] Her self-accusations recall St. Gregory's words concerning Job: 'To anyone this man may seem great in his virtues, to me he appears undoubtedly sublime even in his sins:' for not only was her will and intention to serve God and unite herself to His will, but her soul was filled with that thirst after Him and grief for having offended Him which many can but grieve that they do not possess. 'The longing for solitude,' she writes, 'remained, and I loved to discourse and speak of God; for if I found anyone who could do so, it was a greater joy and satisfaction to me than all the refinements— or rather, to speak more correctly, the real rudeness—of the world's conversation..... I was most deeply penitent for having offended God; and I remember that very often I did not dare to pray, because I was afraid of that most bitter anguish which I felt for having offended God, dreading it as a great chastisement. This grew upon me afterwards to so great a degree that I know of no torment wherewith to compare it; and yet it was neither more nor less because of any fear I had at any time, for it came upon me only when I remembered the consolations of our Lord which He gave me in prayer, the great debt I owed Him, the evil return I made: *I could not bear it.*'[2]

There is nothing exaggerated in this, the strangeness is

---

[1] *Vida,* c. vi. 8.   [2] Ibid. 5.

that it should be rare. She had looked steadily at her own sin and her Lord's love, and the sight wrought in her that suffering of love by which even on earth her gaze was to be purified and strengthened to behold greater things than created beauty can disclose. Who has ever felt any true human love without knowing its suffering also? self-reproach for ingratitude and coldness? In human love we know what St. Teresa describes of celestial love—that we 'do not dare' to admit thoughts and recollections, for very fear of the 'most bitter anguish' which they bring. And who that has felt this with respect to earthly love can doubt that there must come a moment of keenest anguish when the soul first sees her Lord, and herself in the light of His Presence? It may be but a moment—there, where intervals

>   Are measured by the living thought alone,
>   And grow or wane with its intensity;

a moment it may be—with Him in whose sight a thousand years are but as yesterday. Whatever be the mysteries of that purifying love and suffering, Teresa seems to have shared in them on earth.

>   The sight of Him had kindled in her heart
>   All tender, gracious, reverential thoughts;
>   And she was sick with love, and yearned for Him,
>   And felt as though she could but pity Him,
>   That One so sweet should e'er have placed Himself
>   At disadvantage such, as to be used
>   So vilely by a being so vile as she.
>   There was a pleading in His pensive eyes
>   Had pierced her to the quick, and troubled her.

And so she desired

>   To slink away, and hide her from His sight;
>   And yet she had a longing aye to dwell
>   Within the beauty of His countenance.

She had suffered three years from paralysis—from the middle of 1536 to the middle of 1539; and finding earthly help of no avail for her restoration, she had the more earnest recourse to prayer, causing many to be offered for her, especially Eucharistic prayers. She mentions the intercessions which she thus sought as 'prayers that were highly sanctioned;' and says, 'I never liked those other devotions which some people, especially women, make use of with a ceremoniousness to me intolerable, but which move them to be devout.'[1] 'From silly devotions, good Lord, deliver us!' is her exclamation in another part of her life, and it is not difficult to imagine the repulsion which her grand and earnest soul must have felt from some expressions of popular devotion.

Her prayers, and those offered for her, were granted—she was restored to health. She always believed that she owed it in great part to the prayers of St. Joseph, for whom she had an especial love and veneration.

[1] *Vida*, c. vi. 9.

Chapter the Third.

1539—1555.

Only this veyle which Thou hast broke,
  And must be broken yet in me;
This veyle, I say, is all the cloke
  And cloud which shadows me from Thee.
This veyle Thy full-eyed Love denies,
And only gleams and shadows spies.

O take it off! make no delay,
  But brush me with Thy light, that I
May shine into a perfect day,
  And warm me at Thy glorious eye!
O take it off! or till it flee,
Though with no lilie, stay with me.

HENRY VAUGHAN.

ALTHOUGH the desire to serve God better had been Teresa's motive in wishing for recovery, she was no sooner restored to health than she yielded to her old temptation of wasting time, and thought, and heart in unprofitable intercourse; 'waxing cold through conversation with profane men, and through the omission of mental prayer,' say her Bollandist biographers.[1]

[1] *Acta Sanct.* tom. vii. Oct. § vii. 102.

She was but following the usual custom of the convent: there was apparently nothing in its regulations to prevent her spending as much time as she pleased in the locutory, provided she fulfilled certain duties in choir. She was only twenty-four, and had no lack of visitors; her elastic nature rose with brightness and vigour when the weight of suffering was removed, and she used her singular power of charming and interesting for her own amusement; probably feeling greater zest in renewed intercourse with fresh minds from her long-enforced seclusion.

'Who could have said,' she writes, ' that I was so soon to fall, after such great consolations from God—after His Majesty had implanted virtues in me which of themselves made me serve Him—after I had been, as it were, dead . . . after He had raised me up, soul and body, so that all who saw me marvelled to see me alive? . . . So, then, going on from pastime to pastime, from vanity to vanity, from one occasion of sin to another, I began to expose myself exceedingly to the very greatest dangers: my soul was so distressed by many vanities, that I was ashamed to draw near unto God in an act of such special friendship as that of prayer. As my sins multiplied, I began to lose the pleasure and comfort I had in virtuous things; and that loss contributed to the abandonment of prayer. I see now most clearly, O my Lord, that this comfort departed from me because I had departed from Thee. It was the most fearful delusion into which Satan could plunge me—to give up prayer under the pretence of humility. I began to be afraid of giving myself to prayer, because I saw myself so lost. I thought it would be better for me, seeing that in my wickedness I was one of the most wicked, to live like the multitude—to say the prayer which I was bound to say, and that vocally; not to practise mental prayer, nor commune with God so much; for I deserved to be with the devils, and was deceiving those who were about me, because I made an outward show of goodness . . . for with my cunning I so managed matters that all had a good opinion of me, and yet I did not seek this deliberately by simulating devotion, for in all that relates to hypocrisy and ostentation—glory be to God!—I do not remember that I ever offended Him, so far as I know. The very first movements herein gave me such pain, that the devil would depart from me with loss, and the gain remained with me; and thus, accordingly, he never tempted me much in this way. Perhaps, however, if God had permitted Satan to tempt me as sharply herein as he tempted me in other things I should have fallen also into this; but His Majesty has preserved me until now. May He be blessed for evermore! It was rather a heavy affliction to me that I should be thought so well of, for I knew my own secret.'[1]

Even apart from their spiritual interest, who can help being struck with admiration at the almost childlike and transparent simplicity—the tender grace of her words? She fulfils steadily the perilous task (especially to a woman) of speaking of herself, unconsciously revealing the candour and greatness of her soul.

It was not strange that the community thought well of the young nun, since the only thing with which she reproaches herself is the distracting intercourse in which against her conscience she persisted By 'giving up prayer' she does not mean, as will be seen further on, what would be generally understood by the words, but only that she

[1] *Vida*, c. vi. 14; vii. 1, 2.

gave up the practice of regular meditation, of interior communing with God, to which by no earthly guidance she had been led. For she gives as the reason why the nuns did not at this time think her 'so wicked,' that 'they saw that I, who was so young and exposed to so many occasions of sin, withdrew myself often into solitude for prayer, read much, spoke of God, that I liked to have His image painted in many places, to have an oratory of my own, and furnish it with objects of devotion, that I spoke ill of no one, and other things of the same kind in me which have the appearance of virtue. . . . In consequence of this they gave me as much liberty as they did to the oldest nuns, and even more, and had great confidence in me ; for as to taking any liberty for myself, or doing anything without leave, such as conversing through the door, or in secret, or by night—I do not think I could have brought myself to speak with anybody in the monastery in that way, and I never did it—for our Lord held me back.'[1]

She goes on to speak, with greatest good sense of the perils of a nunnery constituted as the Incarnation was at that time. There was no active employment in works of mercy, and as there was no enclosure, and an entire relaxation of rules for a contemplative life, nothing remained, after certain offices of religion had been performed, but to fill up time with gossip either amongst themselves or with those outside. St. Teresa speaks of such a state of things as involving ' the very greatest danger, . . . yea, more, I think it is, for those who will be wicked, a road to hell, rather than a help to their weakness.' Doubtless parents continually placed their daughters in such houses as a merely honourable worldly provision for them, for she

[1] *Vida*, c. vii. 3, 4.

advises such parents to 'marry them to persons of a much lower degree, rather than place them in monasteries of this kind, unless they be of extremely good inclinations,—and God grant that these inclinations may come to good!—or let them keep them at home. . . . Many of them are to be pitied, for they wished to withdraw from the world, and, thinking to escape from the dangers of it, and that they were going to serve our Lord, have found themselves in ten worlds at once, without knowing what to do or how to help themselves.'[1] She goes on deeply to lament the corruption of religious orders, saying that 'the friar and the nun who would really begin to follow their vocation have reason to fear the members of their communities more than all the devils together.'[2]

Returning to her own history, she says, 'When I began to indulge in these conversations, I did not think, seeing they were customary, that my soul must be injured and dissipated, as I afterwards found it must be, by such conversations. I thought that, as receiving visits was so common in many monasteries, no more harm would befall me thereby than befell others whom I knew to be good. I did not observe that they were much better than I was, and that an act which was perilous for me was not so perilous for them; and yet I have no doubt there was some danger in it, were it nothing else but a waste of time.'[3]

She tells us of a vision during one of these conversations by which 'our Lord was pleased to show me that these friendships were not good for me;' but says expressly that she did not see anything outward—it was an intellectual vision. 'Christ stood before me, stern and grave, giving me to understand what in my conduct was offensive to Him.

[1] *Vida*, c. vii. 7.   [2] Ibid. 9.   [3] Ibid. 10.

I saw Him with the eyes of the soul more distinctly than I could have seen Him with the eyes of the body. The vision made so deep an impression upon me that, though it is more than twenty-six years ago, I seem to see Him present even now. I was greatly astonished and disturbed, and I resolved not to see that person again.'[1]

There is a brass tablet in the locutory of the Incarnation at Avila, representing this vision as St. Teresa described it: our Lord bound to the pillar, and 'with a severe countenance reproaching her for refusing her entire heart to Him, representing to her His immense griefs, and His Body torn by the scourge.'[2]

She was perplexed by the vision, for she was too clear-headed and strong-thoughted to imagine that she had seen any outward appearance. She says, 'It did me much harm that I did not then know it was possible to see anything otherwise than with the eyes of the body,' and that Satan suggested to her that she had imagined it, that it was a diabolical vision, &c. But she adds, 'For all this, the impression remained with me that the vision was from God and not an imagination; but as it was not to my liking, I forced myself to lie to myself.' Nor did the warnings of an aged nun, 'a great servant of God and a strict observer of the rule,' avail to make her break off this fault. As in earlier days she had found food in romances for her vivid imagination, so now she sought it in personal intercourse with those who interested and amused her; and, in spite of her resolution, went back to her former conferences with the same person against whose society she had been specially warned, for 'great importunity was used;' and she was assured

[1] *Vida*, c. vii. 11.
[2] *Acta Sanct.* tom. vii. Oct. § vii. 102.

'there was no harm in seeing such a person.' She says, 'I had a great affection for her;' and one to whom such a heart as Teresa's had given itself, would not be likely to consent to separation from her, if it could be prevented.

At this time (about 1541) she had given up mental prayer for more than a year and a half, 'thinking it an act of greater humility to abstain.' Her father used often to come and see her, 'for it was a comfort to him to speak of the things of God;' and she had, five or six years previously, led him to the practice of mental prayer. From the first, the missionary spirit, which was so strong in her, had shown itself, or, as she describes it, 'before I knew how to be of use to myself, I had a very strong desire to further the progress of others: a most common temptation of beginners.' And loving her father so much, 'I longed,' she says, 'to see him in the possession of that good which I seemed to derive myself from prayer.' She thought 'that in this life there could not be a greater good than prayer,' and so 'contrived to make him enter upon it,' giving him books for that purpose. 'He made so great a progress,' she says, 'that I used to praise our Lord for it.'

Nor was he the only person whom she led, even in these early days, to a life of interior communion with God; 'though,' she writes, 'I was walking in vanity myself. When I saw persons fond of reciting their prayers, I showed them how to make a meditation, and helped them and gave them books; for from the time I began myself to pray, as I said before, I always had a desire that others should serve God.'[1]

But now that she had given up the practice herself, she could not endure that her father should come to her to

[1] *Vida*, c. vii. 21.

confer on such matters; for 'it pained me,' she tells us, 'to see him so deceived as to think that I used to pray to God as before. So I told him that I did not pray; but I did not tell him why. I put my infirmities forward as my excuse.'[1] She told him that it was as much as she could do to perform her duties in choir, though that was not 'sufficient reason for giving up a practice which does not require, of necessity, bodily strength, but only love and a habit thereof.' 'And in sickness itself, and amidst other hindrances, true prayer consists, when the soul loves, in offering up its burden, and in thinking of Him for whom it suffers, and in the resignation of the will.'[2]

Her father accepted the reason she gave him for her change of habit, and was only sorry for her; but his death was soon after (in 1541) to be the means of bringing her back to her former devotions.

She went to nurse him, 'more sick in spirit than he was in body;' and believed that she 'rendered him some service in return for what he had suffered' in hers. Indeed, all through life, whatever her own feelings might be, she seems by her very presence to have been a stay and strength to others; and now she concealed her own grief to help her father, reminding him, when suffering from acute pain in the shoulders, of how he had ever devoutly adored our Lord carrying the Cross on His shoulders, and telling him that perhaps our Lord previously wished him to 'feel somewhat of that pain which He then suffered Himself.' After that he did not complain. For three days he became unconscious, but fully recovered his faculties, and bade his children 'serve God always, and consider how all things come to an end.' He died while repeating the Creed. 'It seemed as

---

[1] *Vida*, c. vii. 18.   [2] Ibid. 19.

if my very soul were wrenched asunder,' Teresa writes, ' when
I saw him at the point of death—my love for him was so
deep.' And she speaks of 'losing all the comfort and good
of life' in losing him.

His confessor, F. Vicente Barron, was 'a most learned
Dominican,' and ' a very good man.' To him Teresa confessed, and ' by degrees, beginning to speak to him,' told
him of her way of prayer. He charged her never to omit
it, and, she says, ' took upon himself the task of helping my
soul in earnest, and of making me see the perilous state I
was in.' So she began to return to her former prayer, and
never again gave it up.

Still she halted between two ways,—not giving up the
one thing which she felt hindered communion with God ; so
that she writes, 'my life became most wretched, because I
learned in prayer more and more of my faults.' God would
have all her great heart for Himself, and she suffered much
in prayer, for she was not able, she tells us, ' to shut myself
up within myself—that was my whole method of prayer—
without shutting up with me a thousand vanities at the same
time.' She was troubled ' either when, wasting time with
seculars, she heard a voice within herself complaining of her
neglect of God, or when, in her oratory communing with
God, mind and heart wandered away to profane confabula-
tions and affections.' [1]

The marvel is, as she herself says, how ' anyone could
have borne it without abandoning either the one or the
other. I know well that it was not in my power then to
give up prayer, because He held me in His hand who
sought me that He might show me greater mercies.' The
greatness of God's graces bestowed on her distressed her,

[1] *Acta Sanct.* tom. vii. Oct. § vii. 102.

knowing she was keeping back something from Him. 'O my King,' she exclaims, 'Thou didst administer to me the most delicate and painful chastisement it was possible for me to bear; for Thou knewest well what would have given me the most pain. *Thou didst chastise my sins with great consolations.*' [1]

She exhorts those who are entering on a life of prayer to form friendships and converse familiarly with others who are doing the same thing; advising them not to use too great religious reserve through fear of vain glory, since there is always danger of it in every good work, which yet 'must not be omitted through fear of vain-glory.' For herself she says 'it seems to me that if I had had anyone with whom I could have spoken of all this, it might have helped me not to fall. I might, at least, have been ashamed before him, and yet I was not ashamed before God. . . . . Of myself I may say that, if our Lord had not revealed to me this truth, and given me the opportunity of speaking very frequently to persons given to prayer, I should have gone on falling and rising till I tumbled into hell. I had many friends to help me to fall; but as to rising again, I was so much left to myself that I wonder now I was not always on the ground.' [2]

The next fourteen years (from 1541 to 1555) were the most spiritually suffering of her life. 'I passed nearly twenty years on this stormy sea,' she wrote, 'falling and rising, but rising to no good purpose, seeing that I went and fell again.' In another place she speaks of spending more than eighteen years 'in that strife and contention which arose out of my attempts to reconcile God and the world.' But as this inward strife came to an end in 1555, she

[1] *Vida,* c. vii. 28, 30.   [2] Ibid. 32, 33, 37.

must reckon the period of eighteen or twenty years during which it lasted as beginning with her very first essays in mental prayer, when she indeed loved it, but did not think it needful to give up for its sake intercourse which she also loved. And this was either in the autumn of 1535, when she was taken from the convent to her sister's house, or in the spring of 1536, when she went to Bezedas for her cure. It does not seem quite clear during which of these two journeys she went to her uncle's house, and received from him the book which at once determined her to 'make a beginning of that way of prayer,' with this book as her guide; 'for I had no master,' she says—'I mean, no confessor—who understood me, though I sought for such a one for twenty years afterwards.'

But whether this beginning of prayer was made in 1535 or 1536, the period from either date to 1555 would be the time which she speaks of as 'more than eighteen' and 'nearly twenty' years, during which, the Bollandists say, 'she halted between two sides, accommodating herself by turns to God and to man, giving herself wholly to neither.' Her severe illness and enforced seclusion occupied, however, the first three or four years of this period—until 1539; and on her recovery, as we have seen, she gave up mental prayer for 'a year and more.' Now she had resumed it, never again to let it go; but as she did not let go the distractions which hindered her, she had no comfort in her prayer. If she had had a competent spiritual guide, it would probably have been far otherwise with her, but the very docility of a really great nature was a source of fresh discomfort to her, since she could not shut her ears to the voice of conscience; and yet 'neither could I,' she says, 'entirely believe that those things which my confessors did not make so much of were so wrong as I in my soul felt them to be.'

She describes her life as the most painful 'that can be imagined, because I had no sweetness in God, and no pleasure in the world. When I was in the midst of the pleasures of the world, the remembrance of what I owed to God made me sad; and when I was praying to God, my worldly affections disturbed me. This is so painful a struggle, that I know not how I could have borne it for a month, let alone for so many years. Nevertheless I can trace distinctly the great mercy of our Lord to me, while thus immersed in the world, in that I had still the courage to pray. . . . I may speak of that which I know by experience; and so I say, let him never cease from prayer who has once begun it, be his life ever so wicked; for prayer is the way to amend it, and without prayer such amendment will be much more difficult. Let him not be tempted by Satan, as I was, to give it up, on the pretence of humility; let him rather believe that His words are true who says that, if we truly repent, and resolve never to offend Him, He will take us into His favour again, give us the graces He gave us before, and occasionally even greater, if our repentance deserve it.'[1]

'Oh, that I knew how to describe the captivity of my soul in those days!' she exclaims. 'I understood perfectly that I was in captivity, but I could not understand the nature of it.'[2] She needed help to make her break once for all with the obstacle which kept her back, and she received only hindrance from those who should have guided her. One of her confessors, she says, 'told me that, even if I were raised to high contemplation, those occasions and

[1] *Vida*, c. viii. 2, 6.   [2] Ibid. 15.

conversations were not unfitting for me.' Her discernment in spiritual things was plainly in advance of that of her directors; for, she adds, 'when they saw my good desires, and how I occupied myself in prayer, I seemed to them to have done much; but my soul knew that this was not doing what I was bound to do for Him to whom I owed so much. I am sorry for my poor soul even now, because of its great sufferings, and the little help it had from anyone except God, and for the wide door that men opened for it, that it might go forth to its pastimes and pleasures, when they said that these things were lawful.'[1]

Still she persevered. Through suffering, through aridity, through imperfections, through ill advice, through her own inconsistencies and resistance to concience—still she held fast to prayer. God had said to her heart, 'Seek My face;' and her heart said unto Him, 'Thy face, Lord, will I seek.' 'Very often, for some years,' she writes, ' I was more occupied with the wish to see the end of the time I had appointed for myself to spend in prayer, and in watching the hour-glass, than with other thoughts that were good. If a sharp penance had been laid upon me, I know of none that I would not very often have willingly undertaken, rather than prepare myself for prayer by self-recollection. . . . The sadness I felt on entering the oratory was so great, that it required all the courage I had to force myself in. They say of me that my courage is not slight, and it is known that God has given me a courage beyond that of a woman; but I have made a bad use of it. In the end, our Lord came to my help; and then, when I had done this violence to myself, I found greater peace and joy than I sometimes had when I had a desire to pray.'[2]

[1] *Vida*, c. viii. 16.   [2] Ibid. 10.

In this manner, 'now dry, now bedewed with divine consolations, she passed her days.'[1] 'I sought for help, but it must be that I did not understand how all is of little profit if we do not root out all confidence in ourselves, and place it wholly in God. I wished to live, but I saw clearly that I was not living, but rather wrestling with the shadow of death; there was no one to give me life, and I was not able to take it. He who could have given it me had good reasons for not coming to my aid, seeing that He had brought me back to Himself so many times, and I as often had left Him.'[2]

'My soul was now grown weary,' she writes. But the time of refreshing was at hand. Going one day into the oratory, where so many hours of persevering prayer had been passed, she saw a picture which had been put by there, after having been used during 'a certain feast observed in the house.' 'It was,' she tells us, 'a representation of Christ most grievously wounded; and so devotional, that the very sight of it, when I saw it, moved me, so well did it show forth that which He suffered for us. So keenly did I feel the evil return I had made for those wounds, that I thought my heart was breaking. I threw myself on the ground beside it, my tears flowing plenteously, and implored Him to strengthen me once for all, so that I might never offend Him any more.'[3]

Only love could entirely subdue a heart like hers, absorbing the love of anything which could offend Him; and from this time a desire 'to withdraw from the occasions of sin' began to grow within her; and she says, 'as soon as I had done so, I turned lovingly to His Majesty at once. . . .

---

[1] *Acta Sanct.* § viii. 120.   [2] *Vida*, c. viii. 18.
[3] Ibid. c. ix. 1.

Entire Conversion.

I do not think I had yet perfectly disposed myself to seek His service when His Majesty turned towards me with His consolations.'[1]

Often before this, during the weary years that were gone, she used to think of the conversion of the Magdalene, longing for such love as hers, especially at Communion. 'As I knew for certain,' she tells us, 'that our Lord was then within me, I used to place myself at His feet, thinking that my tears would not be despised. I did not know what I was saying; only He did great things for me, in that He was pleased I should shed those tears, seeing that I so soon forgot that impression. . . . But this last time, before that picture of which I am speaking, I seem to have made greater progress, for I was now very distrustful of myself, placing all my confidence in God.'[2]

At this time also the 'Confessions of St. Augustine' were given to her. Their influence upon her has already been mentioned; and she says, 'I used to find great comfort in those saints whom, after they had sinned, our Lord converted to Himself. I thought they would help me, and that, as our Lord had forgiven them, so also He would forgive me. One thing, however, there was that troubled me—I have spoken of it before: our Lord had called them but once, and they never relapsed, while my relapses were now so many. This it was that vexed me. But calling to mind the love that He bore me, I took courage again. Of His mercy I never doubted once, but I did very often of myself. O my God, I am amazed at the hardness of my heart amidst so many succours from Thee! I am filled with dread when I see how little I could do with myself, and how I was clogged, so that I could not resolve to give myself entirely to God.'[3]

---
[1] *Vida*, c. ix. 10.   [2] Ibid. 2, 3.   [3] Ibid. 8, 9.

But now she had finally resolved to forsake all for His sake. 'God Himself,' she confesses, 'came to my aid, and helped me to turn away from them.' At this point of her history she writes, 'Henceforth it is another and a new book,—I mean, another and a new life. Hitherto my life was my own; my life since . . . is the life which God lived in me,—so it seems to me; for I feel it to be impossible that I should have escaped in so short a time from ways and works that were so wicked. May our Lord be praised, Who has delivered me from myself.'[1]

'Thus was she brought forth into a place of liberty; He brought her forth, even because He had a favour unto her. Royal-hearted, she turned once for all from whatever might come between her soul and Him—if perchance her eyes might even on earth see the King in His beauty, might behold the land that is very far away. She had said, speaking of that fervent prayer in her oratory, 'It seems to me that I said to Him then that I would not rise up till He granted my petition.' She had wrestled with the 'Traveller unknown,' the Angel of Great Counsel, and had conquered.

> In vain Thou strugglest to get free,
>   I never will unloose my hold;
> Art Thou the Man that died for me?
>   The secret of Thy love unfold.
> Wrestling, I will not let Thee go
> Till I Thy Name, Thy Nature know.
>
> Yield to me now, for I am weak,
>   But confident in self-despair;
> Speak to my heart, in blessings speak;
>   Be conquered by my instant prayer!
> Speak, or Thou never hence shalt move,
> And tell me if Thy Name be Love?

[1] *Vida*, c. xxiii. 1.

'Tis Love! 'tis Love! Thou diedst for me!
  I hear Thy whisper in my heart!
The morning breaks, the shadows flee;
  Pure universal Love Thou art!
To me, to all, Thy bowels move;
Thy Nature and Thy Name is Love!

My prayer hath power with God; the grace
  Unspeakable I now receive;
Through faith I see Thee face to face,
  I see Thee face to face, and live:
In vain I have not wept and strove;
Thy Nature and Thy Name is Love.

Chapter the Fourth.

*Ya, Jesus, mi corason
No sabe mas de llorar ;
Que le ha convertido en mar,
El mar de vuestra pasion.*   LOPE DE VEGA.

ALTHOUGH, as we have seen, old things had passed away,—that henceforth Teresa stood fast in the liberty wherewith she had been made free,—yet this new era in her life was marked in its beginning by fresh trials,—doubts, chiefly suggested from without by well-meaning friends, as to the source and reality of the graces wherewith God enriched her soul.

But in order to understand these trials, and her subsequent history, it is necessary to pause, and to examine, if it be possible, what was that 'prayer,' of which she makes continual mention, and which is the key to all the sorrows and all the joys of her life,—to its trials, consolations, labours, strength—to all that she attempted or that she achieved.

And now, indeed, we are 'at the mouth of a labyrinth,' or rather, as one straining eye and ear when the skylark is pouring its full heart 'from heaven, or near it.' The painter-monk of San Marco prayed before he painted, and painted kneeling. Yet he expressed but the outer light—the beam cast upon the outward shape. And in himself that light and saintly grace burned so keenly that it is no marvel it was reflected upon his canvas; and that he should be alone and unapproachable in the special gift and inheritance which he has left to Christendom—the portraiture of the beauty of holiness shining in the lines of saintly forms, upon which he had himself looked steadfastly until he saw each face as it had been the face of an angel.

But—to try with weak utterance and faltering pen to express the inner life of such a one—of one who soared 'on seraph wings of ecstasy' far beyond the regions to which most attain—this would be a hopeless task, condemned at once by its own presumption, if it were attempted otherwise than by a reverent and careful selection and arrangement of her own words. Even thus it is a task full of difficulty for several reasons. There is, first, the great quantity of material to be dealt with. And there is also this difficulty, which is noticed both by the Bollandists and by Ribera, that her description of her way of prayer and interior life is scattered diffusely through her writings, mixed up with other matter, and often without method in the relation.

Besides, in spite of the candour and even childlike simplicity of St. Teresa's words, they are often 'dark with excess of light;' and the soul faints and wearies even in the attempt to dwell on the subjects of which she writes. Yet it is also allured and led on by the 'intensely human outpouring of affection, in its most diversified and purest forms, affection fastening itself with the most natural freshness and simplicity on things unseen; so exulting, yet so reverent; so tender, yet so strong, and manly, and severe; so frank and unconstrained in its fears and griefs and anxieties; so alive to its weakness, yet so willing to accept the discipline of affliction, and so confident of the love behind it.'

Still it must be remembered that in attempting any true sketch of Teresa de Ahumada we are passing from ordinary to extra-ordinary history, from that which can be proved, as we say, by common experience, to that incapable of such proof, because far above it. If it be permitted to quote noble words lately spoken, 'we have faculties which enable us to know the phenomena of sense and of the outward world. We have faculties different from them, which enable us to know the truths of mathematics. Have we anything else? . . . In music, in painting, in poetry, we say that we *know*. There are powers in human nature and in the human mind of dealing with these subjects, powers of the greatest activity and energy, most subtle and most delicate, yet most real, undoubting of themselves and undoubted in their effects, of which no one makes any question; *certain* within limits of what they know and do, but which yet in their tests of certainty are absolutely different from mathematical or physical knowledge, and absolutely impatient of the verifications which are indispensable in sensible and mathematical proof. As a man might be the greatest physicist and the greatest mathematician, while all their marvellous regions were to him absolutely a blank; though his mind was one to which, say music, its meaning and its laws, were absolutely incomprehensible, the most impossible of puzzles. He might not know a false note in music from a true one; he might be utterly unable to see the difference between what is noble and base in it, or to distinguish the greatest work of Handel or Beethoven from any other collection of sounds. And yet the musician *knows*: he knows the glory and the truth, and the ordered perfection of which he speaks. . . . The world of music is a most real world; man has faculties for reading it and judging of it; and the evidences of its reality are in the domain of fact and history.'

'Is there in human nature such a faculty, separate from the faculties by which we judge of the things of sense and the abstractions of the pure intellect, but yet a true and trustworthy faculty, for knowing God—for knowing God in some such way as we know the spirits and souls, half disclosed, half concealed under the mask and garment of the flesh, among whom we have been brought up, among whom we live? Can we know Him in such a true sense as we know those whom we love and those whom we dislike; those whom we venerate and trust, and those whom we fear and shrink from? Is there a faculty in the human soul for knowing its Maker and God—knowing Him, though behind the veil—knowing Him, though flesh and blood can never see Him—knowing Him, though the questioning intellect loses itself in the thought of Him?'[1]

'That I may know Him, and the power of His resurrection, and the fellowship of His sufferings;' these words are the key to St. Teresa's spiritual history; nay, her life, her words, her work are contained in them. There are two Books of Holy Scripture continually in our mind as we read her writings—the Psalms and the Epistles of St. Paul. She had realized, as few have done, the great idea which the Psalms, in manifold tones, express; the idea that the soul 'can have secret yet real access, everywhere, every moment, to Infinite compassion, Infinite loving-kindness, Infinite and all-sufficing goodness, to whom, as into the heart of the tenderest of friends, it could pour out its distresses, before whom, as before the feet of a faithful Comforter and Guide, it could lay down the burden of its care and commit its way.'

[1] Dean Church, *Sacred Poetry of Early Religions*.

Ribera, who was her confessor, says in his 'Life' of her, 'I will not follow my own imaginations, nor torture my ingenuity, nor report exaggerations concerning things which I never saw, nor such things as spiritual men, treating of this subject, desire to see; but I will simply relate those things which the great Lord gave to be seen in this holy virgin, and which we ourselves knew and saw in familiar intercourse with her. . . . And I think it will be pleasing and useful for all to describe in this place those steps by which He led her to that highest kind of prayer to which she attained.'[1]

> O luce eterna, che sola in Te sidi,
> Sola T' intendi, e da Te intelletta,
> Ed intendente Te ami ed arridi,

dost Thou yet desire that mortal man should know and love Thee, and in Thee find beatification!

Long before the 'new life' had begun in Teresa—the life which she is not afraid to say 'God lived in me'—she had had what she calls 'certain commencements' of it. She tells us, 'When I formed those pictures within myself of throwing myself at the feet of Christ . . . and sometimes even when I was reading, a feeling of the presence of God would come over me unexpectedly, so that I could in no wise doubt either that He was within me, or that I was wholly absorbed in Him. It was not by way of vision. . . . The will loves; the memory, so it seems to me, is as it were lost; and the understanding, so I think, makes no reflections—yet is not lost: . . . it is not at work, but it stands as if amazed at the greatness of the things it understands; for God wills it to understand that it understands nothing whatever of that which His Majesty places before it.'[2]

[1] *Ribera*, lib. iv. c. i. 10.   [2] *Vida* c. x. 1.

Ribera says that her life of prayer began when she received from her uncle the 'Terca Abecedario;' but it is perplexing to find one whose childhood had been devout, and who had entered a religious order, speaking of herself as not having 'prayed' hitherto: afterwards she speaks of leaving off 'prayer.' What we should gather from many passages in her works is that she had been entirely in the habit of using vocal prayers; and, though doubtless in a devout spirit, without so using them with heart and all powers of soul and mind as to turn them into mental prayer. This, indeed, it would have been hardly possible for her to do, since she tells us that she did not understand the Latin of the Divine Offices, which according to her rule she recited. And the recital of prayers, however carefully done, she does not call 'praying,' and therefore speaks of herself as having given up prayer, though fulfilling all prescribed devotions of her rule.

There are many ways of praying, short of high experiences, which we are used to think of as food for the soul, and which doubtless are so. We may follow common prayer with others, speaking to God with soul and intelligence, as well as with lips and intention—making the words of others our own by hearty lifting of the soul to God; what we think of, in short, as the opposite of 'wandering' in church. Or we may do the same with prayers we say out of a book at home. Or, even without previous meditation, we may pray to God out of our hearts, telling Him what we want either in words which come at the moment, or without words.

But certainly of the two first ways of praying there is no recognition in St. Teresa's 'Life'; the impression which on the whole remains is, that though fulfilling devoutly public offices of religion, she did not in them find communion of the soul with God (at least not until after she had mastered the science of mental prayer), probably, for one reason, because she did not always attach a definite meaning to the words she was using. For Ribera, speaking on this subject, says: 'Although vocal prayer be one thing, which is said by the mouth, and mental another, which is accomplished by the intellect and will, without the voice, yet if vocal prayer be what it ought, mental is included in it; since he who speaks with God ought to consider with Whom he is speaking, and Who it is that Himself speaks, in order that he may know fully after what manner he ought to bear himself towards so great a Lord, and converse with Him. On these two points very much depends.'[1] And though she speaks of the advantages of using a book in private, it seems to have been as spiritual reading, as something to lead to prayer, not as contenting herself by using the words of others to speak to God.

She says indeed that in the beginning a book was 'all her comfort;' 'for God never endowed me with the gift of making reflections with the understanding, or with that of using the imagination to any good purpose: my imagination is so sluggish, that even if I would think of, or picture to myself, as I used to labour to picture, our Lord's Humanity, I never could do it.'[2] She seems to have passed at once from the use of devoutly recited forms of prayer to high communion of the soul with God, although, as we have seen, this communion was for nearly twenty years, more or less, interrupted and overclouded. But she had 'spent nearly nine months in the practice of solitude,' when she received the book which became her teacher, and says that even then 'our Lord began to comfort me so much in this

---

[1] *Ribera*, lib. iv. c. iv. 74.   [2] *Vida*, c. iv. 10.

way of prayer, as in His mercy to raise me to the prayer of quiet, and now and then to that of union, though I understood not what either the one or the other was, nor the great esteem I ought to have had of them. It is true that the prayer of union lasted but a short time: I know not if it continued for the space of an *Ave Maria*; but the fruits of it remained; and they were such that, though I was not then twenty years of age, I seemed to despise the world utterly.'[1]

Here, in the very beginning, she touches at once upon 'mystical theology;' yet all her relations of high states of prayer are mingled with such simple and childlike sentiments, that it cannot be unprofitable to try to understand something of what God did for her soul. It must be remembered that all she wrote of her own experiences was at the command of her superiors. 'I speak from my own experience,' she says, when entering upon the subject, 'as I have been commanded; and if what I say be not correct, let him[2] to whom I send it destroy it, for he knows better than I do what is wrong in it. I entreat him, from the love of my Lord, to publish abroad what I have thus far said of my wretched life, and of my sins. I give him leave to do so; and to all my confessors also,—of whom he is one. . . . But as to that which I am now going to say, I give no such leave; nor, if it be shown to anyone, do I consent to its being said who the person is whose experience it describes, nor who wrote it. . . . I have, as it were, to steal the time, and that with difficulty, because my writing hinders me from spinning. . . . If, then, I should say anything that is right, our Lord will have it said for some good purpose; that which is wrong will be mine, and your reverence will strike it out.'[3]

[1] *Vida*, c. iv. 9.   [2] F. Ybañez.   [3] *Vida*, c. x. 10, 11.

'So then,' she continues, 'everything here beyond the simple story of my life your reverence must take upon yourself,—since you have so pressed me to give some account of the graces which our Lord bestowed upon me in prayer, —if it be consistent with the truths of our holy Catholic faith; if it be not, your reverence must burn it at once,—for I give my consent.'[1]

She, whose 'Life' was to become a Spanish classic, seems not to have had any consciousness of her own literary ability. 'It is enough that I am a woman,' she wrote, 'to make my sails droop : how much more, then, when I am a woman, and a wicked one? . . . If indeed our Lord had given me greater abilities and a better memory, I might then profit by what I have seen and read ; but my abilities are very slight.'[2] Ribera tells us, however, that she used to wish she could write with four hands at once instead of with one, so slow did the process of writing seem to the overflowing heart and brain.

Perhaps it will be best to take her own kind of parable to help us to distinguish, in some measure, the different conditions of which she writes. She says herself : 'How clear soever I may wish to make my account of that which relates to prayer, it will be obscure enough for those who are without experience. . . . I shall have to make use of a comparison ; I should like to avoid it, because I am a woman, and write simply what I have been commanded. But this language of spirituality is so difficult of utterance for those who are not learned, and such am I. . . . Your reverence will be amused when you see my stupidity.'[3]

She then goes on to say that a beginner must look upon himself as making a garden, wherein our Lord may take His

[1] *Vida*, c. x. 13. [2] Ibid. 11. [3] Ibid. c. xi. 9.

delight,—that the soil abounds in weeds and is unfruitful, but that our Lord roots up the weeds and plants good herbs,—that this is already done when a soul is determined to give itself to prayer and has begun to practise it,—and that our part is, as good gardeners, 'by the help of God, to see that the plants grow, to water them carefully, that they may not die, but produce blossoms, which shall send forth much fragrance, refreshing to our Lord; so that He may come often for His pleasure into this garden, and delight Himself in the midst of these virtues.'[1]

'Let us now see,' she continues, 'how this garden is to be watered, that we may understand what we have to do.... It seems to me that the garden may be watered in four ways: by water taken out of a well, which is very laborious; or with water raised by means of an engine and buckets, drawn by a windlass,—I have drawn it this way sometimes,—it is a less troublesome way than the first, and gives more water; or by a stream or brook, whereby the garden is watered in a much better way,—for the soil is more thoroughly saturated, and there is no necessity to water it so often, and the labour of the gardener is much less; or by showers of rain, when our Lord Himself waters it, without labour on our part,—and this way is incomparably better than all the others of which I have spoken.'[2]

'The water that I shall give him shall be in him a well of water springing up into everlasting life.' Ribera says that St. Teresa used to insist much, *et quidem acriter ac vehementer*, on the importance of firmly and generously determining with oneself not to rest until that water of life which God gives, is given us to drink, 'for by this name she calls supernatural prayer, which we cannot procure for ourselves

[1] *Vida,* c. xi. 10.   [2] Ibid. 11.

by our own industry and diligence, although for the rest she was not ignorant that whatever kind of prayer is acceptable is a supernatural work.'[1]

She compares these 'four ways of irrigation by which the garden is to be maintained,' to four degrees of prayer. 'Of those who are beginners in prayer, we may say that they are those who draw the water up out of the well,—a process which, as I have said, is very laborious; for they must be wearied in keeping the senses recollected, and this is a great labour, because the senses have hitherto been accustomed to distractions. It is necessary for beginners to accustom themselves to disregard what they hear or see, and to put it away from them during the time of prayer. . . . They must strive to meditate on the life of Christ, and the understanding is wearied thereby. . . . This is beginning to draw water up out of the well. God grant there may be water in it! That, however, does not depend on us; we are drawing it, and doing what we can towards watering the flowers. So good is God, that when, for reasons known to His Majesty,—perhaps for our greater good,—it is His will the well should be dry, He Himself preserves the flowers without water, —we, like good gardeners, doing what lies in our power,— and makes our virtues grow. By water here I mean tears; and if there be none, then tenderness and an inward feeling of devotion.'[2]

'What, then, will he do here who sees that, for many days, he is conscious only of aridity, disgust, dislike, and so great an unwillingness to go to the well for water, that he would give it up altogether, if he did not remember that he has to please and serve the Lord of the garden? . . . He must rejoice to take comfort, and consider it as the greatest

[1] *Ribera*, lib. iv. c. iv. [2] *Vida*, c. xi. 13, 14.

CH. IV. *Desire to glorify God by Prayer.* 63

favour to labour in the garden of so great an Emperor; . . . his purpose must be not to please himself, but Him, . . . let him help Him to carry the cross, and let him think how He carried it all His life long; let him not seek his kingdom here, nor ever intermit his prayer; and so let him resolve, if this aridity should last even his whole life long, never to let Christ fall down beneath the cross.'[1]

Words worthy of her who had found the true motive for prayer, not in the sweetness which it brought to her, but in the glory which it brought to God,—in helping her Lord to bear His cross! Words well befitting her whose 'love was so immense, that though she thought herself imperfect in other things, yet she was ever conscious of being borne into God by ardent love (*se in Deum ardenti amore ferri*): and this grew from day to day. She used to say that she should exult to see others gifted in Heaven with greater glory than herself, but she did not know if she could rejoice to know that another loved God more than she did.'[2]

'The time will come when he shall be paid once for all,' she continues, speaking of those who persevere in prayer through aridity. 'Let him have no fear that his labour is in vain: he serves a good Master, whose eyes are upon him.... These labours have their reward. I know it, for I am one who underwent them for many years. When I drew but one drop of water out of this blessed well, I considered it was a mercy of God. I know these labours are very great, and require, I think, greater courage than many others in this world; but I have seen clearly that God does not leave them without a recompense, even in this life; for it is very certain that in one hour, during which our Lord gave me to taste His sweetness, all the anxieties which I had to bear when

[1] *Vida*, c. xi. 15, 16.   [2] *Ribera*, lib. iv. c. iv. 101.

persevering in prayer seem to me ever afterwards perfectly rewarded.'[1]

She dwells at great length, in writing of this first degree of prayer, on the duty of not caring much whether sweetness and tenderness fail the soul, saying that those who are content to be without them have already travelled a great part of the road; and that she believes our Lord frequently sends these trials 'to try those who love Him, and to ascertain if they will drink the chalice, and help Him to carry the cross, before He intrusts them with His greater treasures.' She says that when God gives the wish to converse with Him in solitude, 'the greater part of the work is done. Give praise to His Majesty for it, and trust in His goodness Who has never failed those who love Him. Close the eyes of your imagination, and do not ask why He gives devotion to this person in so short a time, and none to me after so many years. . . . He shows us mercy enough when it is His pleasure we should be willing to dig in His garden, and to be so near the Lord of it. He certainly is near to us. . . . It is certain that the love of God does not consist in tears, nor in this sweetness and tenderness which we for the most part desire, and with which we console ourselves; but rather in serving Him in justice, fortitude, and humility. That seems to me to be a receiving rather than a giving of anything on our part.'[2] She speaks in this place of the consolations she had received as having been necessary for one so 'weak and infirm of purpose;' adding, 'but when the servants of God, who are men of weight, learning, and sense, make so much account, as I see they do, whether God gives them sweetness in devotion or not, I am disgusted when I listen to them.'[3]

The remarkable common sense with which she treats

[1] *Vida*, c. xi. 17.   [2] Ibid. 19, 20.   [3] Ibid. 21.

the most mystical subjects causes her to dwell at length on the frequent confusion made between *feelings* and the will, saying that people are 'distressed, thinking they are doing nothing; the understanding ceases from its acts, and they cannot bear it. Yet perhaps at that very time the will is feeding and gathering strength, and they know it not.'[1] She insists upon the truth that what God seeks in us is the resolution to be always thinking of Him and loving Him; and also that the apparent want of profit from prayer often is caused by bodily indisposition. 'I have had very great experience in the matter,' she writes, 'and I know it is true . . . for we are so wretched, that this poor prisoner of a soul shares in the miseries of the body. The change of the seasons and the alterations of the humours very often compel it, without fault of its own, not to do what it would, but rather to suffer in every way.'[2] Her opinion was that 'the more we force the soul on these occasions, the greater the mischief and the longer it lasts. Some discretion must be used, in order to ascertain whether ill health be the occasion or not. . . . Let those who thus suffer understand that they are ill; a change should be made in the hour of prayer, and oftentimes that change should be continued for some days. . . . It is very often the misery of one that loves God to see itself living in such wretchedness, unable to do what it would, because it has to keep so evil a guest as the body.'[3]

'Take care, then, of the body, for the love of God,' is her advice, and also that the soul should not be tormented 'to the doing of that which is out of its power;' adding, that 'no one should distress himself on account of aridities, or because his thoughts are restless and distracted; neither

[1] *Vida,* c. xi. 22.   [2] Ibid. 23.   [3] Ibid.

should he be afflicted thereat, if he would attain to liberty of spirit, and not be always in trouble.'[1] Her natural greatness of mind and unselfishness purified by grace made her unselfish and great-minded in prayer; seeing the obstacles and difficulties in the way in their true light, as hindrances which would change into helps if rightly regarded. She said that prayer was the royal road to heaven, and that a great treasure was provided for those who walked in it, and yet that for a very little we choose to stop short in it; although the time will come when it will be manifest that what we weigh against so precious a thing—is nothing.[2] She compared a soul living without mental prayer to one whose body is paralysed, and who has no use of hands or feet, although possessing those members; and in like manner she says that certain souls are sick and ill affected, so that of themselves they cannot walk, although richly gifted by nature, and able to converse with God. And that such souls, if they do not sedulously watch and will not be cured of their disease, are changed as it were into statues of salt.[3]

In thus describing the 'beginnings of devotion,' St. Teresa says we are able in some degree to help ourselves by thinking of, and pondering on, the sufferings of our Lord for our sake. She advises the soul which God does not raise to a higher state than this 'not to try to rise of itself,' but to 'remain in His presence continually, and to speak to Him; pray to Him in its necessities, and complain to Him of its troubles; be merry with Him in its joys, and yet not forget Him because of its joys.'[4] She speaks strongly against a kind of pride in seeking to ascend higher

---

[1] *Vida*, c. xi. 25.   [2] *Via Perf.* cap. xxi.
[3] *Mansiones*, l. c. i. (quoted by Ribera).   [4] *Vida*, c. xii. 3.

of ourselves, saying that the foundation of the whole building of prayer being humility, 'the nearer we draw unto God, the more this virtue should grow; if it does not, everything is lost.' With her usual clear-sighted sense she warns against the attempt to bring about of ourselves that suspension of the mental faculties upon which the Quietists were inclined to insist as the condition of true communion with God. She knew well what that true suspension is, when 'the understanding ceases from its acts, because God suspends it;' but she knew also that any attempt to fancy or force ourselves into this condition would be unreal and mischievous.[1] 'This is what I say must not be done,' she writes, 'for in that case we shall be stupid and cold, and the result will be neither the one nor the other. For when our Lord suspends the understanding, and makes it cease from its acts, He puts before it that which astonishes and occupies it. . . . To have the powers of the mind occupied, and to think that you can keep them at the same time quiet, is folly. . . . Again I repeat my advice: it is of great moment not to raise our spirit ourselves, if our Lord does not raise it for us; and if He does, there can be no mistaking it. For women it is specially wrong, because the devil can delude them,—though I am certain our Lord will never allow him to hurt anyone who labours to draw men unto God in humility.'[2]

[1] 'God alone can and may bid the reason to be silent in time of prayer. He endowed the soul with powers, in order that they might be used so long as He grants free disposal of them; and it is a false and heretical doctrine of Molinos, that man ought to annihilate them himself, may reduce them, that is, to inaction. Inaction, thus produced, would render us a prey to every freak of the imagination, and every delusion of the heart.'—From *Maximes Spirituelles*, by Père Grou.

[2] *Vida*, c. xii. 8, 9, 12.

Before going on to speak of what she calls the second degree of prayer, St. Teresa enlarges at some length on the trials, difficulties, and dangers of beginners, and especially on the necessity of humility, courage, and distrust of self. 'His Majesty seeks and loves courageous souls,' she writes, 'but they must be humble in their ways, and have no confidence in themselves.' She says that she derived profit from that saying of St. Augustine: 'Give me, O Lord, what Thou commandest, and command what Thou wilt;' and also from 'thinking how St. Peter lost nothing by throwing himself into the sea, though he was afterwards afraid.' She had courageously cast herself on the great sea of mental prayer, leaving all, if only on the midnight ocean she might approach nearer to her Lord; and she tries with tender earnestness to help others who, seeing the wind boisterous, might be afraid, and might sink in the waves which, trodden in faith and humility, would surely uphold their feet. She warns them against the false humility which would make the wish to imitate the saints seem presumptuous, exhorting them to strive after generous desires. 'Our hearts,' she says, 'are so mean that we think the earth would fail us under our feet, if we were to cease to care even for a moment for the body, and give ourselves up to spirituality. Then we think that to have all we require contributes to recollection, because anxieties disturb prayer. It is painful to me that our confidence in God is so scanty, and our self-love so strong, as that any anxiety about our own necessities should disturb us.'[1] Such anxiety, she considers, betrays the desire 'that we may not miss our ease in this world, and yet have the fruition of God in the next.' 'And so it will be,' she continues, 'if we walk according to justice, clinging

[1] *Vida*, c. xiii. 6.

CH. IV. *Courage and Generosity in Prayer.* 69

to virtue; but it is the pace of a hen—it will never bring us to liberty of spirit.'[1]

She also strongly warns against over-anxiety as to health, saying that when Satan sees us a little anxious about it, 'he wants nothing more to convince us that our way of life must kill us, and destroy our health.' She had passed herself through this temptation, but says her health had been much better since she ceased to look after her ease and comforts. Another temptation of beginners is the desire to teach others, and lead them in the way of mental prayer, before they are themselves endowed with solid virtues. This, she tells us, was a fault in herself, causing temptation to others; 'for, on the one hand, they heard me say great things of the blessedness of prayer, and, on the other, saw how poor I was in virtue, notwithstanding my prayers.'[2]

She advises those who can make use of the understanding in meditation not to spend the whole time in that way; but to pause in their use of the intellect, giving it 'a Sunday or a time when no work ought to be done,' to 'place themselves in the presence of Christ, and, without fatiguing the understanding, converse with Him, and in Him rejoice, without wearying themselves in searching out reasons.'[3] She reminds them also that whatever graces have been given to them, they must never forget self-examination, 'for there is no soul so great a giant on this road but has frequent need to turn back, and be again an infant at the breast. . . . The knowledge of our sins and of our own selves is the bread which we have to eat with all the meats, however delicate they may be, in the way of prayer.'[4] And the subject to which all should turn again and again for meditation is 'the

[1] *Vida*, c. xiii. 7. [2] Ibid. 11.
[3] Ibid. 17. [4] Ibid. 23.

Passion and Life of Christ, the Source of all good that ever came, and that ever shall come.'[1]

Our own sins and the merciful and dearly-bought remedy for those sins—these are the two subjects to which one so profoundly versed in spiritual love as St. Teresa would have us ever return and dwell upon. She often mentions our Lord bound to the pillar as a subject for mental prayer, and says that in such a meditation 'it is well we should make reflections for a time, and consider the sufferings He there endured, for whom He endured them, Who He is Who endured them, and the love with which He bore them. . . . But a person should not always fatigue himself in making these reflections . . . let him employ himself in looking upon Christ, Who is looking upon him . . . let him humble himself, and delight himself in Christ, and keep in mind that He never deserved to be there.'[2]

St. Teresa had suffered too much herself from inexperience in her directors not to caution beginners against dangers from this cause. Prudence, experience, and learning are the three qualities which she considers necessary in a spiritual guide if he is not to do more harm than good. Learning she especially insists upon, saying that even if a learned director have not much experience in mental prayer himself, he will be a far safer guide than a silly and unlearned director who should pretend to more spirituality. For as she says, with one of her sharp touches of common sense, 'a spirituality, the foundations of which are not resting upon the truth, I would rather were not accompanied with prayer. . . . Every Christian should continue to be guided by a learned director if he can, and the more learned the better. They who walk in the way of prayer have the greater need

---

[1] *Vida*, c. xiii. 20.   [2] Ibid. 31.

Learning in Spiritual Guides.

of learning, and the more spiritual they are, the greater is that need. Let them not say that learned men not given to prayer are not fit counsellors for those who pray :[1] that is a delusion. I have conversed with many ; and now for some years I have sought them the more, because of my greater need of them. I have always been fond of them, for though some of them have no experience, they do not dislike spirituality, neither are they ignorant of what it is, because in the sacred writings with which they are familiar they always find the truth about spirituality. I am certain myself that a person given to prayer, who treats of these matters with learned men, unless he is deceived with his own consent, will never be carried away by any illusions of the devil. . . . Blessed be Thou, O Lord, who hast made me so incapable and so useless ; but I bless Thee still more for this—that Thou quickenest so many to quicken us. Our prayer must therefore be very earnest for those who give us light. What should we be without them in the midst of these violent storms which now disturb the Church ? May it please our Lord to hold them in His hand, and help them that they may help us.'[2]

[1] It must be remembered that St. Teresa is here speaking of the practice of *mental* prayer.
[2] *Vida*, c. xiii. 24, 26, 30.

Chapter the Fifth.

A thousand liveried angels lackey her,
Driving far off each thing of sin and guilt;
And, in clear dream and solemn vision,
Tell her of things that no gross ear can hear.

MASQUE OF COMUS.

IN attempting to give any clear impression, however slight, of St. Teresa's spiritual history, we are continually met by the difficulty of omitting, of compressing into a space which may leave room for anything else, her own rich and discursive narrative. We feel as though vainly attempting to catch the song of the skylark and imprison it in a musical box. And this feeling increases as we pass to her account of the second state of prayer, which she likens to the 'machine of wheel and buckets, whereby the gardener may draw more water with less labour, and be able to take some rest without being continually at work.' She calls it 'the prayer of quiet,' and speaks of it as 'touching on the supernatural,' as 'a gathering together of the faculties of the soul within itself,' yet in such a way that those faculties 'are not lost, neither are they asleep; the will alone is occupied in such a way that, without knowing how it has become a captive, it gives a simple consent to become the prisoner of God; for it knows well what it is to be the captive of Him it loves.' She describes the memory and understanding as sometimes hindering the will at such times, 'like doves which are not satisfied with the food the master of the dovecot gives them without any labouring for it on their part, and which go forth in quest of it elsewhere, and so hardly find it that they come back.' We gather from her description of this 'oracion de quietud' that the soul is then, through the quiet of the will by God's grace, enjoying the fruition of that after which at other times it labours by previous use of memory and understanding; while the latter 'must be thinking that they are of some service to the will; and now and then the memory or the imagination, seeking to represent to it that of which it has the fruition, does it harm.'

Such words may seem too mystical; yet since memory and understanding must ordinarily be used in meditation as the means of feeding upon spiritual truths, it almost necessarily, and *naturally*, if we may here use such a word, follows, when it pleases God to feed the soul without such labour, and to hold it employed in pure adoration and contemplation (for which consent of the will only is needful), that the other powers of the soul should, from very habit, seek employment, not perceiving, as it were, that the end for which they are ordinarily used has been reached; and that they can but fold their wings unless they would trouble the soul. And so far this can be no uncommon experience, although not analysed, and often almost unconscious.

St. Teresa describes at length the great increase of spiritual insight gained at such seasons, and how easily the soul then acquires a true estimate of the sources of joy, losing the desire of earthly things. 'And no wonder,' she writes, 'for it sees clearly that, even for a moment, this joy is not to be had on earth; that there are no riches, no dominion, no honours, no delights, that can for one instant, even for the twinkling of an eye, minister such a joy; for it is a true satisfaction, and the soul sees that it really does satisfy.'[1] She says that at the time there is no disappointment in this joy; 'God in His great mercy will have the soul comprehend that His Majesty is so near to it that it need not send messengers to Him, but may speak to Him itself, and not with a loud crying, because so near is He already that He understands even the movements of its lips.[2] . . . He seems to be filling up the void in our souls occasioned by our sins.'

She speaks of having suffered greatly herself, and lost much time, because she did not know what to do, and writes, 'I am very sorry for those souls who find themselves alone when they come to this state; for though I read many spiritual books, wherein this very matter is discussed, they threw very little light upon it.'[3] On this account, that she might help others, she considered it a very great advantage to be in this state of prayer while writing of it, 'for where our Lord gives the Spirit, it is more easily and better done; it is then as with a person working embroidery with the pattern before her.'

Returning to her simile, she writes : ' It was a great joy to consider my soul as a garden, and our Lord as walking in it. I used to beseech Him to increase the fragrance of the little flowers of virtues,—which were beginning, as it seemed, to bud,—and preserve them, that they might be to His glory, for I desired nothing for myself.'[4] But she warns other souls that when all seems parched—when our Lord ' will have the poor gardener suppose all the trouble he took

[1] *Vida*, c. xiv. 7.   [2] Ibid.
[3] Ibid. 10.   [4] Ibid. 13.

in maintaining and watering the garden to have been taken to no purpose'—is really the time 'for weeding and rooting out every plant, however small it may be, that is worthless, in the knowledge that no efforts of ours are sufficient, if God withholds from us the waters of His grace ; despising ourselves as being nothing, and even less than nothing.'[1]

Her experience, she tells us, is that many attain to the 'prayer of quiet ;' and few go farther, partly it would seem because the satisfaction and peace, 'attended with very great joy and repose of the faculties and most sweet delight, wherein the soul is established,' make it wish for nothing further. She calls the prayer of quiet 'a little spark of the true love of Himself, which our Lord begins to enkindle in the soul,' and expresses belief that when a soul has advanced so far, by God's mercy, He will not fail to be more merciful still, if there be no shortcomings on our part. And therefore she implores those to whom so great a grace has been given 'to know and make much of themselves, with a humble and holy presumption,' lest, through entangling themselves amidst distractions and cares, they fall back. But above all things she exhorts, 'let there be no giving up of prayer ; it is by prayer they will understand what they are doing, and obtain from our Lord the grace to repent and strength to rise again.'

'What the soul has to do,' she writes, 'at those seasons wherein it is raised to the prayer of quiet is nothing more than to be gentle and without noise . . . quietly and wisely understanding that it is not by dint of labour on our part that we can converse to any good purpose with God, and that our own efforts are only great logs of wood, laid on without discretion to quench this little spark ; and let it

[1] *Vida*, c. xiv. 14.

confess this, and in humility say, O Lord, what can I do here? and what has the servant to do with her Lord, and earth with heaven? or words of love that suggest themselves now . . . and let it make no account of the understanding, which is simply tiresome. . . . A little straw—and it will be less than straw if we bring it ourselves—laid on with humility, will be more effectual here, and will help to kindle the fire more than many fagots of most learned reasons, which, in my opinion, will put it out in a moment.'[1]

Therefore the saint advises that even learned men should not 'spend the time in making applications of passages of the Scriptures,' for though learning, she says, 'could not fail to be of great use to them, both before and after prayer, still, in the very time of prayer itself there is little necessity for it, in my opinion, unless it be for the purpose of making the will tepid; for the understanding then, because of its nearness to the light, is itself illuminated. . . . So then, when the soul is in the prayer of quiet, let it repose in its rest, let learning be put on one side. The time will come when they may make use of it in the service of our Lord—when they that possess it will value it so highly as to be glad that they had not neglected it even for all the treasures of the world, simply because it enables them to serve His Majesty. But in the eyes of Infinite Wisdom, believe me, a little striving after humility, and a single act thereof, are worth more than all the science in the world. This is not the time for discussion, but for understanding plainly what we are, and presenting ourselves in simplicity before God, Who will have the soul make itself a fool—as indeed it is—in His presence.'[2]

As for false illusions of Satan trying for his own ends

---

[1] *Vita*, c. xv. 9, 11.   [2] Ibid. 12, 13.

to produce this prayer of quiet, St. Teresa says that the soul can gain little harm by them, if it 'direct unto God the joy and sweetness it then feels;' humbling itself on account of that joy and sweetness. 'Satan will not often repeat his work when he sees that he loses by it.' She is never weary of enlarging on humility as the guardian of prayer, reminding that ' a time may come when they whose will is so wrapt up in the will of God, that they would undergo torture and suffer a thousand deaths rather than fall into a single imperfection, will find it necessary, if they would be delivered from offending God, and from the commission of sin, to make use of the first armour of prayer, to call to mind how everything is coming to an end, that there is a heaven and a hell, and to make use of other reflections of that nature.'[1] This she speaks of as belonging to her own experience, seeing that the growth of the soul is not like that of the body, which ' does not ungrow nor lessen in size;' and that it must be so ' in order to humble us for our greater good, and to keep us from being careless during our exile; seeing that he who has ascended the higher has the more reason to be afraid and to be less confident in himself.'[2]

Such is St Teresa's picture of the 'prayer of quiet;' in which 'a certain serenity, joined with humility and fear concerning our salvation, casts out servile fear at once from the soul, and in its place plants a loyal fear of more perfect growth. . . . It is the beginning of all good; the flowers have so thriven that they are on the point of budding.'[3] It is a fair picture even if we can only gaze upon it from outside, and makes us acquainted with the fair soul of her who painted it, and who interrupts her description to break forth into thanksgiving to Him Who had thus spoken to her heart.

[1] *Vida*, c. xv. 20.   [2] Ibid.   [3] Ibid. 22, 23.

'O my Lord and my God!' she exclaims, 'I cannot utter these words without tears, and rejoicing in my soul . . . because Thou rejoicest in us; for Thou hast told us that Thy delight is to be with the children of men. . . . Even out of my ingratitude Thine infinite goodness has brought forth some good; and the greater my wickedness, the greater the splendour of the great mercy of Thy compassions . . . mercies which draw me out of myself continually, that I may praise Thee more and more! for remaining in myself, without Thee, I could do nothing, O my Lord, but be as the withered flowers of the garden. . . . Let it not be so, O Lord! let not a soul which Thou hast purchased with so many labours be lost—one which Thou hast often ransomed anew. You, my father, must forgive me for wandering from the subject. What I write is what my soul has understood; and it is very often hard enough to abstain from the praises of God when, in the course of writing, the great debt I owe Him presents itself before me.'[1]

St. Teresa's account of the third state of prayer, or that 'of union,' is the most difficult to understand of all her spiritual relations, since it is not trance or rapture, and yet nearly approaches to it. She says herself, 'I never understood it, and never could explain it; and so I was resolved, when I should come thus far in my story, to say very little or nothing at all.' But the day that she wrote these words she tells us that after Communion she was admitted to this state of prayer, and seemed to learn therein how to speak of it. Her words in describing it are amongst the most beautiful and exalted that she wrote, 'words that burn,' so that even through the veil of a translation they deeply touch and warm the heart, as it catches faint glimpses of her meaning.

[1] *Vida*, c. xiv. 15 18.

We know that we are listening to one who had been brought into the clefts of the rock, into the secret places of the stairs, and who is trying, in all simplicity and truthfulness, to tell us of the things which she had seen and known.

She compares the 'oracion de la union de las potencias' to 'water running from a river or from a brook, whereby the garden is watered with very much less trouble, although there is some in directing the water;' and she describes it as 'a sleep of the powers of the soul, which are not wholly lost, nor yet understanding how they work.' 'The pleasure, sweetness, and delight are incomparably greater,' she writes, ' than in the former state of prayer; . . . to me it seems nothing else but a death, as it were, to all things of this world, and a fruition of God. . . . The faculties of the soul now retain only the power of occupying themselves wholly with God ; not one of them ventures to stir, neither can we move one of them without making great efforts to distract ourselves. . . . The understanding is utterly powerless here; the soul longs to send forth words of praise, but it has no control over itself,—it is in a state of sweet restlessness. . . . The joy is so great, that the soul seems now and then to be on the very point of going forth out of the body; and what a blessed death that would be ! . . . It is as if amazed in beholding our Lord taking upon Himself the work of the good gardener, refusing to let the soul undergo any labour whatever but that of taking its pleasure in the flowers beginning to send forth their fragrance. . . . It differs from the prayer of quiet, of which I have spoken, though it does seem as if it were all one with it. In that prayer the soul, which would willingly neither stir nor move, is delighting in the holy repose of Mary ; but in this prayer it can be like Martha also. Accordingly, the soul is, as it were, living the active and contemplative life at once, and is able to apply itself to works of charity and the affairs of its state. Still, those who arrive at this state ... are well aware that the better part of the soul is elsewhere. It is as if we were speaking to one person, and another speaking to us at the same time. ... It happens at times, and indeed very often, that, the will being in union, the soul should be aware of it, and see that the will is a captive and in joy, that the will alone is abiding in great peace; while, on the other hand, the understanding and the memory are so free, that they can be employed in affairs and be occupied in works of charity. I say this, that you, my father, may see it is so, and understand the matter when it sha 1 happen to yourself.'[1]

To many such words will seem but the poetry of spiritual madness, and doubtless St. Teresa knew that they would be accounted folly; but, instead of shrinking from the imputation, she, as it were, goes to meet it, and embraces it. 'It is a glorious folly, a heavenly madness,' she says, 'wherein true wisdom is acquired; and to the soul a kind of fruition most full of delight. ... O my God, what must that soul be when it is in this state? It wishes it were all tongue, in order that it may praise our Lord. It utters a thousand holy follies, striving continually to please Him by whom it is thus possessed. ... It would have all men behold it, and know of its bliss, to the praise of God, and help it to praise Him. It would have them to be partakers of its joy; for its joy is greater than it can bear. It seems to me that it is like the woman in the Gospel, who would, or used to, call in her neighbours. The admirable spirit of David, the royal prophet, must have felt in the same way, so it seems to me, when he played on the harp, singing the praises of

[1] *Vida,* c. xvii. 5, 6.

God. . . . I do not think that I have exaggerated in any way, but rather fallen short, in speaking of that joy which our Lord, of His good pleasure, gives to the soul in this its exile. Blessed for ever be Thou, O Lord! and may all created things praise Thee for ever!'[1]

Yet such words are words of truth and soberness, as well as of burning love. If we were not familiar with the language of the Psalms, perhaps their divine music might seem to us as dark speech upon the harp. We sing such songs as the Psalm *Quemadmodum*, hardly perceiving the deep and mystical chords that we are striking, or the melodies which they awaken. The same strain of heavenly longing breathes in Teresa's words. 'I beseech you, my father,' she exclaims, 'let us all be mad, for the love of Him who for our sakes suffered men to say of Him that He was mad. O my King, seeing that I am now, while writing this, still under the power of this heavenly madness, an effect of Thy mercy and goodness,—and it is a mercy I never deserved,—grant, I beseech Thee, that all those with whom I may have to converse may become mad through thy love. . . . This thy servant, O my God, is no longer able to endure sufferings so great as those are which she must bear when she sees herself without Thee. . . . This my soul longs to be free; eating is killing it, and sleep is wearisome; it sees itself wasting the time of this life in comforts, and that there is no comfort for it now but in Thee . . . for now it desires to live not in itself, but in Thee. . . . O my God, when shall my soul praise Thee without distraction, not dissipated in this way, unable to control itself? I understand now the mischief that sin has done, in that it has rendered us unable to do what we desire—to be always occupied with God!'[2]

[1] *Vida*, c. xvi. 1, 5, 6, 7.   [2] Ibid. 8, 10; xvii. 9.

Her soul was athirst for God, yea, even for the living God. 'When shall I come to appear before the presence of God?' was but the natural utterance of her heart of hearts. Yet in the very midst of these sublime aspirations she pauses and turns, as so often is her custom, to a practical consideration concerning the spiritual welfare of others. She is evidently anxious that her confessor, F. Ybanez, at whose desire she wrote these experiences, should be raised to them himself, believing that through this 'heavenly madness' he will accomplish far more than in colder moods. 'You, my father,' she writes, 'say that you wish me well. I wish you would prove it by disposing yourself so that God may bestow this grace upon you; for I see very few people who have not too much sense for everything they have to do. . . . Even preachers go about arranging their sermons so as to displease no one.[1] They have a good intention, and their work is good; yet still few amend their lives. But how is it that they are not many who, in consequence of these sermons, abstain from public sins? Well, I think it is because the preachers are highly sensible men. They are not burning with the great fire of the love of God, as the Apostles were, casting worldly prudence aside; and so their fire throws out but little heat. I do not say that their fire ought to burn like that of the Apostles, but I do wish it were a stronger fire than I see it is. Do you, my father, know wherein much of this fire consists? In the hatred of this life, in the desertion of its honours, in being utterly indifferent whether we lose or gain anything or everything, provided the truth be told and maintained for the glory of God; for he who is courageously in earnest for God looks upon loss or gain indifferently.'[2]

[1] 'Legant prædicatores' was here written on the margin of Teresa's MS. by F. Dom. Bañez.   [2] *Vida*, c. xvi. 11, 12.

'O grand freedom, to regard it as a captivity to be obliged to live and converse with men according to the laws of the world! It is the gift of our Lord; there is not a slave who would not imperil everything that he might escape and return to his country. . . . May our Lord give us His grace for that end! You, my father, if it shall seem good to you, will tear up what I have written, and consider it as a letter for yourself alone, and forgive me that I have been very bold.'[1]

It is impossible to add anything to this relation concerning the third degree of prayer, for, as the saint says herself, 'It is one grace that our Lord gives grace; and it is another grace to understand what grace and what gift it is; and it is another and further grace to have the power to describe and explain it to others.'

We must pass on to her account of the fourth state of prayer, rapture or ecstatic trance; which she likens to the rain which comes down from heaven 'to fill and saturate in its abundance the whole of this garden with water.' There is, of course, no doubt that such an exceptional condition of communion with God has been bestowed upon His servants, since there are several records of it in Holy Scripture; the only doubt, in any particular instance, would be whether the 'rapture' were real or imaginary. It is, so far, a distincter condition than that of the prayer of union, and seems to us the less mystical—that we are accustomed to the descriptions of it in the Bible, as in the cases of Daniel, Ezekiel, St. Paul, &c. And, therefore, although *entirely* supernatural, mystical, and beyond any common experience, we seem less unable to attach some meaning to words descriptive of it, because familiar with the like from our childhood. Yet it is a higher

---

[1] *Vida*, c. xvii. 11, 12, 13.

state, Teresa tells us, than that of union, during which the soul still 'feels that it is not dead altogether,' but 'retains the sense to see that it is in the world, and to feel its own loneliness;' but now it is carried out of itself, bathed in that flood whose streams make glad the city of God.

> Onde la vision crescer conviene,
> Crescer l' ardor che di quella s' accende,
> Crescer lo raggio, che da esso viene.[1]

'In this fourth state,' Teresa writes, 'there is no sense of anything, only fruition. . . . The senses were permitted before, as I have said, to give some signs of the great joy they feel, but now, in this state, the joy of the soul is incomparably greater, and the power of showing it is still less; for there is no power in the body, and the soul has none, whereby this fruition can be made known. . . . The soul, while thus seeking after God, is conscious, with a joy excessive and sweet, that it is, as it were, utterly fainting away in a kind of trance: breathing, and all the bodily strength fails it, so that it cannot even move the hands without great pain; the eyes close involuntarily, and, if they are open, they are as if they saw nothing; nor is reading possible—the very letters seem strange, and cannot be distinguished—the letters, indeed, are visible, but, as the understanding furnishes no help, all reading is impracticable, although seriously attempted. The ear hears; but what is heard is not comprehended. The senses are of no use whatever, except to hinder the soul's fruition; and so they rather hurt it. It is useless to try to speak, because it is not possible to conceive a word; nor, if it were conceived, is there strength sufficient to utter it; for all bodily strength vanishes, and that of the

---

[1] *Paradiso*, c. xiv.

soul increases, to enable it the better to have the fruition of its joy.'[1]

We know, from St. Paul's account of his own rapture, that in it there was the entire suspension of the life of sense here described; since he could not tell whether his spirit remained in the body, or was carried out of it. 'Let him describe it who knows it,' says St. Teresa; 'for as it is impossible to understand it, much more is it so to describe it. . . . To him who has not had that experience it must appear folly. . . All I am able to say is, that the soul is represented as being close to God; and that there abides a conviction thereof so certain and strong that it cannot possibly help believing so. . . . The restless little butterfly of the memory has its wings burnt now, and it cannot fly.'[2]

She says that if our Lord never ceased to pour down this water, 'the gardener certainly would have plenty of rest' and 'would have his delight therein, but in this life that is impossible. This water from heaven comes down very often when the gardener least expects it. . . . Our Lord advances step by step to lay hold of the little bird, and to lay it in the nest where it may repose. He observed it fluttering for a long time, striving with the understanding and the will, and with all its might, to seek God and to please Him; so now it is His pleasure to reward it even in this life. And what a reward! One moment is enough to repay all the possible trials of this life.'[3]

'This prayer, however long it may last, does no harm—at least it has never done any harm to me; nor do I remember, however ill I might have been when our Lord had mercy on me in this way, that I ever felt the worse for it—on the contrary, I was always better afterwards. But so

---
[1] *Vida*, c. xviii. 14.   [2] Ibid. 18, 19.   [3] Ibid. 12, 13.

great a blessing, what harm can it do? The outward effects are so plain as to leave no doubt possible that there must have been some great cause, seeing that it robs us of our bodily powers with so much joy, in order to leave them greater. . . . It is plain, from the overflowing abundance of grace, that the brightness of the sun which had shone there must have been great, seeing that it has thus made the soul to melt away. And this is to be considered, for, as it seems to me, the period of time, however long it may have been, during which the faculties of the soul were entranced, is very short : if half an hour, that would be a long time. I do not think that I have ever been so long.'[1]

Teresa tells us that when thinking how to write of the condition of the soul in rapture, our Lord had seemed to say to her, 'It undoes itself utterly, My daughter, in order that it may give itself more and more to Me: it is not itself that then lives, it is I.' 'A rapture,' she says, 'is absolutely irresistible. . . . It comes, in general, as a shock, quick and sharp, before you can collect your thoughts, or help yourself in any way, and you see and feel it as a cloud, or a strong eagle rising upwards, and carrying you away on its wings. . . . Yet the weakness of our nature makes us afraid at first, and we require a much more resolute and courageous spirit than in the previous states, in order to risk everything, come what may, and to abandon ourselves into the hands of God, and go willingly whither we are carried, seeing that we must be carried away, however painful it may be ; and so trying is it, that I would very often resist, and exert all my strength, particularly at those times when the rapture was coming on me in public. I did so, too, very often when I was alone, because I was afraid of delusions. Occasionally

[1] *Vida*, c. xviii. 15, 16.

I was able, by great efforts, to make a slight resistance; but afterwards I was worn out, like a person who had been contending with a strong giant. . . . If any earthly thing be then offered to the soul, even though it may be that which it habitually found most sweet, the soul will have none of it; yea, it seems to throw it away at once. The soul sees distinctly that it seeks nothing but God; yet its love dwells not on any attribute of Him in particular, it seeks Him as He is. . . . All my anxiety at these times is that I should die. . . . I forget everything in my eagerness to see God; and this abandonment and loneliness seem preferable to any company in the world. . . . Oh, if we were utterly detached—if we never placed our happiness in anything of this world—how the pain, caused by living always away from God, would temper the fear of death with the desire of enjoying the true life!'[1]

She describes the highest kind of rapture as full of sharpest pain, 'which we can never inflict of ourselves, nor remove when once it has come.' And she says that to this state of pain she had been brought after all the sweetness and delight of soul and body vouchsafed to her in painless rapture. 'Even now,' she writes, 'I have that sweetness occasionally; but it is the pain of which I speak that is the most frequent and the most common. We have no part in causing this pain; but very often there springs up a desire unexpectedly . . . which pierces the soul in a moment . . . so that it rises upwards above itself and above all created things. God then so strips it of everything, that, do what it may, there is nothing on earth that can be its companion. Neither, indeed, would it wish to have any; it would rather die in that loneliness. . . . Though God seems, as it were, far

[1] *Vida*, c. xx. 3, 4, 15, 17; xxi. 9.

away from the soul at that moment, yet He reveals His grandeurs at times in the strangest way conceivable. That way is indescribable; I do not think anyone can believe or comprehend it who has not previously had experience of it. ... In this communication the desire grows, so also does the bitterness of that loneliness wherein the soul beholds itself, suffering a pain so sharp and piercing that, in that very loneliness in which it dwells, it may literally say of itself .... " Vigilavi, et factus sum sicut passer solitarius in tecto." '[1]

What is this pain of which she speaks but the same which was expressed almost in like words by the Psalmist? 'Oh that I had wings like a dove! for then would I flee away and be at rest. I would make haste to escape. I would remain in the wilderness. There is none upon earth that I desire in comparison of Thee. My flesh and my heart faileth, but God is the strength of my heart, and my portion for ever.' St. Teresa tells us that 'it is a sharp martyrdom, full of sweetness;' and that she trembled when she felt it coming on. 'But when I am in them,' she adds, 'I then wish to spend therein all the rest of my life, though the pain be so very great, that I can scarcely endure it.' And whereas rapture in the beginning had left her physically strengthened, now it left her in pain over her whole body, as if her bones were out of joint. So we read that after his great ' vision of the evening and the morning' Daniel 'fainted, and was sick certain days.'[2] 'The soul is tormented also,' she says, 'because the pain has increased so much that it seeks solitude no longer, as it did before, nor companionship, unless it be that of those to whom it may make its complaint.'[3]

[1] *Vida*, c. xx. 12, 13.   [2] Dan. viii. 27.
[3] *Vida*, c. xx. 16, 18.

'See, my father,' she continues, 'what rest I can have in this life, now that what I once had in prayer and loneliness—therein our Lord used to comfort me—has become in general a torment of this kind ; while at the same time it is so full of sweetness, that the soul, discerning its inestimable worth, prefers it to all those consolations which it formerly had. It seems also to be a safer way, because it is the way of the Cross ; and involves, in my opinion, a joy of exceeding worth, because the state of the body in it is only pain. It is the soul that suffers and exults alone in that joy and contentment which suffering supplies.'[1]

She says that in the beginning she was afraid ; but that she was reassured, and bidden to esteem this grace more than all that had been given her ; 'for the soul was purified by this pain—burnished, or refined as gold in the crucible, so that it might be the better enamelled with His gifts.'

If it were necessary for a moment to defend St. Teresa's writings from the charge of expressing hysterical fancies and self-delusions, they would find their best defence in these last words,—in her perfect indifference to sweetness or to pain, except as either might be God's will for her; and in her simple recognition of pain as the safer way, because it was that which Christ chose, and which gave her a portion in His Cross. There is this further answer to any such charges—that she regards special graces from God, and states of high fruition, as means to an end, that end being His glory and the salvation of men. She speaks of them as producing generous resolutions, saying that 'the soul remains possessed of so much courage, that if it were now hewn in pieces for God, it would be a great consolation to it. This is the time of resolutions, of heroic

[1] *Vida*, c. xx. 19.

determinations, of the living energy of good desires, of the beginning of hatred of the world, and of the most clear perception of its vanity. The soul makes greater and higher progress than it ever made before in the previous states of prayer; and grows in humility more and more. . . . It looks upon itself as most unworthy, for in a room into which the sunlight enters strongly not a cobweb can be hid; it sees its own misery; self-conceit is so far away, that it seems as if it never could have had any, for now its eyes behold how very little it could ever do, or rather, that it never did anything. . . . Its past life stands before it then, together with the great mercy of God, in great distinctness. . . . It sees, so far as itself is concerned, that it has deserved hell, and that its punishment is bliss. It undoes itself in the praises of God, and I would gladly undo myself now.' [1]

'The good effects of this prayer abide in the soul for some time. Now that it clearly apprehends that the fruit is not its own, the soul can begin to share it with others. . . . It begins to benefit its neighbours, as it were, without being aware of it, or doing anything consciously: its neighbours understand the matter, because the odour of the flowers has grown so strong as to make them eager to approach them.' [2]

'The greater the growth of love and humility in the soul, the stronger the perfume of the flowers of virtues is for itself and for others. God is the Soul of that soul now; it is He who has the charge of it; and so He enlightens it; for He seems to be watching over it, always attentive to it, that it may not offend Him, giving it grace, and stirring it up in His service. Before the soul fell into the trance, it thought itself to be careful about not offending God, and that it did what it could in proportion to its strength; but now that it

---

[1] *Vida*, c. xix. 2.   [2] Ibid. 4.

has attained to this state, in which the Sun of Justice shines upon it, and makes it open its eyes, it beholds so many motes, that it would gladly close them again. It is not so truly the child of the noble eagle, that it can gaze upon the sun; but, for the few instants it can keep them open, it beholds itself unclean. It remembers the words, "Who shall be just in thy presence?"[1] When it looks on this divine Sun, the brightness thereof dazzles it; when it looks on itself, its eyes are blinded by the dust.'[2]

'It is in rapture that true humility is acquired—humility that will never say any good of self, nor suffer others to do so. The Lord of the garden, not the soul, distributes the fruit thereof, and so none remains in its hands; all the good it has it refers to God; if it says anything about itself, it is for His glory. . . . The soul now seeks not, and possesses not, any other will but that of doing our Lord's will, and so it prays Him to let it be so; it gives to Him the keys of its own will. It sees most clearly how lightly are the things of this world to be esteemed, and the nothingness thereof. . . . This is really the way in which these things come to pass; if the raptures be true raptures, the fruits and advantages spoken of abide in the soul; but if they did not, I should have great doubts about their being from God—yea rather, I should be afraid they were those frenzies of which St. Vincent speaks. I have seen it myself, and I know it by experience, that the soul in rapture is mistress of everything, and acquires such freedom in one hour, and even in less, as to be unable to recognize itself. It sees distinctly that all this does not belong to it, neither knows it how it came to possess so great a good; but it clearly perceives the very great blessing

---

[1] Job iv. 17, 'Numquid homo Dei comparatione justificabitur?'
[2] *Vida*, c. xx. 37; xxi. 10, 13.

which every one of these raptures always brings. No one will believe this who has not had experience of it, and so they do not believe the poor soul. . . . Yet they would not be astonished if they knew that it comes not from the soul, but from our Lord, to Whom it has given up the keys of its will. True revelations—the great gifts and visions—come by ecstasies, all tending to make the soul humble and strong, to make it despise the things of this world, and have a clearer knowledge of the greatness of the reward which our Lord has prepared for those who serve Him.'[1]

With these words St. Teresa ends her celebrated description of the four degrees of prayer; adding this petition: 'May it please His Majesty that the great munificence with which He hath dealt with me, miserable sinner that I am, may have some weight with those who shall read this, so that they may be strong and courageous enough to give up everything utterly for God! If His Majesty repays us so abundantly, that even in this life the reward and gain of those who serve Him become visible, what will it be in the next?'[2]

[1] *Vida*, c. xx. 30, 31, 38; xxi. 15.   [2] Ibid. c. xxi. 16.

Chapter the Sixth.

*It is no flaming lustre made of light;
No sweet concert or well-tuned harmony;
Ambrosia for to feast the appetite,
Or flowery odour mixed with spicery;
No sweet embrace, nor pleasure bodily:
And yet it is a kind of inward feast,
A harmony that sounds within the breast;
An odour, light, embrace, in which the soul doth rest.*
                                        GILES FLETCHER.

IF the attempt to convey, in the foregoing chapters, any notion of St. Teresa's spiritual relations has not entirely failed, it will at least be apparent that her description is of no dreamy rest, or soft indulgence, or excited frenzy. She tells us, indeed, of wholly supernatural and mystical conditions, describes the condition of the soul—

> That hath no eyes to see, nor ears to hear,
> Yet sees and hears, and is all eye, all ear;

and fears not to assert that she herself, while 'leaning on the strong pillar of prayer,' had received high and peculiar graces. But these special gifts and extraordinary communications were amongst the promises made unto the fathers, and fulfilled when heaven was opened to man. To 'dream dreams,' to 'see visions,' to 'prophesy,' were gifts promised when the days should come in which He should pour out His Spirit upon the servants and the handmaidens. The only question is, whether the graces which St. Teresa describes were *false* visions, *false* dreams.

It might, possibly, satisfy us to know the result of the long, anxious, critical, and at first doubting examination made on this point during her life by all best qualified to judge, through learning, experience. saintliness, and intimate acquaintance with the woman, her character and her life; or to know the outward result of her spiritual history—the life and labours which were but the expression of her inner self—of that life which for so many long years was hid with Christ in God, becoming manifest through no intention of hers, though at length shining forth with a brilliancy which makes her one of the most marked and striking figures even in the Spain of the sixteenth century. Is it possible to believe otherwise concerning her? to believe, as many would have us do, that all her labours and marvellous influence on the religious life of her own and other countries were *in spite* of her interior life? Is it possible to believe that this life, up to her forty-fifth year, had been spent in dreamy fancies and profane self-deception?

But, apart from these considerations, is there no inner evidence in her writings which tells us of what manner of spirit she was? It is an evidence which grows upon us the more we read of her works, and the more familiar we become with them. It must not be imagined that chosen morsels have here been sifted from a mass of puerile and worthless writing; the difficulty has been to reject any, where all was beautiful and noble-hearted. What are the qualities which even these short extracts reveal?

There is, first and before all, the deepest humility—a humility so true that it does not shrink from obedience—from telling the story of her soul—knowing that all in it of good was from God—all of short-comings and sins its own. This humility shines through every word she ever wrote, the gift of God, making it possible for her to receive without injury the weight of spiritual benefits with which He crowned her.[1] She interrupts her relation of the states of prayer to break out into a kind of remonstrance with God for giving such graces to one like herself. 'O Lord, consider what Thou art doing; forget not so soon the great evils that I have done. . . . O my Creator, pour not a liquor so precious into a vessel so broken; for Thou hast already seen how on other occasions I allowed it to run to waste. Lay not up treasure like this, where the longing after the consolations of this life is not so mortified as it ought to be; for it will be utterly lost. How canst Thou commit the defence of the city and the keys of its fortress to a commander so cowardly, who at the first assault will let the enemy enter within? Oh let not Thy love be so great, O King Eternal, as to imperil jewels so precious! O my Lord, to me it seems that it becomes a ground for undervaluing them, when Thou puttest them in the power of one so wretched, so vile, so frail, so miserable, and so worthless as I am . . . in short, I am a woman, not good, but wicked. . . . Thou, O

---

[1] When one of her superiors objected to her rather obeying human direction than celestial visions, she instantly answered: 'I may be deceived if I obey visions; but if I obey you, who are over me in God, I cannot be deceived.'—Johannes a Jesu, *Orationes in Nat. S. Teresa*, v. Opera, vol. iii. p. 502.

my God, knowest already that I beg this of Thee with my whole will, from the bottom of my heart, and that I have done so more than once ; and I account it a blessing to lose the greatest blessings which may be had on earth, if Thou wouldst but bestow these graces upon him who will make a better use of them to the increase of Thy glory.'[1] Yet she speaks afterwards of this prayer being 'foolishness and want of humility; for our Lord knoweth well what is expedient.'

'That God in all things may be glorified;' this was the desire which possessed her soul; the burning love of God which consumed her utterly swallowing up self-love. There is deepest contrition and perception of her own vileness, with perfect, unswerving, and cheerful trust in God's mercy through Christ. There is an absolute surrender of her will to the will of God, content to receive sweetness or pain as it pleased Him. There is the true, though rarest, estimation of the real value of earthly things ; with ardent desire to benefit others while yet hardly thinking herself fit to do so.

These are indeed but a few of the various and delicate spiritual graces which breathe through her writings ; can we believe that they were granted to a self-deceiving fanatic? The distinguishing mark of such a one would be a great value for supernatural graces in themselves, and elation at receiving them; while exactly the opposite characterises St. Teresa. She enquires why God passes by 'most holy persons,' to bestow these graces upon her, and says it is because her weakness had need of these succours, while, 'they, being strong, serve Thee without them, and Thou dealest with them as with a strong race, free from all self-

[1] *Vida*, c. xviii. 6, 7.

interest.' And she dwells at great length on her temptation to give up prayer through false humility, imploring others not to fall into the same error, or give it up; 'even if they should fall after our Lord has raised them to so high a degree of prayer . . . they must not be discouraged, unless they would lose themselves utterly. . . . They should know that when I was neglecting it, my life was much worse than it had ever been. . . . How could my spirit be quiet? It was going away in its misery from its true rest. What a proud humility was that which Satan devised for me, when I ceased to lean upon the pillar, and threw the staff away which supported me, in order that my fall might not be great!'[1]

Her writings abound with plain and simple directions for beginners in mental prayer: she is never forgetful, or unable to enter into the needs of, the simplest soul. She used to say, Ribera tells us, 'that no better society can be had than Jesus Christ, and that we should therefore imagine Him present with us. That if we accustom ourselves to have Him present with us, and that He shall see that we do that out of love, and that we desire sincerely to please Him, we shall ever have Him with us; and truly it is a great thing to have such a Friend at our side. That the consideration of the Passion of the Lord was the way of prayer, by which all ought to begin, to continue, and to end, and that that way was most safe and excellent, until God shall lead us to other supernatural paths. She added that we ought not always to reason with the intellect, but to imagine ourselves present with Christ, and without any straining of intellect speak to Him, and take delight in Him (*cum Ipso deliciari*), not tormenting ourselves to form prayers,

---

[1] *Vida*, c. xix. 15, 17.

but only representing to Him our necessities and the causes of our troubles; and this indeed one at one time, and another at another time, lest it should be wearisome to the soul always to taste the same food.'[1]

Ribera adds that she advised those who cannot pray after this manner to place themselves before our Lord, and with humility to entreat Him not to desert them, but to cleave to them as a companion. If in the space of a year they cannot attain to this, then let them persevere longer, nor grieve to employ so much time for a thing in attaining which it is so well spent.'[2]

She was wont to say that, by the consideration of God, we shall the sooner attain to the knowledge of our own condition; for that when we consider divine perfections we see our sins and imperfections the better, as whiteness opposed to blackness appears the whiter; and that our intellect and will are ennobled and made more ready for all good by considering God at one time, and ourselves at another, for that if we never emerge from the slough of our own miseries the stream will ever be turbid. It would be impossible for one who spent most of her time during devotion in self-deceiving fancies to write with such simplicity and truthfulness of the first principles of prayer.

> Giunse al suo principio cose
> Ch' io non intesi, si parlò profondo,[3]

may be true; but it is unreasonable to assume that those profound things are fancies because they pass our comprehension.

There is a very remarkable chapter in her autobiography, full of beauty, in which she combats the opinion advanced

---

[1] *Ribera*, lib. iv. c. iv. 75, 76.   [2] Ibid. 77.   [3] *Paradiso*, c. xv.

by some spiritual writers, that we ought so to withdraw from all bodily imagination, in contemplation of the Divinity, as to put away the consideration even of the Sacred Humanity itself; and that, as the work of contemplation is wholly spiritual, any bodily object whatever must disturb and hinder it. She says that she was misled herself in this matter; but now, she exclaims, 'O Lord of my soul, and my Good! Jesus Christ crucified! I never think of this opinion, which I then held, without pain; I believe it was an act of high treason, though done in ignorance. . . . Is it possible, O my Lord, that I could have had the thought, if only for an hour, that Thou couldst be a hindrance to my greatest good? . . . I did not continue long of this opinion, and so I returned to my habit of delighting in our Lord, particularly at communion. I wish I could have His picture and image always before my eyes, since I cannot have Him graven in my soul as deeply as I wish. . . . To withdraw altogether from Christ, and to compare His divine Body with our miseries, or with any created thing whatever, is what I cannot endure.'[1]

She believed that this theory arose from 'a little absence of humility—so secret and so hidden that we do not observe it;' and asks who is there that 'can possibly imagine himself not to be exceedingly rich, most abundantly rewarded, when our Lord permits him to stand with St. John at the foot of the cross? I know not into whose head it could have entered to be not satisfied with this, unless it be mine, which has gone wrong in every way where it should have gone right onwards. . . . Certainly it is not always that one can bear to meditate on sufferings so great as were those He underwent.'[2] 'But who,' she continues, 'is to hinder us

---

[1] *Vida*, c. xxii. 2, 4, 5.   [2] Ibid. 7, 8.

from thinking of Him risen from the grave, seeing that we have Him to meet us in the sacrament? Behold Him . . . before His Ascension into heaven, without pain, all-glorious, giving strength to some and courage to others. . . . With so good a Friend and Captain ever present, Himself the first to suffer, everything can be borne. He helps, He strengthens, He never fails, He is the true Friend. I see clearly, and since then have always seen, that if we are to please God, and if He is to give us His great graces, everything must pass through the hands of His most Sacred Humanity, in Whom His Majesty said that He is well pleased. . . . So, then, I would have your reverence seek no other way, even if you were arrived at the highest contemplation. This way is safe. Our Lord is He by Whom all good things come to us; He will teach you. Consider His life; that is the best example. What more can we want than so good a Friend at our side, Who will not forsake us when we are in trouble and distress, as they do who belong to this world? Let us consider the glorious St. Paul, who seems as if Jesus was never absent from his lips, as if he had Him deep down in his heart.'[1]

Teresa says that an opposite course 'is making the soul, as they say, to walk in the air: for it has nothing to rest on, how full soever of God it may think itself to be.' She describes it as a 'seeking to be Mary before it has laboured with Martha;' for 'we are not angels, we have a body; to seek to make ourselves angels while we are on the earth, and so much on the earth as I was, is an act of folly. If it be His Majesty's good pleasure to raise us and place us among His chamberlains and secret counsellors, we must go willingly; if not, we must serve Him in the lower offices of His house,

[1] *Vida*, c. xxii. 8, 9, 10.

and not sit down on the upper seats. . . . And now that the soul is permitted to sit at the feet of Christ, let it contrive not to quit its place, but keep it anyhow. Let it follow the example of the Magdalene; and when it shall be strong enough, God will lead it into the wilderness. . . . We may do what we like, but He throws the spirit into a trance as easily as a giant takes up a straw: no resistance is possible.'[1]

She believed that God gave grace to souls according to the measure of their abandonment of themselves into His hands, that He may do with them as He will. 'We never thoroughly believe,' she says, 'that God rewards a hundredfold even in this life. It seems also to me as if His Majesty were going about to try those who love Him . . . revealing Himself in supreme joy, so as to quicken our belief, if it should be dead, in what He will give us, saying, Behold! this is but a drop of the immense sea of blessings. . . . O my soul's Lord, who can find words to describe what Thou givest to those who trust in Thee, and what they lose who come to this state, and yet dwell in themselves!'[2]

We may conclude what has been here said of her interior life by an anecdote told of her by Ribera. 'She was so absorbed in God,' he says, 'that when one of her confessors, a man distinguished for learning, with whom she conferred of her matters, and from whom she concealed nothing, asked her how she divided her time (thinking that she dedicated some hours of the day to prayer and some to the management of affairs), she made answer, 'Could he not imagine a man in suchwise taken captive by the love of another that he could not for one moment depart from the side of the beloved? And that after this manner she loved

[1] *Vida*, c. xxii. 18, 19, 20.   [2] Ibid. 23, 26.

Christ the Lord, ever finding comfort with Him (*sese cum Eo consolando*) and ever speaking with Him and of Him.'[1]

If any of the words that have been gathered from her manifold outpourings of love—the expressions of that—

<blockquote>
concreata e perpetua sete
Del deiforme regno
</blockquote>

which consumed her should seem to some unreal or overstrained, let them but recall for a moment to memory and imagination the purest and deepest sentiments of earthly love, happiness in the presence of one beloved, desire for it in absence, confidence, preference for the ease and comfort of another rather than for our own,—and the vivid picture and remembrance of such affection will make them able to comprehend that divine love may also have power to awaken a response in some hearts, and so fill them with that repose of the soul in the presence of a Beauty before which all other beauty pales, that there should be none upon earth that they desire in comparison of that Incarnate Love, Who presents Himself to the heart of man as an adequate object for its highest affections.

[1] *Ribera*, lib. iv. c. 5, 100.

Chapter the Seventh.

1555—1559.

Oh, dull of heart! enclosed doth lie
In each ' Come, Lord,' an 'Here am I.'
Thy love, thy longing, are not thine,
Reflections of a love divine:
Thy very prayer to thee was given,
Itself a messenger from Heaven.

. . . . . .

All other gifts unto His foes
He freely gives, nor grudging knows;
But Love's sweet smart, and costly pain,
A treasure for His friends remain.

ARCHBISHOP OF DUBLIN.

IN the year 1555 a college of Jesuits was founded in Avila; but some of the fathers of this society had come there, we are told, in 1553, and Teresa 'was greatly attracted by them,' or, rather, by what she had heard of their way of life and prayer.

Born in 1491, and therefore twenty-three years older than Teresa, their great founder died in 1556, before she became known or in any way outwardly remarkable. But she must have been well acquainted with his history and character, since his fame was at its highest during the twenty-two years which she had now passed in the Incarnation.

Nor could she have been without keenest interest in the career of Francis Xavier, who was but ten years older than herself, and had but lately passed to his rest; his ardent spirit, so kindred to her own, quickly burning out its mortal frame in unceasing missionary toil. But the third great saint of the Jésuit order, Francis Borgia, was still alive, and in the year 1554 had been appointed by Ignatius commissary for the affairs of the society in Spain. Thus the order was in the first fresh vigour of its marvellous life, moulded by two of the most distinguished men of that age, instinct with their fervour and devotion, and adorned by the labours and by the death of the greatest missionary of Christendom.

Teresa appears to have turned instinctively to them for sympathy and guidance; but for a time delayed to seek it; not thinking herself 'fit to speak to them, or strong enough to obey them.' Some guidance, however, she now felt that she must have, for she was greatly perplexed; not understanding her own way of prayer, and the rather fearing self-delusion in the matter because a certain nun, Magdalene of the Cross, of Cordova, had lately filled Spain with the fame first of her sanctity and then of her detected impostures.[1]

Teresa had recourse first to a layman, a 'saintly nobleman,' living in Avila, Don Francisco de Salcedo. He was at this time married, but was greatly given to religious practices, and for twenty years had attended theological lectures of the Dominicans. He became a priest after his

---

[1] Popes, Emperors, and Kings used to beg her prayers, and the mother of Philip II. would have his first swaddling clothes blessed by her. In 1546 she unexpectedly confessed her frauds to the Visitor of the Order.

wife's death, was chaplain to St. Teresa's first convent of Reformed Carmelites, and died two years before her, after ten years of priesthood. Through him she became acquainted with Gaspar Daza, 'a man of great sense, and very gentle with all people.' He had lately formed a society of priests in Avila, and had placed them under the direction of F. Baltasar Alvarez, of whom we shall hear further. She revealed to him the state of her soul and her method of prayer, meaning to confess to him and take him for her guide; but he refused to undertake the office on the plea of over-occupation; and she soon found he was unsuited to her case, for 'when I perceived,' she writes, 'that he ordered the affairs of my soul as if I ought to be perfect at once, I saw that much more care was necessary in my case; . . . for the pain it gave me to see that I was not doing—and, as I thought, could not do—what he told me, was enough to destroy all hope, and make me abandon the matter altogether.'[1]

So she arranged with her lay friend, Don Salcedo, to come and see her now and then, and seems for a time to have been really 'directed' by him. Indeed, she says herself that she believed he was, by the pains he took, 'the beginning of salvation' to her soul. He was himself a proficient in mental prayer, 'and all his life was ordered with that perfection which his state admitted.' 'His wife,' Teresa writes, 'is so great a servant of God and so full of charity, that nothing is lost to him on her account—in short, she was the chosen wife of one who God knew would serve Him so well.' They were connected by marriage with the De Cepedas.

He encouraged her to have patience with herself, telling

[1] *Vida*, c. xxiii. 8, 9.

her she must not expect to get rid of every failing at once, or allow such imperfections to trouble devotion. But by degrees he became perplexed at her account of the graces shown to her in prayer, and what she calls her 'great imperfections;' thinking them inconsistent with each other; and 'he could not help being very much afraid,' thinking that the evil spirit might have something to do with the matter. Her unhappiness at this suggestion was extreme. It 'distressed me exceedingly,' she says, 'and I cried; for certainly I was anxious to please God, and I could not persuade myself that Satan had anything to do with it. But I was afraid, on account of my great sins, that God might leave me blind, so that I should understand nothing.'[1] Another distress to her was that she could not clearly describe her state in prayer to her friend. At length, however, she found in the 'Subida del Monte Sion,' by a Franciscan friar, a passage descriptive of it; and, marking it, she gave him the book; begging that he and Daza would consider the matter, and tell her what to do. She determined, if they thought it right, to give up that method of prayer altogether; 'for why,' she writes, 'should I expose myself to danger when, at the end of nearly twenty years, during which I had used it, I had gained nothing, but had fallen into a delusion of the devil? It was better for me to give it up. And yet this seemed to me hard; for I had already discovered what my soul would become without prayer. Everything seemed full of trouble. I was like a person in the middle of a river, who, in whatever direction he may turn, fears a still greater danger, and is well-nigh drowned.'[2]

Another trial was that some of those to whom she applied for advice caused her much pain by discussing her

[1] *Vida*, c. xxiii. 12.   [2] Ibid. 13.

condition, and 'making enquiries one of another, for a good purpose,' so that they 'made things known which might well have remained secret, because not intended for everyone.' But the climax of her distress was when Don Salcedo came to her in much distress, and told her the result of his consultation with Daza; namely, that, in the opinion of both, she was deluded by an evil spirit. They advised her to take counsel with a certain Jesuit father, F. Juan de Padranos, who had just been sent by St. Francis Borgia to found a house in Avila, telling her not to swerve in a single point from his advice, for that she was in great danger if she had no one to direct her.

'This answer so alarmed and distressed me,' writes Teresa, 'that I knew not what to do—I did nothing but cry.' She determined to see F. Padranos, but did not like the nuns to know of it, or see her 'converse with such holy persons as those of the Society of Jesus.' To seek their advice was evidently considered something unusual, implying a desire for greater strictness and holiness; and she shrank from the talk which this would make in the convent, fearing also her own inability to comply with what might be required of her; so she persuaded the sacristan and the portress to tell no one of F. Padranos' visit. The result gives us an amusing little glimpse of the convent and its ways. 'This was of little use, after all,' she wrote; 'for when I was called down there was one at the door, as it happened, who told it to the whole convent.'[1]

To this father she opened her whole soul, and made a general confession of her whole life, having previously written out 'all the evil and all the good,' as clearly as she understood it. He greatly encouraged her; telling her on no

[1] *Vida*, c. xxiii. 17.

account to give up her prayer, for that it was very evidently the work of the Spirit of God; only he bade her to be careful to avoid all imperfections which intercepted God's grace in her soul; and Ribera says, 'exercised her by the usual precepts of prayer which are prescribed in the Exercises of the blessed Ignatius, but not by all of them.' He added, 'Who knows whether perchance God may not will to effect good to many by thee.'[1]

'He made me very much ashamed of myself,' she writes, 'and directed me by a way which seemed to change me altogether. What a grand thing it is to understand a soul! ... After this my confession, my soul was so docile that, as it seems to me, there was nothing in the world I was not prepared to undertake. I began at once to make a change in many things, though my confessor never pressed me—on the contrary, he seemed to make light of it all. I was the more influenced by this, because he led me on by the way of the love of God; he left me free, and did not press me, unless I did so myself, out of love.'[2]

Two things, however, he desired which were hard to her—to resist to the utmost of her power the sensible sweetness and delight poured upon her in prayer; fixing her thoughts on the Sacred Humanity only, and to practise greater outward mortification and penance, which she had hitherto refrained from doing on account of weak health. 'He told me,' she says, 'that certain penances would not hurt me,' and 'ordered me to practise certain acts of mortification not very pleasant for me. I did so, because I felt that our Lord was enjoining it all, and giving him grace to command me in such a way as to make me obedient unto him.'[3]

[1] *Ribera*, i. c. v. 76.   [2] *Vida*, c. xxiii. 18; xxiv. 1.
[3] Ibid. 2.

It may be said here, once for all, with regard to austerities practised by St. Teresa (which were not slight), that there is nowhere the faintest trace of the spirit which is sometimes supposed to prompt such acts—of the attempt to expiate and atone for sin by their means, or to attain through them to peace of conscience and reconciliation with God. Whether they have ever been used, or abused, in this way, it is not necessary here to enquire; certainly the most notable instances in the Church of such strictness have been of persons undoubting of God's love to them, and filled with answering love to Him; as, in our day, we may instance Lacordaire, of whom we are told that from the time of his conversion, no cloud ever darkened the sunshine of his soul, rejoicing in God's love through Christ.

In Teresa's case, such special acts of penance seem to have been inspired by the simple desire to remove all which could hinder the workings of the Holy Spirit, keeping under her body, and punishing herself for faults and imperfections that they might be the sooner amended; and also, chiefly later in life, by the loving longing to join herself the closer, if it might be, to Him Whose sufferings had redeemed her, and on which she ever dwelt in fervent meditation. To consider them, and to be herself without pain or self-denial, was what her loving heart could scarcely bear. 'Who can look upon our Lord,' she writes in one place, 'covered with wounds, and bowed down under persecutions, without accepting, loving, and longing for them?'[1] In the beginning, as we see, she used some penances through obedience. F. Padranos must have seen at once that he had to deal with a soul marvellously gifted by nature, and still more by grace, with one to whom those very gifts of nature

[1] *Vida*, c. xxvi. 7.

presented unusual difficulties and temptations—whose 'sins had been chastised with great consolations,' as she expressed herself, and yet who had clung to certain things which interfered with these divine consolations, producing disorder in her soul. She mentions that even now she dreaded placing herself under F. Padranos; 'for I was afraid,' she writes, 'of my own wickedness, and I thought I should be obliged to cease from it, and give up my amusements.' The 'wickedness' was evidently that which had so long been a snare to her, amusing but unprofitable and distracting intercourse with worldly persons.

It is not, therefore, surprising that her new adviser should have led her to test the reality of the grace and sweetness which she experienced, and of her own correspondence to them, by striving for a time to resist sensible delight, and at the same time to kill and mortify all opposed to God's will for her; thus laying the foundations for a high interior life by penitence and watchfulness—a penitence finding its expression in even stern self-discipline. He was but following the leadings of God's dealings with her, Who had accompanied His spiritual favours with sharp bodily suffering; and he told her, she says, that perhaps God had sent her so much sickness because she had neglected to punish her own faults. 'If we would judge ourselves, we should not be judged,' were almost his words to her; and certainly St. Paul's account of the 'godly sorrow' of his Corinthian penitents has more resemblance to the path of severe repentance—'carefulness,' 'clearing of herself,' 'revenge'—in which Teresa was led, than to the temper of mind which refuses or condemns such self-discipline. 'The days will come when the Bridegroom shall be taken away from them, and then shall they fast in those days,' were the words of the Bridegroom beholding the ages through which the Bride should await His return. If it be right to take 'fasting' as including other modes of self-denial, is it any marvel that the children of the bride-chamber should thus prepare and discipline their souls, finding even a severe joy in suffering which may assist self-conquest ; in pain borne for offences, though forgiven, against Him Whom their soul loveth ; so that at length every thought may be brought into captivity to the obedience of Christ? And if 'in fastings often' has not been a marked characteristic of some branches or of some later ages of the Church, is not that rather a reason for being slow to question or condemn those who have been taught in a severer school?

'I continued thus nearly two months,' St. Teresa writes, 'doing all I could to resist the sweetness and graces that God sent. But our Lord was more careful to show His mercies, and during those two months to reveal Himself more than before, so that I might the better comprehend that it was no longer in my power to resist Him.'[1] Further help and guidance was at hand. She had given up the intercourse which had interested and amused her, and she was rewarded a hundredfold in that very thing she had renounced, rewarded by intercourse with the saints that were in the earth, and the excellent, in whom was all her delight. St. Francis Borgia came at this time (1557) to Avila, and was entreated both by F. Padranos and Salcedo to see Teresa, and pronounce on her way of prayer. *Dictum, factum*, writes Ribera, adding, that when he had heard her, he immediately said that this was the work of the Spirit of God, and that His leadings ought no longer to be resisted ; only advising that she should always begin by meditating on

[1] *Vida,* c. xxiv. 1.

the Passion, and that if she should then be raised up in spirit by God, she ought not to resist, but to allow herself freely to be carried away.

This interview with St. Francis Borgia is the first time that we hear of her being brought into relation with any of the most eminent men of her time; and the advice of one so experienced must have been a great benefit to her. In her eighth Spiritual 'Relation,' written for F. Alvarez, she mentions that condition in which the will is wholly intent upon God, while memory and understanding 'are at liberty to attend to other matters of the service of God—in a word, Martha and Mary together;' and says, 'I asked Father Francis if this was a delusion, for it made me stupid; and his reply was, that it often happened.'

Soon after Francis Borgia's visit, F. Padranos was removed from Avila, to Teresa's great distress, for she thought 'that it was not possible to find another such as he.' She went to stay with a kinswoman, and 'contrived at once to find another confessor, in the Society of Jesus.' At this time her close friendship began with Doña Guiomar de Ulloa, 'a noble lady, a widow, much given to prayer.' She introduced her to F. Balthasar Alvarez, under whose direction Teresa placed herself; but this could not have been until 1558, as Alvarez was not ordained priest until that year.

He told her that she ought to leave nothing undone that she might be wholly pleasing to God; but was, however, 'very prudent and gentle at the same time, especially as to giving up certain friendships;' for Teresa, 'generous in disposition,' as Ribera says, could not bear to pain those who had shown her affection. 'I asked him,' she writes, 'if I must be ungrateful.' He bade her to lay the matter before

God for a few days, and to recite the 'Veni Creator,' that God might enlighten her.

It was while she was saying it one day, having for some time prayed, imploring our Lord to help her to please Him in all things, that for the first time, she tells us, 'the grace of ecstasy' was bestowed upon her. 'I fell into a trance— so suddenly, that I was as it were carried out of myself. I could have no doubt about it, for it was most plain.'

There is a passage in Archbishop Trench's 'Synonyms of the New Testament' in which, speaking of the distinct manifestations of extra-ordinary spiritual forces from above, and from beneath, the Archbishop says that one acted upon by the first 'is, indeed, rapt out of himself; he is "in the Spirit" (Rev. i. 10); he is "in an ecstasy" (Acts xi. 5); he is ὑπὸ Πνεύματος Ἁγίου φερόμενος (2 Pet. i. 21), which is very much more than "*moved* by the Holy Ghost," as we have rendered it. . . . But then he is not *beside* himself; he is *lifted above*, not *set beside*, his everyday self. It is not discord and disorder, but a higher harmony and a diviner order, which are introduced into his soul; so that he is not as one overborne in the region of his lower life by forces stronger than his own, by an insurrection from beneath; but his spirit is lifted out of that region into a clearer atmosphere, a diviner day, than any in which at other times it is permitted him to breathe. All that he before had still remains his, only purged, exalted, quickened, by a power higher than his own, but yet not alien to his own; for man is most truly man when he is most filled with the fulness of God.'[1]

It would be impossible to express in clearer or nobler words, closely resembling her own, the condition which St. Teresa describes. Were the spiritual forces which acted upon

[1] *Synonyms of the New Testament*, § vi. pp. 21, 22.

her from beneath, or from above, is a question to which her character, her life, the Church, have given but one answer; and having lately dwelt upon the subject, it is needless to do more than relate the history which she has left us of her experience.

While in this ecstasy, she tells us that she heard these words: 'I will not have thee converse with men, but with angels.' 'They made me afraid, though, on the other hand, they gave me great comfort. . . . Those words have been fulfilled; for I have never been able to form friendship with, nor have any comfort in, nor any particular love for, any persons whatever, except those who, as I believe, love God, and who strive to serve Him. . . . Accordingly, there was no necessity for laying further commands upon me in this matter. When my confessor saw how much I clung to these friendships, he did not venture to bid me distinctly to give them up. He must have waited till our Lord did the work —as He did Himself. Nor did I think myself that I could succeed; for I had tried before, and the pain it gave me was so great that I abandoned the attempt, on the ground that there was nothing unseemly in those attachments. Now our Lord set me at liberty, and gave me strength also to use it. So I told my confessor of it, and gave up everything, according to his advice. It did a great deal of good to those with whom I used to converse to see my determination. God be blessed for ever! Who in one moment set me free, while I had been for many years making many efforts, and had never succeeded, very often doing such violence to myself as injured my health; but, as it was done by Him Who is Almighty, and the true Lord of all, it gave me no pain whatever.'[1]

A long chapter of St. Teresa's autobiography is devoted

[1] *Vida*, c. xxiv. 7, 8, 9.

to a description of 'divine locutions,' and to warnings against delusions. Here again it is impossible to do more than gather from her own words her experience and belief on this mysterious subject. They will supply the best materials for an answer to the question whether all was but the result of a heated imagination. That God 'spake some time by visions unto His saints' we know; that many have been deluded into imagining themselves thus highly favoured is equally certain. Teresa at least clearly perceived the danger, saying distinctly, that there are locutions which proceed from the evil one, and which have a certain sweetness and joy, by means of which sweetnesses, she writes, 'he may deceive any one who does not, or who never did, taste of the sweetness of God,—by which I mean a certain sweet, strong, impressive, delightsome and calm refreshing. Those little fervid bursts of tears, and other slight emotions . . . I do not call devotion.'[1]

In divine locution, she tells us, 'the words are very distinctly formed; but by the bodily ear they are not heard. They are, however, much more clearly understood than they would be if they were heard by the ear. . . . In this locution of God addressed to the soul there is no escape, for in spite of ourselves we must listen. . . . We should understand that His Will must be done; and He reveals Himself as our true Lord, having dominion over us.'[2] She goes on to explain that what is imagined to be a divine locution 'may be but an apprehension of the understanding,—for that is possible,—or even words which the mind addressed to itself . . . he who has heard the divine locution will see clearly enough what this is, because there is a great difference between the two. If it be anything which the understand-

[1] *Vida*, c. xxv. 14. [2] Ibid. c. xxv. 2.

ing has fashioned, however cunningly it may have done so, he sees that it is the understanding which has arranged that locution, and that it is speaking of itself. . . . The words it forms are something indistinct, fantastic, and not clear like the divine locutions. It is in our power to turn away our attention from these locutions of our own, just as we can be silent when we are speaking; but, with respect to the former, that cannot be done.'[1]

'There is another test more decisive still. The words formed by the understanding effect nothing; but when our Lord speaks, it is at once word and work; and though the words may not be meant to stir up our devotion, but are rather words of reproof, they dispose a soul at once, strengthen it, make it tender, give it light, console and calm it. . . . It may occur, too, when the understanding and the soul are so troubled and distressed that they cannot form one sentence correctly: and yet grand sentences, perfectly arranged, such as the soul in its most recollected state never could have formed, are uttered, and at the first word, as I said, change it utterly. . . . We listen as we do to a person of great holiness, learning, or authority, whom we know to be incapable of uttering a falsehood. And yet this is an inadequate illustration; for these locutions proceed occasionally in such great majesty that, without our recollecting Who it is that utters them, they make us tremble if they be words of reproof, and die of love if words of love.'

'There is no reason, therefore, why I should dwell longer on this matter. It is a wonder to me that any experienced person, unless he deliberately chooses to do so, can fall into delusions. . . . I repeat it, unless a soul be so wicked as to pretend that it has these locutions, which would be a great

[1] *Vida,* c. xxv. 4.

sin, and say that it hears divine words when it hears nothing of the kind, it cannot possibly fail to see clearly that itself arranges the words, and utters them to itself. . . . I end by saying that, in my opinion, we may hear the locutions that proceed from the understanding whenever we like, and think that we hear them when we pray. But it is not so with the divine locutions; for many days I may desire to hear them, and I cannot; and at other times, even when I would not, as I said before, hear them, I must.'[1]

Such words are certainly as unlike those of a deluded fanatic as can well be imagined, especially the distinct perception that what is taken as a voice from God may be but an 'apprehension of the understanding'—the mind speaking to itself. However, Teresa was full of fears herself at this time, whenever she was not occupied in prayer; (when she prayed she *could* not fear) and her scruples and terrors were much increased by her friends, for these matters began now to be talked of,—Alvarez having desired her to make them known to a few, all of them 'very great servants of God.' Five or six of them assembled together; and, she says, 'had many conferences together about my necessities, for they had a great affection for me, and were afraid I was under a delusion.' She went to San Egidio, the Jesuits' church in Avila, to see Alvarez; and there he told her that they were all of opinion that she was deceived by Satan; that she must communicate less frequently, and try to distract herself, and be less alone.

'Why should I not believe them?' she writes. 'I did all I could to believe them. I reflected on my wicked life, and therefore what they said to me must be true. . . . I had not been to Communion for many days, nor had I been

[1] *Vida*, c. xxv. 5, 6, 10, 11, 12.

alone, which was all my comfort. I had no one to speak to, for everyone was against me. Some, I thought, made a mock of me when I spoke to them of my prayer, as if I were a person under delusions of the imagination; others warned my confessor to be on his guard against me; and some said it was clear the whole was an operation of Satan. My confessor . . . always comforted me; and he alone did so. He told me that, if I did not offend God, my prayer, even if it was the work of Satan, could do me no harm; that I should be delivered from it.'[1]

This state had lasted 'about two years' (from 1557 to 1559), and she continually prayed God to lead her by another way. But in her extreme distress after F. Alvarez had told her the opinion of her friends, she left the church, and entered a certain oratory, 'perceiving no consolation,' says Ribera, 'either from heaven or from men; when lo! the Lord, Who never had forgotten her, spake to her innermost heart, saying: "Fear not, my daughter, for I will never desert thee: it is I; fear not."'[2]

She had never been in such distress before as when these words comforted her, for the dread lest the evil one had deluded her left her no peace; and her state in the oratory was such that she says she thought many hours would have been necessary to calm her, and that no one could have done it. 'Yet I found myself,' she writes, 'through these words alone, tranquil and strong, courageous and confident, at rest and enlightened; in a moment my soul seemed changed, and I felt I could maintain against all the world that my prayer was the work of God. . . . Oh, how good is God! . . . He gives not counsel only, but relief as well. His words are deeds. O my God! as He strengthens our

[1] *Vida*, c. xxv. 19, 20.   [2] *Ribera*, l. i. c. v. 81.

faith, love grows. . . . Who is He, that all my faculties should thus obey Him? Who is He, that gives light in such darkness in a moment; Who softens a heart that seemed to be made of stone; Who gives the waters of sweet tears, where for a long time great dryness seems to have prevailed? . . . All things fail; but Thou, Lord of all, never failest! They who love Thee, oh, how little they have to suffer! oh, how gently, how tenderly, how sweetly Thou, O my Lord, dealest with them! . . . It seems as if Thou didst subject those who love Thee to a severe trial; but it is in order that they may learn, in the depths of that trial, the depths of Thy love.'[1]

From this time her fears vanished. 'I do not understand,' she says, 'those terrors which make us cry out Satan, Satan! when we may say God, God! and make Satan tremble. . . . I took up the cross in my hand,—I was changed in a moment into another person; and it seemed as if God had really given me courage enough not to be afraid of encountering all the evil spirits. . . . So I cried out, Come on, all of you; I am the servant of our Lord: I should like to see what you can do against me. And certainly they seemed to be afraid of me, for I was left in peace: I feared them so little, that the terrors which until now oppressed me quitted me altogether. . . . I cared no more for them than for flies. They seem to be such cowards; for their strength fails them at the sight of anyone who despises them. We ourselves put weapons into their hands, that they may assail us; those very weapons with which we should defend ourselves. It is a great pity. But if, for the love of God . . . we embraced the cross, and set about His service in earnest, Satan would fly away before such realities as from the plague.'[2]

[1] *Vida*, c. xxv. 22, 23.   [2] Ibid. 24-27.

Courage was indeed a virtue too congenial to her nature not to be greatly prized by her; and she says that she looked upon the courage which our Lord had implanted in her as one of the very greatest mercies which He had bestowed upon her; 'for a cowardly soul, afraid of anything but sin against God, is a very unseemly thing, when we have on our side the King omnipotent, our Lord most High. . . . There is nothing to be afraid of if we walk, as I said before, in the truth, in the sight of His Majesty, with a pure conscience'[1]

[1] *Vida,* c. xxvi. 1.

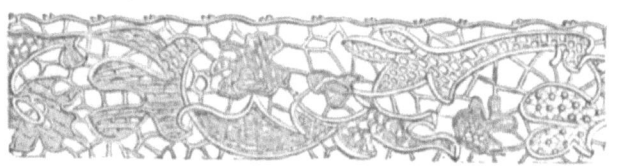

Chapter the Eighth.

1559—1561.

En las internas entrañas
Senti un golpe repentino;
El blason era divino
Porque obró grandes hazañas.
Con el golpe fui herida;
Y aunque la herida es mortal,
Y es un dolor desigual,
Es muerte que causa vida.
Si mata, como da vida?
Y si vida, como muerte?
Como sana cuando hiere?
Y se vé con el unida?
Tiene tan divinas mañas,
Que en un acerbo trance
Sale triunfando de lance
Obrando grandes hazañas.   ST. TERESA.

HE spiritual troubles of Teresa had not, however, ended; she suffered much at this time from her director. Professor Zöckler calls him 'the pious and enlightened, and withal truly humble Jesuit, Baltasar Alvarez;'[1] Sacchinus, the Jesuit chronicler, speaks of him as one not caring to have many

[1] *Zeitschrift für Lutherische Theologie,* 1865: 'Teresia von Avila.'

penitents, but rather striving to make a few better through continual growth; above all things, making a law to himself to speak to his penitents only of divine things; refusing all gifts or allurements of private friendship; and pleased that they should occasionally go to other advisers. He lived at the Jesuit College at Avila from 1559 to 1566, when he was sent to Medina del Campo, and was Teresa's confessor during that time.

She says he 'mortified me greatly, and now and then distressed me; he tried me heavily, for he dispirited me exceedingly, and yet he was the one who, I believe, did me the most good. Though I had a great affection for him, I was occasionally tempted to leave him; I thought that the pain he inflicted on me disturbed my prayer. Whenever I was resolved on leaving him I used to feel instantly that I ought not to do so; and one reproach of our Lord would press more heavily upon me than all that my confessor did. Now and then I was worn out—torture on the one hand, reproaches on the other.'[1]

The Bollandists, quoting Ludovicus de Ponte, ascribe Alvarez's treatment of Teresa at this time partly to deep spiritual trials of his own, and give part of a relation which he made of his condition to the General of the Society, in which he speaks of his own inward desolation and intolerance to others. Teresa's sensitive nature suffered keenly in consequence, especially as it was a difficulty to her to speak at all of special graces vouchsafed to her. 'I was so ashamed of myself,' she says, 'that I felt it more keenly at times to speak of them than I should have done in confessing grave sins. . . . I thought they did not believe me, and that they were laughing at me. I felt it so much—for I

[1] *Vida*, c. xxvi. 4.

look on this as an irreverent treatment of the marvels of God—that I was glad to be silent.'

But the unusual conditions of mental prayer which she experienced only became more frequent during the next two years, in spite of many prayers made on her behalf that she might be led 'by another and a safer way.' She tried to believe what most of her friends told her, that this way 'was so suspicious,' and joined her prayers to theirs, though, she says, 'when I saw the progress I was making, I was unable really to desire a change. . . . I could do nothing but put myself in the hands of God: He knew what was expedient for me: let Him do with me according to His will in all things.' The Lutheran writer, Zöckler, remarks of this period in her history, 'it plainly betokens an advance in her ever more richly unfolding and more and more strengthening inner experience, that a constant vision of the Saviour immediately present with her took the place of the divine locutions which she had previously heard.'[1] It was on St. Peter's day[2] that she had first this 'vision;' but she 'saw nothing with the eyes of the body.' 'Jesus Christ seemed to be by my side continually; and as the vision was not imaginary, I saw no form; but I had a distinct feeling that He was always on my right hand, a witness of all I did; and never at any time, if I was but slightly recollected, or not too much distracted, could I be ignorant of His near presence.'[3]

She was unlike those who have deluded themselves with fanatical fancies in this, that anything which seemed to her an unusual spiritual grace filled her at first with self-distrust. On this occasion she says, 'I went at once to my confessor,

[1] *Zeitschrift für Luther. Theol.* 1865, p. 87.
[2] The Bollandists say that this was in 1559.   [3] *Vida*, c. xxviii. 3.

in great distress, to tell him of it. He asked in what form I saw our Lord. I told him I saw no form. He then said, "How did you know that it was Christ?" I replied that I did not know how I knew it, but I could not help knowing that He was close beside me—that I saw Him distinctly, and felt His presence—that the recollectedness of my soul was deeper in the prayer of quiet, and more continuous—that the effects thereof were very different from what I had hitherto experienced, and that it was most certain.'[1]

Nothing could shake this 'infinite comfortable assurance,' as Zöckler calls it. 'In vain,' he writes, 'did her spiritual advisers . . . suggest faithless doubts. . . . The vision remained her own, yea, and it grew day by day in clearness, and in a penetrating influence upon her heart and spiritual knowledge. . . . And at first it is the crucified, the suffering, the thorn-crowned Saviour Whom she beholds after this manner; but later she almost always sees Him, especially at Mass during meditation before the consecrated Host, as the Risen and Glorified Lord, in His full celestial majesty.' It is difficult to make a choice from her own words, for all are steeped in love and beauty; and this cannot be denied even by those who doubt the source of her joy. 'It is not like that presence of God,' she writes, 'which is frequently felt . . . when we seem, at the very commencement of our prayer, to find Him with Whom we would converse, and when we seem to feel that He hears us by the effects and the spiritual impressions of great love and faith of which we are then conscious. . . . This is a great grace from God . . . but it is not vision. . . . There is so much of heaven in this language, that it cannot well be understood on earth, though we may desire ever so much to explain it, if our Lord will

[1] *Vida*, c. xxvii. 3, 4.

not teach it experimentally . . . He renders Himself present to the soul by a certain knowledge of Himself which is more clear than the sun. . . . God and the soul understand one another, merely because His Majesty so wills it, without the help of other means, to express the love there is between them both.'[1]

'Oh, marvellous goodness of God,' she exclaims, 'in that Thou permittest eyes which have looked upon so much evil as those of my soul to look upon Thee! . . . The joy of this is so far above all conceivable joys, that it may well make us loathe all the joys of earth, for they are all but dross. . . . Those which our Lord gives, what are they? One drop only of the waters of the overflowing river which He is reserving for us. . . . What will be the accidental glory and the joy of the blessed who have entered on it, when they see that, though they were late, yet they left nothing undone which it was possible for them to do for God, who kept back nothing they could give Him. . . . How rich will he be who gave up all his riches for Christ? How honourable will he be who, for His sake, sought no honours whatever, but rather took pleasure in seeing himself abased! How wise he will be who rejoiced when men accounted him as mad!—they did so of Wisdom Itself!'[2]

She breaks out into complaints that 'the grand impetuosities of the Saints' are forgotten, and that 'they are all gone whom people regarded as mad, because they saw them perform heroic acts, as true lovers of Christ;' saying that even if some should take scandal at such actions, 'others are filled with remorse: anyhow, we should have before us some likeness of that which our Lord and His Apostles endured, for we have need of it now more than ever.'

[1] *Vida*, c. xxvii. 5, 6, 8, 12.   [2] Ibid. c. xxvii. 13, 15.

This period of her life, from 1559 to 1561, just before the great outer work of her life began, is especially crowded with visions. Still, she tells us again, 'I never saw with my bodily eyes, nor, indeed, any other, but only with the eyes of the soul.' She says she cannot explain 'how it is that a light so strong can enter the interior sense, or so distinct an image the understanding, so as to seem to be really there; for this must be work for learned men. Our Lord has not been pleased to let me understand how it is. I am so ignorant myself, and so dull of understanding, that although people have very much wished to explain it to me, I have never been able to understand how it can be. . . . One thing, however, I have to say: if in Heaven itself there were nothing else to delight our eyes but the great beauty of glorified bodies, that would be an excessive bliss, particularly the vision of the Humanity of Jesus Christ our Lord. If here below, where His Majesty shows Himself to us according to the measure which our wretchedness can bear, it is so great, what must it be there, where the fruition of it is complete!'[1]

Her state began to be talked about, and almost all her religious friends agreed in telling her she was deluded by Satan. Even one of the fathers at the Jesuits' College, to whom she confessed if F. Alvarez were absent, took this view, and bade her to make signs of contempt and scorn if any vision should appear to her, and to make the sign of the cross. This last she did, but says, 'I did not always make signs of contempt, because I felt that too much. It reminded me of the insults which the Jews heaped upon Him.'

F. Alvarez, however, always stood by her, though she knew that others used to say to him that he must be on his guard against her, and she 'did nothing but weep,' fearing

[1] *Vida*, c. xxviii. 4, 9.

she should at last 'find no one to hear her confession.' Besides this, her friends used to put questions to her, and when 'I answered simply and carelessly,' she says, 'they concluded forthwith that I wished to teach them, and that I considered myself to be a learned woman. All this was carried to my confessor—for certainly they desired my amendment—and so he would reprimand me. This lasted some time, and I was distressed on many sides.'[1]

She prayed much to be delivered from delusions. 'I was always praying to that effect, and with many tears,' she writes; but her prayers were answered by an over-flowing and ever-increasing love of God within her. 'I tried to distract myself; I never ceased to be in prayer; even during sleep my prayer seemed to be continued. . . . I saw myself dying with a desire to see God, and I knew not how to seek that life otherwise than by dying. . . . I never could be sorry that I had had these heavenly visions; nor would I exchange even one of them for all the wealth and all the pleasures of the world.'[2] She takes pains to express the difference between these impetuosities of love; calm through their very strength, and those 'devotional sensations, not uncommon, which seem on the point of causing suffocation, and are beyond control'—agitations which 'should be avoided by gently endeavouring to be recollected;' and by reason drawing in the reins, 'because nature itself may be contributing to it; and we should consider with fear that all this may not be perfect, and that much sensuality may be involved in it.' But in the true love with which 'God wounds the soul,' it 'loses all self-consciousness;' it sees distinctly 'that it never did anything whereby this love should come to it, and that it does come

[1] *Vida*, c. xxviii. 23. [2] Ibid. c. xxix. 5, 9, 10.

from that exceeding love which our Lord bears it. A spark seems to have fallen suddenly upon it, that has set it all on fire.' 'Oh, how often,' she exclaims, 'do I remember, when in this state, those words of David, *Quemadmodum desiderat cervus ad fontes aquarum!* They seem to me to be literally true of myself.'[1]

It was at this time that she had the famous vision which has become identified with her in all representations of her in art,—poor and ignoble as most of them are,—the 'transverberation' of her heart. It is best to give her own account of it without any comment. The Bollandists enquire at great length into its actual physical effect, and the proofs of it; but this we are not here concerned to do. There is, however, enough known beyond all doubt in our own day, as in other times, of the 'reactive power of the spirit, which is the stronger, in moulding and fashioning the flesh, which is the weaker,'[2] to prevent us from calling that which is supernatural impossible, or an imposture.

'I saw an angel close by me,' Teresa wrote, 'on my left side, in bodily form. This I am not accustomed to see, unless very rarely. Though I have visions of angels frequently, yet I see them only by an intellectual vision, such as I have spoken of before. It was our Lord's will that in this vision I should see the angel in this wise. He was not large, but small of stature, and most beautiful—his face burning, as if he were one of the highest angels, who seem to be all of fire: they must be those whom we call cherubim. Their names they never tell me; but I see very well that there is in heaven so great a difference between one angel and another, and between these and the others, that I cannot

[1] *Vida*, c. xxix. 11, 14.
[2] Archbishop Trench, *Lecture on the Mendicant Orders*.

explain it. I saw in his hand a long spear of gold, and at the iron's point there seemed to be a little fire. He appeared to me to be thrusting it at times into my heart, and to pierce my very entrails; when he drew it out, he seemed to draw them out also, and to leave me all on fire with a great love of God. The pain was so great that it made me moan; and yet so surpassing was the sweetness of this excessive pain, that I could not wish to be rid of it. The soul is satisfied now with nothing less than God. The pain is not bodily, but spiritual; though the body has its share in it, even a large one. It is a caressing of love so sweet which now takes place between the soul and God, that I pray God of His goodness to make him experience it who may think that I am lying. During the days that this lasted I went about as if beside myself. I wished to see, or speak with, no one, but only to cherish my pain, which was to me a greater bliss than all created things could give me.'[1]

After this, pondering within herself, says her Bollandist biographer, what reward she should give unto the Lord for all the benefits that He had done unto her, she formed the resolution in all things to take utmost care not to offend God by the very slightest sin; and this was followed by her celebrated vow, never in any action to do that which was the less perfect, but always what seemed to her the most pleasing and acceptable to God. Yepes says of this vow, 'suited rather to the virtue of Seraphim than of men,' that he believed she fulfilled it; and that many bore witness that as long as they lived with her they could perceive nothing in her contrary to perfection. The vow, however, became before long a source of scruples both to her and to her confessors; apparently amid multiplicity of business and work they could not

---

[1] *Vida*, c. xxix. 16, 17.

always determine what *was* the most perfect course, and she was advised to apply to the Provincial of her Order for absolution from her vow. She obediently made the necessary application ; and the following document was sent to Avila : 'F. Angelo de Salazar, Principal in the Province of Castile of the Order of the Blessed Virgin of Mount Carmel. By the tenor of these letters we give and commit our authority to the Rev. Father Prior of our Convent of Avila, and to the Rev. Father Garcia of Toledo, of the Order of Preachers, by which either of them, administering the Sacrament of Penitence to our most dear sister Teresa of Jesus, Prioress of the nuns of St. Joseph, may release her from any vow made by her, or alter the same, according as it may appear to them the rather to serve the honour of God and the quietness of mind of our aforesaid sister. For which cause, as we have said, the power and authority which we have from our office we grant to the said Fathers. Given at Toledo, the second day of March, 1565.'

To this document F. Garcia of Toledo added with his own hand as follows : 'Having heard thy confession, as the Father Provincial requires, I, both because I believe it to be for the peace and quiet of thy soul, and also, which in this case is the same thing, serviceable to thy confessors, abolish and extinguish the vow made by thee. In the Name of the Father and of the Son and of the Holy Ghost. Amen. The way, however, in which it appears to me that the vow may be afresh made by thee, is this : that thou shouldest surely vow, when thou treatest of any matter with thy confessor in the sacred tribunal, to carry into execution whatever he shall declare to thee to be of greatest perfection, etc.' [1]

To return, however, to the time when she made her vow,

[1] *Acta Sanct.* t. vii. Oct. § xiii. 231, 232.

1560. 'Amidst trials and perplexities,' she writes, 'our Lord was pleased to succour me in a great measure,—and, for the moment, altogether, — by bringing to the place where I was that blessed friar, Peter of Alcantara.'[1] He was at this time amongst the foremost of those who were seeking to revive earnest piety and reform abuses in the Spanish Church. Born in 1499, at Alcantara in Estramadura, he studied as a boy at Salamanca, for he was only fourteen when recalled to Alcantara: but even then his whole time had been divided between the schools, the church, the hospital, and his closet. He renounced the career open to him in the world, and at sixteen took the Franciscan habit in the solitary convent of Manjarez, situated among the mountains that divide Castile and Portugal, where he gave himself up to a life of continual prayer and severe austerity. 'He spoke of it to me and to another person, from whom he kept few or no secrets,' Teresa says in one of the additions to her autobiography. 'He told me, I think, that for forty years he slept but an hour and a half out of the twenty-four; and that the most laborious penance he underwent, when he began, was this of overcoming sleep. For that purpose, he was always either kneeling or standing. When he slept, he sat down, his head resting against a piece of wood driven into the wall. Lie down he could not, if he wished it, for his cell, as everyone knows, was only four feet and a half in length. In all these years he never covered his head with his hood, even when the sun was hottest or the rain heaviest. He never covered his feet; the only garment he wore was made of sackcloth, and that was as tight as it could be, with nothing between it and his flesh: over this he wore a cloak of the same stuff. He told me

[1] *Vida*, c. xxx. 2.

that in the severe cold he used to take off his cloak, and open the door and the window of his cell, in order that when he put on his cloak again, after shutting the door and the window, he might give some satisfaction to his body in the pleasure it might have in the increased warmth. His ordinary practice was to eat but once in three days. He said to me, "Why are you astonished at it? It is very possible for anyone who is used to it." . . . He was an aged man when I made his acquaintance; and his weakness was so great that he seemed like nothing else but the roots of trees. With all his sanctity he was very agreeable, though his words were few, unless when he was asked questions; he was very pleasant to speak to, for he had a most clear understanding.'[1]

He was made superior of the Franciscans at Badajos when only twenty-three, and at twenty-five received priest's orders by the command of his superiors. But as his earnest desire for retirement continued, he was sent to the lonely convent at Lapa, near Soriana, where he composed his 'Golden Book' on Mental Prayer, esteemed a masterpiece by St. Luis de Granada, St. Teresa, St. Francis de Sales, &c. Forced from his retreat by John III. of Portugal, who would fain have kept him as his spiritual adviser, he contrived to leave him to appease some divisions in his native city, and was soon after chosen Provincial of Estramadura, where his work of reform began. He drew up strict rules, which were accepted; but not content with this, after eminent services and reforms of his Order both in Spain and Portugal, he established in 1555, near Pedroso, in the diocese of Palentia, a congregation of friars under a still severer rule, who were the beginning of the reformed institute of Franciscan Friars, called Barefooted, or 'of the strictest observance

[1] *Vida,* c. xxvii. 18, 19.

of St. Peter of Alcantara,' and which, as we shall see later, suggested the first thought of Teresa's reform. They slept on boards or mats, and only the sick used either flesh, fish, eggs, or wine. They insisted especially that both their convents and churches should be extremely small and poor, and that they should receive no remuneration for saying mass. Three hours were spent daily in mental prayer.

Charles V. in vain sought to retain St. Peter of Alcantara as his confessor at St. Just: he refused the office, saying that it would interfere with devotion and with ministrations to others.

The friendship which sprung up between this remarkable man and Teresa was of the warmest. Belonging to an older generation and to a somewhat different school of thought from herself, at least less deeply imbued with mysticism, his was exactly the mind upon which she could lean at this period of her life, and the judgment to which she could trust. The first ' Relation ' of her spiritual state was written for him, in 1560, and describes her method of prayer, her trances, and condition of mind. ' When I see anyone who knows anything about me,' she writes in this Relation, ' I wish to let him know my whole life, because my honour seems to me to consist in the honour of our Lord, and I care for nothing else. . . . Nor can I believe it of God, though I have deserved to fall into delusions because of my sins, that He has left unheeded so many prayers of so many good people for two years; and I do nothing else but ask everybody to pray to our Lord that He would show me if this be for His glory, or lead me by another way.'

Nothing could be more comforting than her intercourse with St. Peter of Alcantara: he bade her ' not be distressed, but to praise God, and to abide in the full conviction that this was the work of the Spirit of God.' Thirty-three reasons for believing this were found amongst her papers, written, the Bollandists say,[1] in Peter of Alcantara's handwriting. They are given by Ribera,[2] and are very remarkable for a calm common sense united with sympathetic discernment. For instance, alluding to her extra-ordinary graces, he writes under the fourth head, 'She has never prayed for nor wished for them ; all she wishes for is to do the will of God our Lord in all things.' And again : '17. They are in her the cause of the deepest humility; she understands that what she receives comes to her from the hand of our Lord, and how little worth she is herself. 25. She cannot bear to be directed by anyone who will not tell her of her faults, and rebuke her : all that she accepts with great humility. 29. . . . She has put far away from herself all the littleness and silliness of women. She is singularly free from scruples, and most sincere.'

'He was greatly comforted in me,' writes St. Teresa; 'was most kind and serviceable, and ever afterwards took great care of me, and told me of his own affairs and labours ; and when he saw that I had those very desires which in himself were fulfilled already—for our Lord had given me very strong desires—and also how great my resolution was, he delighted in conversing with me.'[3]

He appears to have been more generally kind and sympathetic than anyone she had as yet consulted, and he was, she says, 'extremely sorry' for her. 'He told me that one of the greatest trials in this world was that which I had borne—namely, the contradiction of good people—and that more was in reserve for me. I had need, therefore, of some

---

[1] *Acta Sanct.* Oct. t. vii. p. 710.   [2] *Ribera*, l. iv. c. iv.
[3] *Vida*, c. xxx. 5.

one—and there was no one in this city—who understood me; but he would speak to my confessor, and to that married nobleman, already spoken of, who was one of those who tormented me most.'[1] Alvarez was easily satisfied; 'not so the nobleman.' However, her new friend left her 'in the greatest consolation and joy,' bidding her 'continue her prayer with confidence, and without any doubt that it was the work of God.'

Still, she suffered—grievously at times in body, and also in mind; it seems at this time, as if she were tried by an almost morbid self-introspection. She says herself it was false humility. Losing sensible sweetness, she fancied herself so wicked, as to have been the cause, by her sins, 'of all the evils and all the heresies that had sprung up;' whereas, as she says, 'true humility is not attended with trouble; it does not disturb the soul; it causes neither obscurity nor aridity: on the contrary, it consoles . . . bringing with it calm, sweetness, and light.' She describes interior aridity as only one who had felt its sharpest pangs could describe it. 'The soul truly believes all that the Church holds; but its profession of the faith is hardly more than an outward profession of the mouth. . . . Temptations seem to press it down, and make it dull, so that its knowledge of God becomes to it as that of something which it hears of far away. So tepid is its love that, when it hears God spoken of, it listens and believes that He is what He is, because the Church so teaches; but it recollects nothing of its own former experience. Vocal prayer or solitude is only a greater affliction, because the interior suffering—whence it comes, it knows not—is unendurable.'[2]

Her confessors seem to have had a hard time of it with her

[1] *Vida*, c. xxx. 6.   [2] Ibid. 14.

just now. She thought she was deceiving them, and used to go to them and 'caution them very earnestly to be on their guard against' her. One of them told her, at last, not to distress herself, for that even if she wished to deceive him, he had sense enough not to be deceived. 'This,' she naïvely says, 'gave me great comfort.' She did not find comfort in friends, since, she says, 'to converse with anyone is worse, for the devil then sends so offensive a spirit of bad temper, that I think I could eat people up; nor can I help myself. I feel that I do something when I keep myself under control; or rather our Lord does so, when He holds back with His hand anyone in this state from saying or doing something that may be hurtful to his neighbours and offensive to God.'[1] Still, she almost always found sensible comfort in Communion. 'As I drew near to the most Holy Sacrament,' she writes, 'all at once my soul and body would be so well, that I was amazed. It seemed to be nothing else but an instantaneous dispersion of the darkness that covered my soul: when the sun rose, I saw how silly I had been.' She was also comforted by watching her understanding, when she could not keep it fixed upon God, and leaving it alone 'to see what it would do. Glory be to God! for a wonder, it never runs on what is wrong, but only on indifferent things, considering what is going on here, or there, or elsewhere.'[2]

Then she believed herself to be specially tormented by evil spirits, and at other times grieved when people made much of her. 'It is not so,' she says, 'when I am persecuted; . . . my soul seems then to be a queen in its kingdom, having everything under its feet. . . . Once when I was much distressed . . . our Lord said to me, What was

[1] *Vida*, c. xxx. 15.   [2] Ibid. 16, 19.

CH. VIII. *Need for Action.* 137

I afraid of? one of two things must happen—people would either speak ill of me, or give glory to Him. . . . This made me quite calm, and it comforts me whenever I think of it.'[1]

The time for action was near; a mind like hers could not much longer continue without some outward expression of the earnestness and zeal which were preying upon themselves. She thought at this time of leaving the Convent of the Incarnation and going to another monastery, where enclosure was more strictly observed; thinking that it would be a great consolation to her to live where she was not known; but her superiors would never let her go. And she says that she perceived later that 'all these little fears and distresses, and semblance of humility, were mere imperfections, . . . for a soul left in the hands of God cares nothing about evil or good report, if it clearly comprehends, when our Lord is pleased to bestow upon it His grace, that it has nothing of its own.' As for evil report, she speaks of it as useful, inasmuch as 'that it tolerates no faults in good people, and helps them to perfection by dint of complaints against them. Perfection is not attained to at once, yet the world, when it sees anyone beginning to travel on that road, insists on his becoming perfect at once; . . . and the more men respect such an one, the more do they forget that he is still in the body; . . . and so, though the poor soul have not yet begun to walk, the world will have it fly.'[2]

The last marked event of her spiritual life before her outward work began must be given in her own words. 'I was,' she writes, ' one day in prayer, when I found myself in a moment, without knowing how, plunged apparently into hell. . . . It was but a moment, but it seems to me impossible I should ever forget it, even if I were to live many

[1] *Vida*, c. xxxi. 13, 15.   [2] Ibid. 18, 19.

years. ... But as to what I then felt, I do not know where to begin, if I were to describe it: it is utterly inexplicable. I felt a fire in my soul. I cannot see how it is possible to describe it. My bodily sufferings were unendurable. I have undergone most painful sufferings in this life, and, as the physicians say, the greatest that can be borne, such as the contraction of my sinews when I was paralysed, ... yet all these were as nothing in comparison with what I felt then, especially when I saw that there would be no intermission, nor any end to them. These sufferings were nothing in comparison with the anguish of my soul, a sense of oppression, of stifling, and of pain so keen, accompanied by so hopeless and cruel an infliction, that I know not how to speak of it. If I said that the soul is continually being torn from the body, it would be nothing, for that implies the destruction of life by the hands of another; but here it is the soul itself that is tearing itself in pieces. I cannot describe that inward fire or that despair, surpassing all torments and all pain. I did not see who it was that tormented me, but I felt myself on fire, and torn to pieces, as it seemed to me; and, I repeat it, this inward fire and despair are the greatest torments of all. ... There was no light, but all was thick darkness. I do not understand how it is: though there was no light, yet everything that can give pain by being seen was visible. ... I know not how it was, but I understood distinctly that it was a great mercy that our Lord would have me see with mine own eyes the very place from which His compassion saved me. I have listened to people speaking of these things, and I have at other times dwelt on the various torments of hell, though not often, because my soul made no progress by the way of fear. ... But all is as nothing before this—it is a wholly different matter. In short, the one is a reality, the other a picture; and all burning here in this life is as nothing in comparison with the fire that is there.

'I was so terrified by that vision—and that terror is on me even now while I am writing—that, though it took place nearly six years ago, the natural warmth of my body is chilled by fear even now when I think of it. And so, amid all the pain and suffering which I may have had to bear, I remember no time in which I do not think that all we have to suffer in this world is as nothing. It seems to me that we complain without reason. I repeat it, this vision was one of the grandest mercies of our Lord.'[1]

It increased her zeal and vehement desire both for more devoted service herself and for the salvation of others. She could no longer be satisfied with the usual convent life. Even before this she tells us how she had suffered from 'the inward stirring of love' urging her 'to do something for the service of God;' and of how such love is like a great fire, which requires fuel continually, in order that it may not burn out.' Yet, 'I am not able,' she writes, 'to do more than adorn images with boughs and flowers, clean or arrange an oratory, or some such trifling acts, so that I am ashamed of myself.' She says that one 'who has learning, ability, and power to preach, to hear confessions, and to draw souls unto God,' 'neither knows nor comprehends the blessing he possesses, unless he knows by experience what it is to be powerless to serve God in anything, and at the same time to be receiving much from Him.'[2]

No words could bring the saint more vividly before us at this time in her life, with her burning love, her great soul and mind, now ripened and matured—unconscious of all

[1] *Vida*, c. xxxii. 7.   [2] Ibid. c. xxx. 26.

that God had put in her power, unknowing of her own strength and influence—but feeling oppressed and hemmed in by the poverty of her outer life. Yet when wrought up to the highest point by the terrible vision which she records, her profound common sense and simplicity were not overclouded.[1] 'I tried to think what I could do for God,' she says, 'and thought that the first thing was to follow my vocation to a religious life, which His Majesty had given me, by keeping the rule in the greatest perfection possible.'[2]

Thus she returns, unblinded and unbewildered by fancy, genius, or extraordinary gifts, to the simple obedience of a child. To do her duty in that state of life unto which it had pleased God to call her,—this, she perceives, is the most acceptable service she can render. She says that she 'was in spirit restless,' yet with a restlessness 'not harassing, but rather pleasant. I saw clearly that it was the work of God, and that His Majesty had furnished my soul with fervour, so that I might be able to digest other and stronger food than I had been accustomed to eat.'[3]

She had more outward hindrances than most in the way of living strictly, being much sought for; 'the rule being kept, not in its original exactness, but according to the custom of the whole Order, authorized by the Bull of Mitigation;' so that 'this inconvenience of going out,' she writes, 'though it was I that took most advantage of it, was a very grievous one for me; for many persons, to whom my

---

[1] 'Je ne sais si l'on trouverait un plus parfait modèle d'une vertu fort recommandée aux personnes pieuses, et qui est peut-être la plus rare, la simplicité. Elle découvre son âme, et on y reconnaît les grandes lignes de la nature humaine.'—*Rousselot: Les Mystiques Espagnols.* Paris, 1867, p. 334.

[2] *Vida,* c. xxxii. 11.   [3] Ibid.

superiors could not say no, were glad to have me with them. My superiors, thus importuned, commanded me to visit these persons; and thus it was so arranged that I could not be long together in the monastery.'[1]

But now the fire was kindled; the inward life and spiritual experience which had slowly and painfully ripened through long years of struggle were soon to find expression in work and writings which rank amongst the most considerable influences in Christendom in the sixteenth century, effecting a wide-spread and lasting practical reform, and giving a new method to 'the only philosophy then possible in Spain—Catholic Mysticism.'

[1] *Vida,* c. xxxii. 12.

Chapter the Ninth.

1561, 1562.

*Non temer, chè venne al mondo
Gesù, d'eterno ben largo ampio mare
Per far leggiero ogni gravoso pondo.
Sempre son l'onde sue più dolci et chiare
A chi con umil barca in quel gran fondo
Dell' alta sua bontà si lascia andare.*

VITTORIA COLONNA.

ON a certain night,[1] Ribera tells us,[2] several of her cousins and relatives were assembled in Teresa's cell in the Incaruation; some of them being nuns, and others persons living in the world. Amongst them were Juaña de Suarez, her old friend, and Maria de Ocampo, with her sister Eleonora, granddaughters of Teresa's eldest uncle, Francisco Alvarez de Cepeda. The elder, who afterwards became Maria of St. John Baptist, and Prioress of the Reformed Carmelites at Valladolid, had ever been especially beloved by Teresa, in spite of her apparently light and worldly nature. She had a passion for dress, which she indulged to excess, using great ingenuity and industry in fresh devices for personal adornment. She was staying at the convent, drawn thither by

---

[1] In July 1561.   [2] *Ribera,* l. i. c. vii.

her affection for her aunt (as a father's first cousin was called in Spain); and on this evening in her cell the little company began to talk, 'in a kind of play and joke,'[1] of the hindrances and vexations belonging to the kind of life which they were leading at the Incarnation, on account, as it seemed to them, of the great number in the community.[2] We have seen the disquiet and restlessness with which her present life had of late filled St. Teresa; but the first spark which kindled her longings into action came from her light-hearted young cousin. Maria de Ocampo exclaimed: 'Why, then, should not all of us here present agree to begin another kind of life, which after the fashion of the old anchorites may breathe the spirit of greater solitude?'

Her words pleased them all, and the night was spent in mutual discourse, and discussion as to the possibility of founding a convent into which few should be admitted, and of the expense required for the undertaking. Maria immediately offered a thousand ducats of her own inheritance for the purpose; and Ribera speaks of the joy of Teresa 'when she heard one, hitherto almost wholly absorbed by worldly vanities, discuss with such ardour the beginning of this new kind of life.'

Never was a great work begun with less thought of doing anything great. There was no intention of reforming the order; none present seem to have known anything of its history, and it was not till some time later that even Teresa knew that in the original Rule she would find all they required. She had recourse now to her friend Doña Guiomar de Ulloa, who had been so helpful to her on many

[1] *Ribera.*
[2] St. Teresa says in a letter that there were 180 nuns at the Incarnation during the twenty-five years she had lived there.

occasions, and said to her, half playfully: 'These maidens have been recently talking much of a new convent to be founded by us in imitation of the Barefooted Franciscans, and have been making many plans about it.'[1] Doña Guiomar did not take the words in jest, but 'began to consider how to provide a revenue for the home.'

And now for a moment Teresa held back, filled with loving thoughts of the home where she had so long dwelt, and taking, she says, 'the greatest delight in the house in which I was then living, because it was very pleasant to me, and in my own cell most convenient for my purpose.' But one day, after Communion, she could not doubt that she was called to this work; and, in spite of her longings to do something, 'suffered most keenly,' she says, 'because I saw in part the great anxieties and troubles that the work would cost me, and I was also very happy in the house I was in then; and though I used to speak of this matter in past times, yet it was not with resolution nor with any confidence that the thing could ever be done.'

Alvarez neither encouraged her nor absolutely forbade the attempt; referring her to the Provincial of the Carmelites, Angelo de Salazar. He was pleased with the project, promising Doña Guiomar to acknowledge the new house. Teresa then laid the matter before 'the holy priest, Peter of Alcantara,' who strongly advised her going forward in the work, and gave 'his sanction on all points.' She also consulted St. Luis Bertrand, 'a bright star of the renowned Order of Preachers,' who after three or four months wrote thus to her:—

'Mother Teresa, I have received thy letter; and because the business about which thou hast consulted me pertains to the service of God, I wished first to commend it to His

[1] *Ribera*, L. i. c. vii. 99.

divine Majesty by my poor prayers and sacrifices: for which cause I have delayed my answer. Now, in the Name of the same Lord, I say to thee to take courage in the accomplishment of so great a work, for God will help and protect thee; and in His Name I certify to thee that fifty years shall not have passed, before thy Order shall be one of the most illustrious which the Church of God possesses, Who, etc.

'From Valentia, etc.'[1]

But the affair became scarcely known when there arose, Teresa writes, 'a violent persecution, which cannot be very easily described—sharp sayings and keen jests. People said it was folly in me, who was so well off in my monastery; as to my friend, the persecution was so continuous that it wearied her.... Among people of prayer, and indeed in the whole neighbourhood, there was hardly one who was not against us, and who did not think our work the greatest folly. There was so much talking and confusion in the very monastery wherein I was, that the Provincial began to think it hard for him to set himself against everybody; so he changed his mind, and would not acknowledge the new house.'[2]

The whole town of Avila seems to have taken upon itself to meddle and be interested in the affair. Doña Guiomar's confessors even refused to give her absolution unless she gave up the scheme; whereupon she had recourse to a learned and holy Dominican, F. Pedro Ibanez; and to him Teresa also gave an account of all she intended to do, and of some of her motives. 'I never said a word of any

---

[1] *Acta Sanct.* Oct. t. vii. § xv. 283. About two years after this letter was written, St. Luis went to America: he was commonly called 'The Apostle of the Indies.'

[2] *Vida*, c. xxxii. 16, 17.

revelation whatever,' she wrote, 'speaking only of the natural reasons which influenced me; for I would not have him give an opinion otherwise than on those grounds.' He asked for eight days before he answered, having already heard the popular cry, and being disposed to think the plan mere folly; but pondering on the matter he 'became convinced it was greatly for the service of God,' and his answer was that they ought to hasten to settle the matter; bidding them to send objectors to him, and he would answer them; and telling them how and in what way the thing was to be done.

This answer was a great comfort to them, especially as it pacified many good people who had taken alarm; amongst them Teresa's old friends, Francis de Salcedo and Gaspar Daza. The former 'admitted that the work might be of God,' and Daza gave them his assistance; so that, 'always with the help of many prayers,' a house was purchased in a convenient spot, and all seemed nearly concluded, when— the very day before the papers were to be signed—the Provincial changed his mind, refusing to permit the new foundation. He was apparently moved to this opposition by her own community, for, Teresa writes, 'I was now very much disliked throughout the whole monastery, because I wished to found another with stricter enclosure. It was said that I insulted my sisters; that I could serve God among them as well as elsewhere, for there were many among them much better than I. . . . Some said I ought to be put in prison; others—but they were not many—defended me in some degree. . . . In other respects God was most merciful unto me, for all this caused me no uneasiness; and I gave up our design with much readiness and joy, as if it cost me nothing. . . . I had done, as it seemed to me, all that was in my power, . . . and so I remained in the house where I was, exceedingly happy and joyful; though, at the same time, I was never able to give up my conviction that the work would be done.'[1]

She was, however, greatly distressed by a letter from F. Alvarez, finding fault with her, since she thought consolations ought to have come from him; and this 'was a greater affliction' to her 'than all the others together.' He told her she ought to recognize in the result that it was all a dream; and 'to lead a new life by ceasing to have anything to do for the future with it, or even to speak of it any more, seeing the scandal it had occasioned;' making other remarks, 'all of them very painful.' She began to consider whether all her 'visions were illusions,' all her 'prayers a delusion;' and her friends tried to frighten her by telling her the times were dangerous, and she might be taken before the Inquisitors. This only made her laugh; 'for I knew well enough,' she writes, 'that in matters of faith I would not break the least ceremony of the Church, that I would expose myself to die a thousand times rather than that anyone should see me go against it, or against any truth of Holy Writ.'[2]

So she remained quiet for five or six months, 'neither thinking nor speaking of the matter;' but the Dominican, F. Ibanez, and Doña Guiomar carried the matter by letters to Rome. She found that she could rely upon Ibanez, told him all her inner history; 'and I begged him,' she says, 'to consider the matter well, and tell me if there was anything therein at variance with the Holy Writings, and give me his opinion on the whole matter.' He reassured her much, and, as so often happened, was deeply impressed himself by the recital, retiring soon after for two years to a lonely monastery

---

[1] *Vida*, c. xxxiii. 2, 3. [2] Ibid. 6.

of his order, 'that he might apply himself more effectually to prayer.'[1]

At this time a new rector, Gaspar de Salazar, was appointed to the Jesuits' College at Avila, 'of great spirituality, high courage, strong understanding, and profound learning.' F. Alvarez wished Teresa to consult him. 'And so it was,' she writes, 'when I went into the confessional, I felt in my soul something, I know not what. . . . It was a spiritual joy, and a conviction in my soul that his soul must understand mine, that it was in unison with it, and yet, as I have said, I knew not how. . . . My relations with him were in every way of the utmost service to me and my soul. . . . I saw that he had a pure and holy soul, with a special grace of our Lord for the discernment of spirits. He gave me great consolation.'[2] F. Alvarez had tried her much, especially by his irresolution in the matter of the new house; so that she says she felt her chains extremely heavy, yet never swerved from his directions. He seems scarcely to have had nobility and freedom of spirit sufficient to comprehend his royal-hearted penitent; but his new superior bade him in future to console her, and not to direct her along a road so narrow, but 'to leave the operations of the Spirit of God alone, since there was nothing to be afraid of.'

She now began to return to the affair of the new foundation, laying her reasons before the rector and Alvarez. The former, she says, 'never had a doubt of its being the work of the Spirit of God,' and did not dare to hinder it, and Alvarez at last gave her leave to prosecute the work with all her might. Determined not to be again hindered if possible,

---

[1] To him first Christendom is indebted for her *Life*; he was the first to perceive that it ought to be written, and to desire her to undertake the task. [2] *Vida*, c. xxxiii. 11, 12.

and knowing that if she spoke of it to her superiors 'all was lost,' she took the course of asking no leave, since she 'made it a great point to do nothing against obedience.' Her brother Lorenzo had sent her some money from America, and she contrived that her sister Juaña, the wife of Juan de Ovalle, should buy a house and prepare it as if for herself. Teresa feared it was too small; but thinking that our Lord had not where to lay His head, she was angry with herself, and, she writes, 'I went to the little house, arranged the divisions of it, and found that it would make a sufficient though small monastery. I did not care now to add to the site by purchase, and so I did nothing but contrive to have it prepared in such a way that it could be lived in. Everything was coarse, and nothing more was done to it than to render it not hurtful to health—and that must be done everywhere.' [1]

Fair visions comforted her,—she believed that St. Clara appeared to her, and afterwards the Blessed Virgin,—encouraging her—

> Pure lilies of eternal peace,
> Whose odours haunt her dreams.

She longed never to part from such joys; but before the weary pilgrim lay the Hill of Difficulty, and she returned to earth, 'left in great loneliness,' she says, 'though so comforted and raised up, so recollected in prayer and softened, that I was for some time unable to move or speak—being, as it were, beside myself.'

Meanwhile, in spite of all the secrecy observed, her work began to be suspected: 'some believed in it, others did not.' She was in great fear lest the Provincial should be spoken to about it, and order her to give it up before any answer had

[1] *Vida,* c. xxxiii. 14.

arrived from Rome. But, instead of this, he desired her, in virtue of her obedience, to go immediately with one companion to Toledo, to a lady in great affliction on account of her husband's death—Doña Luisa de la Cerda, sister of the Duke of Medina-Cœli, who had been married to Arias Pardo, Marshal of Castile. She had heard of Teresa, whose repute was evidently at this time beginning to spread, and being 'in such extreme affliction, that fears were entertained about her life, she much desired to see her, thinking that her presence' would be a consolation to her, and that she could not be comforted otherwise.

As she knew the Provincial well, she obtained her wish; and St. Teresa writes, 'A visible improvement was the immediate result: she was comforted every day more and more. Our Lord must have done this in answer to the many prayers which the good people of my acquaintance made for me, that I might prosper in my work. She had a profound fear of God, and was so good, that her devotion supplied my deficiencies. She conceived a great affection for me: I, too, for her, because of her goodness. But all was as it were a cross for me; for the comforts of her house were a great torment, and her making so much of me made me afraid. I kept my soul continually recollected; I did not dare to be careless; nor was our Lord careless of me . . . I believe that this lady, notwithstanding that she was one of the chief personages of the realm, was a woman of great simplicity, and that few were more humble than she was. I was very sorry for her, for I saw how often she had to submit to much that was disagreeable to her, because of the requirements of her rank.'[1]

At Toledo she met with the priest, Vicente Barron,

[1] *Vida*, c. xxxiv. 4, 6.

who had attended her father's death-bed, and been of use to herself afterwards : now it was her turn, unconsciously, to teach him. She felt irresistibly impelled to speak to him, longing 'to know the state of his soul,' and 'that he should be a great servant of God.' 'We began by asking one another of our past lives,' she writes. 'I told him that my life had been one in which my soul had had many trials. He insisted much on my telling him what those trials were.' She tried to refuse, but he answered that the Dominican Ibanez was a great friend of his, and he could learn all from him, so she had better tell him herself. Upon this she 'told him all in confession;' and the result was a powerful impression made upon his own soul, so that he 'resolved with great earnestness to give himself to prayer.' Teresa was filled with passionate desires for his spiritual advancement. 'I considered,' she says, 'what high gifts and endowments for great services he had, if he gave himself wholly unto God. . . . I never saw anyone who pleased me much without wishing at once he were given wholly unto God ; and sometimes I feel this so keenly that I can hardly contain myself. . . . He asked me to pray much for him to God. . There was no necessity for his doing so, because I could not do anything else ; and so I went back to my place where I was in the habit of praying alone, and began to pray to our Lord, being extremely recollected, in that my simple, silly way, when I speak without knowing very often what I am saying. It is love that speaks, and my soul is so beside itself, that I do not regard the distance between it and God. . . . I remember I said, "O Lord, Thou must not refuse me this grace ; behold him,—he is a fit person to be our friend."'[1]

[1] *Vida*, c. xxxiv. 9, 10.

Her prayers were fully answered, so that she says if she had not seen it she could never have believed 'that our Lord would have given him in so short a time graces so matured, and filled him so full of God.' 'May His Majesty hold him in His hand!' she exclaims. 'If he will go on ... he will be one of the most distinguished servants of God, to the great profit of many souls, because he has in a short time had great experience in spiritual things ... All these blessings, I believe, came to him through the graces our Lord bestowed upon him in prayer; for they are real. ... I was in the greatest joy, beholding that soul. It seemed as if our Lord would have me see clearly the treasures He had laid up in it. ... I thought much of the graces our Lord had given him, and held myself as indebted for them more than if they had been given to myself. So I gave thanks to our Lord when I saw that His Majesty had fulfilled my desires and heard my petition that He would raise up persons like him. And now my soul, no longer able to bear the joy that filled it, went forth out of itself, losing itself that it might gain the more.'[1]

While she was with Doña Luisa, a widow, Maria de Jesu heard of her, and came from a long distance to see her. She had been a novice in a Carmelite convent of Granada; and moved with earnest desires for the Reform of the Order, had gone on foot, and barefooted, to Rome to obtain the necessary faculties. St. Teresa never knew before speaking to her the original constitutions of the Order, and was ignorant, she says, 'that the Rule, before it was mitigated, required of us that we should possess nothing; nor was I going to found a monastery without revenue, for my intention was that we should be without anxiety about all that was necessary for

[1] *Vida*, c. xxxiv. 14, 18, 21.

us, and I did not think of the many anxieties which the possession of property brings in its train. . . . She showed me Briefs she brought from Rome, and during the fortnight she remained with me we laid our plan for the founding of these monasteries.'[1]

Thus her enforced leisure at Toledo was really helping forward the work of her Reform; but she met with nothing but opposition to her new notion of founding a house without revenue. Alvarez, Ibanez, and all the 'learned men' to whom she spoke were against it. She wrote to Ibanez, and he sent back 'two sheets by way of reply, full of objections and theology' against her plan. But her mind could never descend to anything which seemed to her a lower view, when once the higher had been presented to it. 'I answered him,' she says, 'that in order to escape from my vocation, the vow of poverty I had made, and the perfect observance of the counsels of Christ, I did not want any theology to help me. . . . They gave me so many reasons the other way that I did not know what to do; but when I saw what the Rule required, and that poverty was the more perfect way, I could not persuade myself to allow an endowment. And though they did persuade me now and then that they were right, yet, when I returned to my prayer, and saw Christ on the Cross, so poor and destitute, I could not bear to be rich, and I implored Him with tears so to order matters that I might be poor as He was.'[2]

In this difficulty, Peter of Alcantara came again to her help. Doña Luisa had never seen him, but 'it pleased our Lord to bring him to her house.' Having been a great lover of poverty, 'he knew well the treasures it contains,' says Teresa, 'and so he was a great help to me; he charged me

[1] *Vida*, c. xxxv. 1, 2.   [2] Ibid. 4, 5.

on no account whatever to give up my purpose. Now, having this opinion and sanction—no one was better able to give it, because he knew what it was by long experience—I made up my mind to seek no further advice.'

Her Provincial, at this time, withdrew the order for her remaining with Doña Luisa, leaving her at liberty to remain there, or to return to Avila, as it pleased her. The triennial elections were taking place at the Monastery of the Incarnation; and hearing that many wished to elect her as Superior, she was greatly troubled, wrote to her friends asking them not to vote for her, and intended to stay awhile where she was. But her confessor (probably at Toledo) desired her to return at once, only telling her that, as the heat was very great, she might wait a few days, for it would be time enough if she returned before the elections. Her conscience became uneasy at shrinking from trouble, and she determined to go at once. 'I thought,' she writes, 'I was failing in obedience to the commandments of our Lord, and that, as I was happy and contented where I was, I would not go to meet trouble. All my service of God there was lip-service. . . . If I died on the road, let me die. Besides, my soul was in great straits, and our Lord had taken from me all sweetness in prayer. In short, I was in such a state of torment that I begged the lady to let me go. . . . I told her, among many other reasons, that my going away tended greatly to His service, and held out the hope that I might possibly return. She gave way, but with much sorrow. . . . So the pleasure I had in pleasing God took away the pain of quitting that lady, whom I saw suffering so keenly, and others to whom I owed much, particularly my confessor of the Society of Jesus,[1] in whom I found all I needed. But

[1] Garcia of Toledo.

the greater the consolations I lost for our Lord's sake, the greater was my joy in losing them.'[1]

She left Toledo in the beginning of June 1562, and 'travelled in great joy,' clearly perceiving that she was 'going to carry a heavy cross;' 'though I never thought,' she says, 'it would be so heavy as I afterwards found it to be.' She was now 'distressed not to be in the fight, since it was our Lord's will' she should be in it. But she beheld the steep ascent before her 'as a royal road, and not a pathway.' 'It is well seen,' she writes, 'that Thou feignest to make Thy law difficult.[2] I do not see it, nor do I feel that the way that leadeth unto Thee is narrow.'

On the night of her arrival at Avila came also the long-expected Brief from Rome, addressed to Doña Guiomar and her mother. It was dated in the February of that year, 1562, the third of Pius IV., and placed the new monastery under the direct authority of the Bishop, not of the Superior of the Carmelites. Teresa found the Bishop at Avila, and also Peter of Alcantara, who was staying with her old friend Don Francis de Salcedo. They persuaded the Bishop to accept the monastery; 'which was no small thing,' Teresa says, 'because it was founded in poverty. . . . It was the approbation of the holy old man,[3] and the great trouble he took to make now this one, now that one, help us, that did the whole work. If I had not come at the moment, as I have just said, I do not see how it could have been done; for the holy man was here but a short time,—I think not quite eight days,—during which he was also ill; and almost immediately afterwards our Lord took him to Himself. It

---

[1] *Vida*, c. xxxv. 10, 11.
[2] *Ps.* xciii. 20: (Vulg.) 'Qui fingis laborem in præcepto.'
[3] St. Peter of Alcantara.

seems as if His Majesty reserved him till this affair was ended, because now for some time—I think for more than two years—he had been very ill.'[1]

All this time Teresa's doings were not known at the Incarnation, 'though some persons had their suspicions.' Her brother-in-law, Juan de Ovalle, in whose name the new house had been taken, was ill; and in his wife's absence Teresa was permitted to remain with him and nurse him in this very house, which gave her opportunity to superintend the arrangements, and 'obtain from the workmen the hasty preparation of the house, so that it might have the form of a monastery.'

At length, on August 24 (St. Bartholomew's Day), 1562, the new monastery of St. Joseph was formally opened, with great simplicity, quietness, and secrecy. St. Teresa was there to give the habit to 'four poor orphans,' who were the first of the new community, with two of her cousins, nuns, like her, of the Incarnation, who happened just then to have leave of absence from it. Mass was said by Gaspar Daza; Salcedo was also present, as well as the priest Julian of Avila,[2] Don Juan de Ovalle, and his wife, Teresa's youngest sister Juaña. It seems marvellous, and reveals a strange condition of things in the Convent of the Incarnation, that it should be possible for a simple nun to carry out such a scheme without even the knowledge of the Prioress or the Provincial, yet with the approval of the Bishop, and of the

---

[1] *Vida*, c. xxxvi. 1. He died at Arenas in October of this year, 1562. When his end was close at hand he repeated the Psalm *Latatus sum*, and rising on his knees calmly expired. He was canonized in 1669.

[2] He was brother to Maria of St. Joseph, one of the four first novices, and became one of Teresa's most devoted assistants, both in the direction of St. Joseph's, and in her later journeys.—*Ribera*, lib. ii. c. ii. Annot.

many good men who aided her. Knowing that it was hopeless to gain the co-operation of her immediate superiors, she avoided the difficulty by not asking their permission. ' Everything was done in the utmost secrecy,' she writes, 'and if it had not been so, I do not see how anything could have been done at all; for the people of the city were against us, as it appeared afterwards. . . . I saw that everything depended on haste, for many reasons, one of which was that I was afraid I might be ordered back to my monastery at any moment. . . . As the house which thus became a monastery was that of my brother-in-law (I said before that he had bought it, for the purpose of concealing our plan), I was there myself with the permission of my superiors; and I did nothing without the advice of learned men, in order that I might not break, in a single point, my vow of obedience. As these persons considered what I was doing to be most advantageous for the whole Order, on many accounts, they told me—though I was acting secretly, and taking care my superiors should know nothing—that I might go on. If they had told me that there was the slightest imperfection in the whole matter, I would have given up the founding of a thousand monasteries,—how much more, then, this one! I am certain of this; for though I longed to withdraw from everything more and more, and to follow my rule and vocation in the greatest perfection and seclusion, yet I wished to do so only conditionally; for if I should have learnt that it would be for the greater honour of our Lord to abandon it, I would have done so, as I did before on one occasion, in all peace and contentment.' [1]

Her happiness was extreme. She says that she 'felt as it were in bliss,' seeing that the house was actually begun, and

[1] *Vida*, c. xxxvi. 2, 3, 4.

four maidens received without dowry. They all added some religious appellation to their baptismal name,—as 'Antonia of the Holy Ghost,' 'Maria of St. Joseph,' &c., which custom seems henceforth to have prevailed amongst St. Teresa's disciples. She had hitherto signed herself, and been styled, 'Doña Teresa d'Ahumada,' but from this time assumed the name of Teresa of Jesus.

'When all was done—it might have been about three or four hours afterwards'—came the reaction. She was filled with 'distress, obscurity, and darkness of soul,' with fears that she had done wrong, and failed in obedience, 'in having brought it about without the commandment of the Provincial;' and that he would be angry at her having placed the house under the jurisdiction of the Bishop. Then she was troubled lest the nuns should not be contented to live in so strict a house, lest they should not always find food, and feared she had 'done a silly thing.' 'The devil also would have me ask myself how I could think of shutting myself up in so strict a house, when I was subject to so many infirmities; how could I bear so penitential a life, and leave a house large and pleasant, where I had been always so happy, and where I had so many friends? Perhaps I might not like those of the new monastery. I had taken on myself a heavy obligation, and might possibly end in despair. . . . When I found myself in this state, I went and placed myself before the most Holy Sacrament, though I could not pray to Him; so great was my anguish, that I was like one in an agony of death.'[1] 'O my God,' she exclaims, 'how wretched is this life! No joy is lasting; everything is liable to change. Only a moment ago, I do not think I would have exchanged my joy with any man upon earth;

[1] *Vida*, c. xxxvi. 6, 7.

and the very grounds of that joy so tormented me now, that I knew not what to do with myself.'

But the agony of struggle was short; she promised before leaving the chapel to do all in her power to obtain permission to enter the new house, and embrace the stricter life. She immediately became calm and peaceful; 'and I have continued so ever since,' she says, 'and the enclosure, penances, and other rules of this house are to me, in their observance, so singularly sweet and light, the joy I have is so exceedingly great, that I am now and then thinking what on earth I could have chosen which should be more delightful.'[1]

The troubles of the day were not at an end. When her mental struggle was over, she wished to rest herself a little after dinner, having scarcely rested at all the previous night, or for many nights, 'while every day was full of toil.' But their doings could no longer be concealed, the news spread through the city, and reached the Incarnation. The Prioress sent desiring her to return immediately; and she obeyed, 'persuaded,' she says, 'that I should be put in prison at once; but this would have been a great comfort, because I should have nobody to speak to, and might have some rest and solitude, of which I was in great need; for so much intercourse with people had worn me out.'

However, when she told the Prioress what she had done, 'she was softened a little.' The Provincial was sent for, and the whole matter laid before him; Teresa confessing her fault, 'as if I had been very much to blame,' she says, 'and so I seemed to everyone who did not know all the reasons.' He rebuked her sharply, but the nuns seem to have been most incensed, saying she was 'giving scandal in the city, and setting up novelties.'

[1] *Vida*, c. xxxvi. 9.

'At last,' she writes, 'the Provincial commanded me to explain my conduct before the nuns; and I had to do it. As I was perfectly calm, and our Lord helped me, I explained everything in such a way that neither the Provincial nor those who were present found any reason to condemn me. Afterwards I spoke more plainly to the Provincial alone; he was very much satisfied, and promised, if the new monastery prospered, and the city became quiet, to give me leave to live in it.'[1]

Both the Provincial and the nuns of the Incarnation seem to have been in great awe and fear as to what would be said in the city, where, indeed, 'the outcry was very great.' That the towns-people should have so concerned themselves about the proceedings of a few poor women, who desired greater seclusion and strictness, in order the better to pray to God, seems extraordinary; but, two or three days after, the governor and members of the city council came together, and resolved that the new monastery should not be allowed to exist, that 'it was a visible wrong to the state,' and that they would not suffer Teresa and her friends to go on in any way with their work.

They then called together two learned men from each religious Order at Avila, to give their opinion on the matter. Most of them condemned the new foundation; but F. Domingo Bañes (the commentator on St. Thomas) represented that there was no need for haste, and that it was the affair of the Bishop. The last consideration seems obvious; but the people of Avila apparently thought otherwise, and 'were so excited,' Teresa says, 'that they talked of nothing else: everyone condemned me, and hurried to the Provincial and to my monastery.... The informations taken were

[1] *Vida*, c. xxxvi. 14.

sent up to the King's council, and an order came back for a report on the whole matter. Here was the beginning of a grand lawsuit; the city sent delegates to the Court, and some must also be sent to defend the monastery: but I had no money, nor did I know what to do. Our Lord provided for us; for the Father Provincial never ordered me not to meddle in the matter. He is so great a lover of all that is good, that, though he did not help us, he would not be against our work.'[1]

He would not let Teresa return to her house until he saw how it would end. The new-made novices were left alone, and 'did more by their prayers,' she says, 'than I did with all my negotiations, though the affair needed the utmost attention.' But she carried on all the business peacefully; for she had said to God, 'O Lord, this house is not mine; it was founded for Thee; and now that there is no one to take up the cause, do Thou protect it.'

Gaspar Daza, who had celebrated mass at the opening of St. Joseph's, and received the novices, was violently attacked; but he was a great help to St. Teresa, as was also Salcedo, and Gonzalo de Aranda, a priest, 'a very great servant of God, and a lover of all perfection.' He went to Court about her business. 'To relate in detail the heavy trials we passed through would be too tedious,' she writes. 'I wondered at what Satan did against a few poor women, and also how all people thought that merely twelve women, with a prioress, could be so hurtful to the city.'[2]

At last a compromise was proposed: the city would tolerate the new monastery if it was endowed; and to this Teresa consented, thinking 'it would not be amiss, till the people were pacified, to accept an endowment.' That night,

[1] *Vida*, c. xxxvi. 15-17.   [2] Ibid. 19.

she writes, as 'I was in prayer, . . . the holy friar, Peter of Alcantara, appeared to me. He was then dead. But he had written to me before his death . . . that he was glad the foundation was so much spoken against: it was a sign that our Lord would be exceedingly honoured in the monastery, seeing that Satan was so earnest against it; and that I was by no means to consent to an endowment. He urged this upon me twice or thrice in that letter, and said that, if I persisted in this, everything would succeed according to my wish. . . . I will now say no more than that he showed himself severe on this occasion; he merely said that I was on no account to accept an endowment, and asked why it was I did not take his advice. He then disappeared.'[1]

Teresa told Salcedo next day that the lawsuit must go on, for she could not consent to the endowment. He was pleased, and told her afterwards how much he had disliked the compromise. 'Writing thus briefly,' she says, 'it is impossible for me to explain what took place during the two years[2] that passed between the beginning and the completion of the monastery: the last six months and the first six months were the most painful.' Fra Pedro Ibañez never ceased to exert himself on her behalf, and in the end 'prevailed, by some means, on the Father Provincial' to permit her to return to St. Joseph's, and take with her some nuns from the Incarnation, who were willing to join her, 'for the performance of the Divine office, and the training of those who were in the house.'

A second Brief had arrived from Rome, dated December 9, 1562, authorizing the new nuns to be without revenues. The Bollandists say it is not clear by whose means or inter-

---

[1] *Vida*, c. xxxvi. 20, 21.
[2] From July 1561 to Mid-Lent 1563.

cession Teresa obtained this Brief; that she gives the credit
of persuading the Provincial to F. Ibañez, but that it ought
not to be forgotten that one day, while Angelo was still vacil-
lating, St. Teresa suddenly exclaimed, 'See to it, my Father,
that we resist not the Holy Spirit,' and that these words
worked an immediate change in him. They also say that
she took nothing with her from the Incarnation except a
straw palliasse, an old patched habit, a discipline, and a
cilicium made of iron chains.[1] Ribera tells us that the four
nuns who chose to accompany her were 'Anna of St. John,
Anna of the Angels, Maria Isabel, and Isabel of St. Paul,'
first cousin of Maria de Ocampo, and niece, as she would
be called in Spain, of St. Teresa, being the daughter of her
first cousin, Geronimo de Cepeda.

'The day of our coming was a most joyful day [2] for me,'
she writes. No ambition or self-seeking mingled with this
joy; she went there as a simple nun, appointing Anna of
St. John Prioress; although soon after the latter, with all
the sisters, insisted upon Teresa undertaking the office herself. All in the monastery 'breathed the utmost poverty,
not only in the cells and offices, but even in the little
church.'[3] She arranged 'in that little house a very small
church with a narrow double grate of wood, thick and with
very small apertures, through which the nuns could hear
mass. To the church she caused a small vestibule to be
made, in which was the door both of the monastery and
church. Over the door she placed two small statues, of the
Blessed Virgin and of St. Joseph.' The bell, which was
placed in a niche of the wall, weighed less than three pounds.
It was taken from Avila in 1624 by order of F. Stephen,

---

[1] *Acta Sanct.* t. vii. Oct. § xix.   [2] In Lent 1563.
[3] *Acta Sanct.* t. vii. Oct. § xix. 366.   [4] Ibid.

General of the Order, to the monastery of Pastrana, where the general chapters were held; and was used to summon them together, as a reminder of the poverty and simplicity which marked the reform of the Order.

'When we had begun to sing the Office,' Teresa writes, 'the people began to have a great devotion to the monastery: more nuns were received, and our Lord began to stir up those who had been our greatest persecutors to become great benefactors, and give alms to us. In this way they came to approve of what they had condemned; and so, by degrees, they withdrew from the lawsuit. . . . And now there is not one who thinks it would have been right not to have founded the monastery; so they make a point of furnishing us with alms; for, without any asking on our part, without begging of anyone, our Lord moves them to succour us; and so we always have what is necessary for us, and I trust in the Lord it will always be so. As the sisters are few in number, if they do their duty, as our Lord at present by His grace enables them to do, I am confident they will always have it, and that they need not be a burden nor troublesome to anybody; for our Lord will care for them, as He has hitherto done.'[1]

Her account of her own feelings, in reviewing her work, is too beautiful, in its simplicity and humility, to omit. 'During one of those days,' she writes, 'when this monastery, which seems to have cost me some labour, was fully founded by the arrival of the Brief from Rome, which empowered us to live without an endowment; and I was comforting myself on seeing the whole affair concluded, and thinking of all the trouble I had had, and giving thanks to our Lord for having been pleased to make some use of me

[1] *Vida*, c. xxxvi. 25.

—it happened that I began to consider all that we had gone through. Well, so it was; in everyone of my actions, which I thought were of some service, I traced so many faults and imperfections, now and then but little courage, very frequently a want of faith; for until this moment, when I see everything accomplished, I never absolutely believed; neither, however, on the other hand, could I doubt what our Lord said to me about the foundation of this house. . . . In short, I find that our Lord Himself, on His part, did all the good that was done, while I did all the evil. I therefore ceased to think of the matter, and wished never to be reminded of it again, lest I should do myself some harm by dwelling on my many faults. Blessed be He Who, when He pleases, draws good out of all my failings! Amen.'[1]

[1] *Vida,* c. xxxix. 20.

Chapter the Tenth.

Spain, above all other things, is skilled in war, feared, and very bold in battle; light of heart, loyal to her lord, diligent in learning, courtly in speech, accomplished in all good things. Nor is there a land in the world that may be accounted like her in abundance, nor may any equal her in strength, and few there be in the world so great. And above all doth Spain abound in magnificence, and more than all is she famous for her loyalty. O Spain! there is no man can tell of thy worthiness!
                    CRONICA DE ESPAÑA (*of the 13th Century*).

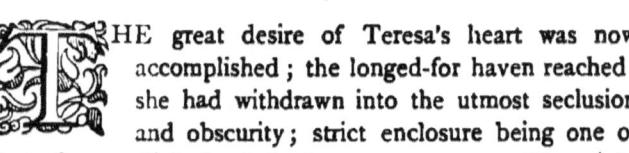HE great desire of Teresa's heart was now accomplished; the longed-for haven reached: she had withdrawn into the utmost seclusion and obscurity; strict enclosure being one of the reforms which she judged most necessary. She might well have argued with herself that the liberty which the mitigated rule allowed gave her large means of doing good to others, and that by giving it up she was sacrificing continual opportunities for that influence which she was conscious of possessing, and which she had so often exercised with profit to others. But there was something greater in her than even the prudence and wisdom which distinguished her,—a response of the soul to divine instincts, a reaching upward, with singleness of aim, to the highest ideal which had

been presented to her. It is not the least remarkable part of the great story of Spain in the sixteenth century that the genius of an obscure nun, illuminated by sanctity, and breaking forth in spite of herself from the retreat she had chosen, should fill her country with its light, and that she should obtain the highest place in its affection and enthusiasm,—declared the second patron saint of Spain by the Cortes[1] even before her canonization, and in 1812 actually named 'Generalissima' of the Spanish armies in the war of independence.

It is the more striking because her light certainly was not made brilliant by surrounding darkness. It shone in the very noontide of her country's glory, during that brief period when Spain held politically the first place in Europe, and when Cervantes and Ignatius Loyola were among her sons. Very rarely can any one country have produced in the same century three works which in different ways have had such wide-spread renown, and exercised such lasting influences, as 'Don Quixote,' the 'Spiritual Exercises of St. Ignatius,' and the 'Life of St. Teresa.'

Nor did Spain at this time appear great because other countries were poor in life and vigour. It is true that her monarch 'wore half the crowns of Europe;' but the period of her eminence was also that of the great revival of thought and learning, when Christendom entered into the full possession of much which had been slowly gained through the Middle Ages; the period of perfection in art which has never since been approached, and of great movements which altered the destinies and constitutions of nations.

To name St. Teresa's contemporaries is almost to name great schools of thought and action. Neither, if she became

[1] In 1617.

one of the leading spirits in that great religious revival which cannot be called a reaction from Lutheranism, since it was simultaneous with it, but which was certainly a *counter*-action to it, was this caused by any lack of bright contemporaneous stars in the calendar of the saints. It was the age of Francis Borgia, Xavier, Las Casas, of St. Thomas de Villanova, St. Charles Borromeo, St. Philip Neri, besides a host of lesser lights who would have been distinguished in an age of less spiritual heroism.

The life of St. Teresa comprised almost all the completest and most brilliant epoch of Spanish history. Born the year before the accession of Charles V., she lived through his reign, when he so used the famous body of infantry formed by the 'Great Captain' that for renown of arms Spain was foremost in Europe. The seeds of decay, which lay deep in the national character, had already begun to germinate, but through the first prosperous years of Philip II. decay was as yet imperceptible; Teresa rejoiced in the glories of Lepanto, but did not live to mourn the defeat of the Armada. 'In less than thirty years,' says Ticknor, 'Charles V., who had inherited not only Spain but Naples, Sicily, and the Low Countries, and into whose treasury the untold wealth of the Indies was already beginning to pour, was elected Emperor of Germany, and undertook a career of foreign conquest such as had not been imagined since the days of Charlemagne. Success and glory seemed to wait for him as he advanced. In Europe he extended his empire till it reached the hated power of Islamism in Turkey; in Africa he garrisoned Tunis and overawed the whole coast of Barbary; in America Cortez and Pizarro were his bloody lieutenants, and achieved for him conquests more vast than were conceived in the dreams of Alexander; while beyond the wastes of the Pacific he stretched his discoveries to the Philippines, and so completed the circle of the globe. This was the brilliant aspect which the fortunes of his country offered to an intelligent and imaginative Spaniard in the first half of the sixteenth century. For, as we well know, such men then looked forward with confidence to the time when Spain would be the head of an empire more extensive than the Roman, and seem sometimes to have trusted that they themselves should live to witness and share its glory.'[1]

It is hardly possible to understand St. Teresa's position and influence without a brief glance at the circumstances which tended to produce that school of thought and religious philosophy of which she is the very flower and perfectest expression; for if the fall of Granada is the central point in Spanish history, the religious character of Christian Spaniards had received an ineffaceable impress from the struggle which it crowned and ended.

During nearly eight centuries Spain had sat almost solitary in Europe, occupied with her own solemn contest— the rampart of Christendom against the miscreant invaders. 'The Spaniards always felt their warfare to be peculiarly that of soldiers of the Cross; they always felt themselves, beyond everything else, and above everything else, to be Christian men contending against misbelief. Their religious sympathies were, therefore, constantly apparent, and often predominated over all others; so that, while they were little connected with the Church of Rome by those political ties which were bringing half Europe into bondage, they were

[1] Ticknor's *Spanish Literature*, vol. i. p. 418. 'Un Monarca, un Imperio, y una Espada,' wrote a soldier-poet much favoured by Charles V.

more connected with its religious spirit than any other people of modern times.'[1]

The heroic elements of the national genius were first, and before all, religious. Although shut up for so many centuries within the narrow limits of the Peninsula with their certainly very tolerant conquerors, the 'sons of the Goths' never faltered in antipathy to the unbeliever, whose graceful and brilliant civilization exercised little or no influence upon them, in spite of unavoidable intercourse, of frequent treaties and intervals of peace.[2] The power and grace of their early literature was entirely their own. The poem of the 'Cid,' which was written two centuries earlier than the 'Canterbury Tales,' is throughout national, Christian, and chivalric, giving a vivid picture of the 'true-heartedness of the people, and of the wide force of a primitive religious enthusiasm; while the early Spanish ballads, the very voice of the people's heart, are entirely original and Christian.'[3] A translation of the Bible is amongst the works of Alfonso the Wise, who died in 1284, and was one of the chief founders of Spanish literature, distinguished both in poetry and prose; and another translation of the Bible was made by Boniface, a

[1] *History of Spanish Literature*, vol. i. p. 314.
[2] 'With the spirit which so long sustained their forefathers against the power of Rome, and which has carried their descendants through a short but hardly less fierce contest against the power of France, they maintained, to a remarkable degree, their ancient manners and feelings, their religion, their laws, and their institutions; and, separating themselves by an implacable hatred from their Moorish invaders, they there, in those rude mountains, laid deep the foundations of that national character which has subsisted down to our own times.'—Ibid. p. 6.
[3] 'Not a single Arabic original has been found for any one of them; nor, so far as we know, has a single passage of Arabic poetry, or a single phrase from any Arabic writer, entered directly into their composition.'—Ibid. p. 98.

brother of St. Vincent Ferrer, and general of the Carthusian Order in the fifteenth century.

There is a certain shrewdness and humorous sharpness (continually noticeable in St. Teresa's writings) among the elements of that fervid and devout genius which had ripened amidst wars and tumults; and not unfrequently a strange profaneness seems to have mingled itself with the faith and knightly loyalty which are the most prominent traits of early Spanish writings; as for instance in the poems of the Arch-Priest of Hita, a writer of note in the fourteenth century. In an allegorical story describing the contest between Doña Quaresma (Lent) and Don Carnaval, the latter calls in Don Amor as his ally, who is joyfully received by a procession in which clergy, friars, and nuns are conspicuous; and the Arch-Priest does not shrink from the blasphemy of representing the procession as singing parodies of the most sacred hymns of the Church, applied to Don Amor, as the *Benedictus qui venit*.[1]

[1] Perhaps the most striking instance of this mingled devotion and profanity was the rude mummery which accompanied the most solemn of all processions on Corpus Christi Day. It was preceded by a monstrous figure, half serpent in form, called the *Tarasca*: men were concealed inside, and it was surmounted by another figure, representing the Woman of Babylon. Hats and caps were snatched from the poor country people by the beast, to their terror and wonder. 'Then followed a company of fair children, with garlands on their heads, singing the litanies of the Church; and sometimes companies of men and women with castanets, dancing the national dances. Two or more Moorish or negro giants, made of pasteboard, came next, jumping about grotesquely. . . . Then, with much pomp and fine music, appeared the priests, bearing the Host under a splendid canopy; and after them a long and devout procession, where was seen, in Madrid, the king with a taper in his hand. . . . Last of all came showy cars filled with actors from the public theatres.'—*Spanish Literature*, vol. ii. p. 250. As so often happens, the common name for the ceremony expressed that

Probably the chivalry of the Middle Ages lasted longer in Spain than in any other country; even in the time of Ferdinand and Isabella, their Secretary, Fernando del Pulgar, mentions several noblemen, known to him, who had gone abroad 'in order,' he says, 'to try the fortune of arms with any cavalier that might be pleased to adventure it with them, and to gain honour for themselves, and the fame of valiant and bold knights for the gentlemen of Castile.' Pulgar had richly earned this fame for himself, and now sleeps where, in the centre of a city in arms, he knelt as he affixed an Ave Maria with the sign of the Cross to the door of the chief mosque in Granada, before it had yielded to the besieging Christian forces; a knightly deed, breathing the very spirit of chivalry. And if the age of chivalry closed magnificently with the fall of Granada, the peculiar genius of Spanish piety was well represented by the two sovereigns, in whom were united the various crowns of Spain; while knightly prowess and religious devotion are marked characteristics of their two greatest subjects, Gonzalvo de Cordova and Christopher Columbus. The latter was indeed a Spaniard in all but birth; 'his loyalty,' says Ticknor, 'his religious faith and enthusiasm, his love of great and extraordinary adventure, were all Spanish rather than Italian, and were all in harmony with the Spanish national character, when he became a part of its glory. His own eyes, he tells us, had watched the Silver Cross, as it slowly rose, for the first time, above the towers of the Alhambra, announcing to the world the final and absolute overthrow of the infidel power in Spain.'[1]

which took most hold of the people's mind, so that, instead of being called, as in France, 'La Fête du bon Dieu,' it was named in popular phrase, 'La Fiesta de los Carros.'

[1] *Spanish Literature*, vol. i. p. 187.

Ferdinand succeeded, by his astute and determined policy, in consolidating the royal power, hitherto more limited in Spain than in any other country in Europe, and transmitted to his grandson an authority far greater than he had himself received. It is true that this was only accomplished by inflicting deepest wounds on the liberties of his country, and on the independence of the nobles and the cities ; while the introduction of the Inquisition in 1481, through the mistaken piety of Isabella, cut at the very roots of any healthy life and growth in the nation. The proud liberty of Aragon in vain opposed its introduction ; but it could never have flourished as it did in Spain had it not itself been in accordance with the general spirit of Spanish piety. It was the spirit of the country which made the Inquisition what it was. 'Familiar del Santo Ufizio' was held an honourable office ; and the greatest dramatist of Spain was careful to place the words after his name on the title-pages of his books. And if almost all the greatest in the Spanish Church of that age suffered sooner or later from its suspicion, or active persecution, nothing is more striking than the submission and loyalty with which they acknowledge its right to all the power it claimed, and bow to its decrees. It was not, like the policy of Charles I. or James II. in England, alien to the general life of the people ; but, in spite of the terror which its vast and noiseless power must have excited, it was justified and accepted by the nation, which had been formed out of bands of mountain warriors, each loyal and obedient to its own chief, but extremely jealous of the royal authority. The hatred of misbelief, which had been nourished through that long struggle, and which was intensified and kept fresh by the sufferings of Christian captives in Algiers, led them to sacrifice everything to the hope of crushing it ; and the scene of the forcible baptism of four thousand by Cardinal Ximenes was but a type of that blind zeal for faith which would fain *force* souls to enter or remain within the fold of the Church.[1]

But the Inquisition cannot be said to have crushed Lutheranism in Spain, for it is not possible to believe that any form of Protestantism would have lived there. It would have been powerless to satisfy the spiritual needs of a religious Spaniard. 'If ever a country was hostile to all novelties,' writes M. Rousselot, 'to all which approached heresy, it was Spain. If France, which had had her Albigenses and Vaudois—if the France of Abelard, the country of rationalism, refused to become Lutheran or Calvinist, what chance was there that Catholicism would have run more risks in Spain?'[2]

Malon de Chaide, an Augustinian monk, born about 1530, and whose doctrine of divine love in his 'Conversion de la Magdalena' has much in common with St. Teresa's, severely rebukes the immorality and practical irreligion of

[1] 'In 1525, when a large number of Moors at Valencia had been baptized only by *absolute physical violence*, it was adjudged, in a decree of Charles V., that they and their children, from the day when this solemn mockery was practised on them, were to be accounted Christians, and to be subjected to the punishments of the Inquisition if they were found to fail in Christian faith or Catholic observances.— Sayas, *Anales de Aragon*, 1667, folio, c. cxxiii. pp. 777, sqq. Ticknor, vol. i. p. 410, *note*.

[2] *Les Mystiques Espagnols*, p. 59. ' L'Espagne n'aurait pu s'accommoder du culte trop simple des églises réformées, elle ne l'aurait pas même compris. . . . . Remplacez cet éclat, ce luxe, cette fête ininterrompue, par un rite monotone et grave, des temples froids et nus, des ministres à la robe sombre, et ces vives imaginations vont s'éteindre ; la foi ne parlera plus aux cœurs quand les symboles ne parleront plus aux yeux.' —Ibid. p. 60.

those who observe religious duties. He complains that one who seeks revenge, a homicide, a robber of the poor, thinks himself a good Christian because he goes to confession, provided he has a fashionable confessor. He describes him arriving at the father's cell, his page arranging a cushion for him, lest he should be tired, &c.; and after all, if he is rebuked, he rises in anger, saying a personage of his quality cannot live like a monk, and goes away satisfied that all is well. Then every young girl has a romance in her pocket when she can scarcely walk, and women go to mass decked as for a wedding. 'But in the midst of their bitterest invectives neither Venegas nor Malon de Chaide seem to be disquieted about Protestantism in their country; they address themselves to bad Catholics, but who yet have no thought of changing their accustomed religion.' Nor is there any trace in the writings of St. Teresa of a sense of *danger* from Lutheranism in Spain. She is filled with an immense compassion for Lutherans, and mourns over their progress in France, but she does not fear them. Even the Inquisition did not disquiet itself on that point; it needed to be stimulated by the Government, by the letter of alarm written from St. Just by Charles V., and by the fears of Philip II., for whom heretic and rebel meant the same thing. Eleven years after the first 'Autos da fé,' in 1559, Protestantism had ceased to exist in Spain, and the Inquisition employed itself in tormenting and crushing the most distinguished Spanish Churchmen.

But in spite of her devoted Catholicism, Spain could not stand apart from the intellectual activity of Europe, from the craving for thought, discussion, and even innovation,—least of all in the age that followed the discovery of America and the fall of Granada. She satisfied these needs by a movement which was at once her reform and her philosophy —Catholic Mysticism. It was not the result of many generations of thinkers; it did not spring from their audacities or their doubts; and if her chief mystics felt the action of the Renaissance, it was always subordinate to religious sentiment.[1] The genius of Spain needed an outcome for its ardour and natural vehemence, especially in an age when new elements were introduced into her social condition, and when, as at the end of the reign of Ferdinand and Isabella, a long course of national prosperity seemed open to her; and all her most ardent souls, exaggerating the perils of thought, and suffering from excess of repression, cast themselves into mysticism as a safe refuge to troubled hearts and unquiet intellects.

Of this mystic theology St. Teresa is the greatest teacher and noblest representative,—the solitary instance of any school of thought, Christian or Pagan, finding its completest expression in a woman. It would be impossible, probably, in any school where feeling, sentiment, and instinct did not predominate; but the great men amongst mystic teachers never attained to her mingled passion and simplicity. If St. John of the Cross was more impetuous, he was less broad and serene. The difference between her and her followers

[1] 'Grâce à eux, la renaissance platonicienne pénètre en Espagne. De tous les systèmes de l'antiquité, en effet, c'est à celui de Platon que les mystiques recourent le plus volontiers, lorsqu'ils n'excluent pas de parti pris tout rationalisme. Les Espagnols auraient pu connaître Platon directement, même ceux d'entre eux qui n'auraient pas su le lire dans l'original, puisqu'il était traduit en Latin, ainsi que Plotin, dès la seconde moitié du XVe siècle, et il est à croire que plusieurs d'entre eux, surtout Malon de Chaide, Louis de Grenade, Louis de Léon, étaient initiés à ses doctrines autrement que par Boëce, Saint Augustin et les Pères.'—*Les Mystiques Espagnols*, p. 453.

has been compared to that between a majestic river and a rushing torrent or impoverished streamlet; while the immense height at which she stands above mystics of her own sex can only be felt by comparing her with such as Madame Guyon, the Spanish nun Maria d' Agrèda, or the Protestant Antoinette Bourignon.[1]

Separated widely from quietism by the practical character of her teaching, she is preserved both from it and from any danger of pantheism by her intensely vivid realization of the Person of her Lord, 'the Mystic Spouse, Who permits—nay, commands—love to men.' She possesses, in common with other Spanish mystics, 'the virtue which everyone in the sixteenth century lacked,—Luther as well as the Duke of Alva, Leo the Tenth equally with Calvin,—pity.'[2] 'God is not satisfied with words and thoughts, my sisters,' she wrote in her 'Mansiones' and 'Via Perfectionis,' 'He requires effects and actions. If, therefore, you see a sick person whom you can in any way relieve, leave your devotions courageously to do so. Have compassion for what she suffers, and let her suffering be as your own. . . . The love of God does not consist in shedding tears, nor in that satisfaction and tenderness which we ordinarily desire because they are consoling: it consists in serving God with courage, in acting justly, in practising humility.'

[1] 'Plus instruite, plus docile, plus simple, d'un jugement plus droit, d'une imagination plus contenue, elle n'a pas les "ambitions epithalamiques" de Mme. Guyon ; jamais elle ne s'est posée comme la pierre angulaire de l'Église . . . . comme l'épouse de Jésus enfant, au-dessus même de la mère du Christ ; jamais elle n'a osé dire que c'est "aux serviteurs de prier et non à l'épouse." La présomption est le péché mignon des mystiques, a-t-on dit. Exceptons Ste. Thérèse: elle a trop d'humilité, humilité qui procède de sa foi, mais aussi d'un rare bon sens.'—Rousselot, *Les Mystiques Espagnols*, p. 309.

[2] Ibid. p. 368.

She continually warns her nuns against perilous excesses of spirituality, vain reveries, deceitful imaginations; teaching them that 'to love is not to abandon oneself to a vague and inert languor: it is to act.' And with all her submission to the Church, and desire for direction, she preserves liberty of conscience, and says that she was never able to abandon the direction of her soul to an unskilful guide.[1]

'Do you see Teresa of Jesus?' F. Alvarez said of her. 'What sublime graces has she received of God! and yet she is like the most tractable little child with regard to everything I can say to her.' But although she became, notwithstanding this docility, the leading spirit amongst the remarkable men who were her friends, and insensibly ended by directing her directors, yet the influence of many who preceded and were contemporaneous with her must not be left out of account, since they were eminent masters of the mystic theology which found in her so remarkable an expression. The serenity and moderation of their teaching divides it sharply from quietism; Juan D'Avilla[2] seems to have had a prevision of their errors in his rebukes to those who, fancying they had surrendered themselves to God, mistook the impulses of their own hearts for His inspiration. 'If they do not feel moved,' he writes in his 'Audi Filia,'

---

[1] 'On conçoit aisément la nécessité d'une sage direction dans la vie mystique; que Jean D'Avilla, Louis de Grenade, directeurs eux-mêmes, théologiens instruits, s'en préoccupent, rien de plus naturel; mais ce souci chez une femme qui est une des plus puissantes expressions du mysticisme, n'est-il pas l'indice d'un fond inaltérable de rectitude et de bon sens?'—Rousselot, *Les Mystiques Espagnols*, p. 330.

[2] Alban Butler writes, 'Juan D'Avila or D'Avilla'—the latter spelling has been here adopted, since he was not a citizen of Avila, and had no connection with it. Davilla was his family name; but it is incorrect to translate his name, as is sometimes done, John of Avila. *Julian* of Avila, Teresa's friend, was rightly so called, being her fellow-citizen, and of plebeian birth.

'they do not act, even to do good works; if they feel themselves moved to act, they do not hesitate to carry out a work, though it may be evil, and contrary to the commandments of God, attributing it to divine inspiration, and the liberty of the Spirit.'

Malon de Chaide has been already mentioned. Juan de los Angeles, the friend of St. Francis Borgia, who flourished in the first half of the sixteenth century, seems to have brought exact learning and severe analysis into his treatment of mystical subjects; and it is this severity and strength which at once strike the most casual reader as distinguishing the Spanish school from the later teaching of St. Francis de Sales and Fénélon ; the former appearing far nearer to the teaching of the Imitation, 'that immortal code of a practical and reasonable mysticism.' Nor is there any other example of a mysticism which remained so entirely faithful to Catholicism, while at the same time so general and widespread. Free-will and moral responsibility in man are never lost sight of in its teaching, and love and adoration of God lead with them to love and respect for men. It must be remembered also that they had not only to teach mystical theology, but to guide and restrain it as a prevailing popular religious sentiment, which, far from being confined to the cloister, was continually feeding it with ardent souls. A striking instance of this wisdom is the judgment of Juan d'Avilla on 'St. Teresa's Life,' sent to him by Doña Luisa de la Cerda, though it may seem almost cold in its guarded circumspection. He says he has 'been comforted by it;' but that 'the book is not fit to be in the hands of everybody, for it is necessary to correct the language in some places, and explain it in others; and there are some things in it useful for your spiritual life, and not so for others who might adopt them, for the special ways by which God leads some souls are not meant for others. . . . They are unreasonable who disbelieve these things merely because they are most high things, and because it seems to them incredible that Infinite Majesty humbles Himself to these loving relations with one of His creatures.' He ends by bidding her 'go on her road, but always suspecting robbers,' and begging her to 'burden herself with a prayer for him.'

Juan D'Avilla, a man revered by all Spain, and called *El Apostol de la Andalucia*, may also be almost called the father of the Spanish saints of his time. He it was who preached the funeral sermon of the once lovely Empress Isabella, and to whom, the same afternoon, the young Duke of Gandia poured out the heart and conscience which had been moved to their depths by one glance at what Death could work. It was a sermon of his also, and his subsequent counsel, which converted St. John of God, founder of the Order of Charity; and his book 'Audi Filia' was an exhortation written to a young girl of rank, Sancha de Carrillo, who on her way to Court, where she had been appointed maid of honour to the Queen, had sought him for confession. She said afterwards that he had sharply rebuked her for approaching the sacred tribunal in rich attire. What passed besides is unknown; but she suddenly gave up all to devote herself to a religious life. The treatise which he addressed to her was a commentary on the verse, *Audi filia, et vide, et inclina aurem tuam: et obliviscere populum tuum et domum patris tui.* The whole spirit of its teaching seems to be, 'to flee from the world, and give oneself to God, far less out of fear of the world than from love to God.'

His teaching on mental prayer in many ways resembles St. Teresa's. Notwithstanding a life entirely devoted to

God, and seeking only the good of souls, he did not escape the suspicion of the Inquisition. Interrogated by it in 1534, he succeeded in justifying himself; but Llorente says that one of his works was put on the *Index* in 1559.

His biographer was his greatest disciple, Luis de Granada, whose own book, the ' Guide to Sinners,' brought him into trouble with the Inquisition, and was prohibited until 1570. This could not prevent the immense popularity of his numerous works, which were translated into Latin, English, Italian, French, and even Japanese. Charles V. kept his 'Treatise on Prayer' amongst his small collection at St. Just; and Gregory XIII. wrote him a letter of congratulation on his 'Greater Catechism.' Yet this son of St. Dominic was regarded with suspicion by the Inquisition during the whole of the short war of extermination against Lutheranism in Spain; although he had never been even disturbed by it, regarding it with indifference and without fear. But he saw plainly the evils in his Church, and says in his Preface to the ' Tratado de la Oracion' that 'the origin of all our disorders does not proceed so much from want of faith as from not considering with sufficient attention the mysteries of the faith.' He seeks to provide subjects for meditation, forms of prayer, nourishment to the soul and the interior life for those unable to find them out for themselves, disdaining no details which might be helpful. ' He is distinguished,' writes M. Rousselot, ' by a great soberness of style, gentleness, and an inexpressible and inimitable charm : there are no theories, no learned disquisitions, nothing which smells of the schools. . . . Responding to a profound and sincere sentiment, satisfying keen religious needs, the "Guia de Pecadores" instructed without repelling, and moved without terrifying.' [1]

[1] *Les Mystiques Espagnols*, pp. 181 and 182 : ' Remarquable

He sought to preserve the spiritual life from excess of mysticism, which seemed to him dangerous to morality, but he taught that the progress of the soul is measured rather by its love than by its comprehension, and that therefore ' it is better to love divine things than to know them, and to know human things than to love them.' Still, feeling deeply, like Lacordaire, that Christianity was not meant to destroy intelligence, he knew how much faith would gain if his countrymen, more enlightened, were taught to employ mind and reason in the service of the religion which they blindly ollowed.

Luis de Granada died in the same year, 1582, as St. Teresa. If he is the greatest and most learned writer among the mystics, his pupil, Luis de Leon, is, perhaps, the most personally interesting. Born at Belmonte in 1527, of a distinguished family, he entered the order of the Hermits of St. Augustine (to which Luther belonged) at the age of seventeen, after a brilliant course at the University of Salamanca. His talents gained for him, when only thirty-four, the chair of St. Thomas Aquinas, and later that of Sacred Literature, but they also drew upon him the envy of many; and it was the time when private enmity found a ready agent in the Inquisition, and when ' it was almost an act of courage in an enlightened priest to dare to preach the word of God,' —when St. Teresa wrote to the Provincial of the Reformed

exemple du sage tempérament que sut garder Louis de Grenade: en servant la religion, il se préservait et cherchait à préserver autrui des excès d'un mysticisme outré, et il sentait, que pour cela les lumières de l'intelligence n'étaient point méprisables. Mais favoriser, même dans la plus étroite mesure, le développement intellectuel au point de vue religieux, n'entrait pas dans le plan de conduite de l'Inquisition. Quoi de surprenant que le guide des pécheurs ait porté ombrage à une puissance plus facile aux soupçons qu'aux scrupules?'

Carmelites, F. Gratian, 'Be very careful as to what you say in your sermons.'

Luis de Leon gave a handle to his enemies by his independence of thought and open speech concerning dangers to faith through general ignorance, especially the ignorance of the clergy.[1] Like Malon de Chaide, he wrote strongly of the evil caused by bad books and romances, maintaining that the remedy was to be found in good books composed in Spanish, 'drawn from Holy Scripture, in accordance with it, and faithful to its spirit.'

He was arrested March 27, 1572, charged with having made a vernacular translation of the Canticles, and with having treated it as a pastoral eclogue. For five years he was kept in the prisons of the Inquisition, and was summoned more than fifty times before his judges, his enemies urging every plea against him, especially that 'his great biblical learning was fast leading him to heresy, if indeed he were not already at heart a Protestant.' Notwithstanding all his declarations of unconditional submission to the doctrines of the Church and to the authority of the Holy Office, four of his judges voted (in September 1576, four years and a half after he had been imprisoned) that he should be put to the rack, 'to ascertain his *intentions* in relation to whatever had been indicated and testified against him;' while two voted that he should be forbidden in future to teach publicly, and should confess before the whole University that certain propositions of his were 'suspicious and ambiguous.'

[1] 'Voilée chez Louis de Grenade et chez Malon, respectueuse chez Ste. Thérèse, la plainte, libre et hardie dans sa bouche, va droit aux plus coupables, aux prêtres, à qui la science est nécessaire ; obligés qu'ils sont d'instruire les hommes.'—*Les Mystiques Espagnols*, p. 216.

But the Supreme Council of the Inquisition at Madrid overruled this judgment, or rather, passing it over in silence, declared him, on December 7, 1576, fully acquitted. His office in the University had not been filled up, and, on December 30, he reappeared in the chair of Sacred Literature, before a crowded audience filled with sympathy for his sufferings. They looked in vain for some allusion to them: with a noble and beautiful self-restraint, he began his lecture where he had ended the last, with the words *Deciamos ahora*, 'We have said just now;' passing over the five years of his persecutions as though they had not existed.

He lived for fourteen years after his release, but never recovered the effects of his imprisonment. To him was committed the task of editing and publishing the works of St. Teresa, after her death. 'I never saw nor knew the blessed mother Teresa of Jesus,' he wrote, 'while she lived in this world; but now, when she lives in heaven, I know her, and do in reality see her continually in two living images of herself, which she left amongst us—viz. her daughters and her books.' He undertook to write her life a few months before his death, but only a few pages of it were finished.

In his 'Commentary on the Book of Job,' written after his release, he seems unconsciously to have expressed his own moral history, and the impression made upon his soul by his sufferings and wrongs. But he must have been almost more remarkable as a poet than as a prose writer; even through the veil of translation his delicate feeling for beauty in nature is full of charm.[1] A small farm near

---

[1] 'Poète d'un mysticisme dont les Grenade, les Thérèse, les Jean de la Croix sont les docteurs, Louis de Léon serait à son rang parmi les grands lyriques non seulement de son pays, mais du monde.'—*Les Mystiques Espagnols*, p. 214.

Salamanca, belonging to his community, supplied all that this sentiment required. He loved to retire to it, and in his prison dwells on all the little details which sufficed to charm him—

> Earth and sky,
> And some flowers to bloom and die.[1]

If in common with some poets of our time he turned for refreshment to the calm beauties of creation, yet for him Nature had no profound sadness, not even the gloom and silence of night, since *Cæli enarrant gloriam Dei.*[2]

---

[1] 'Le moindre objet il le connaît, il l'aime, le regrette ; nul détail ne lui échappe, ni le moulin, ni la source qui se promène parmi les pierres de la jetée, ni le bateau qui conduit dans l'île, ni le "haut peuplier," témoin fréquent de ses méditations, et sous l'ombrage duquel il placera volontiers ses interlocuteurs. Si ceux-ci ne nous transportaient dans un monde différent, nous nous croirions aux bords de l'Ilissus, à l'abri de ce platane si connu de Phèdre, et si admiré de Socrate.'—*Les Mystiques Espagnols*, p. 284.

[2] There are so few hymns on the Ascension, that the insertion here may be forgiven of Ticknor's graceful translation of Luis de Leon's lovely hymn beginning, *Y dexas, Pastor santo* :—

> And dost Thou, holy Shepherd, leave
>   Thine unprotected flock alone,
> Here, in this darksome vale, to grieve,
>   While Thou ascend'st Thy glorious throne?
>
> Oh, where can they their hopes now turn,
>   Who never lived but on Thy love?
> Where rest the hearts for Thee that burn,
>   When Thou art lost in light above?
>
> How shall those eyes now find repose
>   That turn, in vain, Thy smile to see?
> What can they hear save mortal woes,
>   Who lose Thy voice's melody?
>
> And who shall lay his tranquil hand
>   Upon the troubled ocean's might?
> Who hush the winds by his command?
> Who guide us through this starless night?

'Putting aside poets,' M. Rousselot writes, 'who are the true geniuses of Spain in the sixteenth century, the golden age of literature? The mystics.'[1] But the great masters of this mysticism were followed by a crowd of lesser men, who attempted to formalise what, in its first teachers, had been spontaneous, until mysticism became, to use an expression frequently employed by them, *methodus amandi Deum*.[2]

Amongst these St. John of the Cross is not of course to be reckoned: rather he may perhaps represent the extreme of mysticism before its decline. But even of him St. Teresa, with her usual penetration, wrote, 'He is too subtle; he spiritualises to excess.' It is necessary to resume the narrative of her life and work, which had so remarkable an influence upon his.

> For Thou art gone! that cloud so bright
> That bears Thee from our love away,
> Springs upward though the dazzling light,
> And leaves us here to weep and pray!

[1] *Les Mystiques Espagnols*, p. 454. 'Il n'y a donc pas d'exagération à regarder les mystiques comme les vrais philosophes de l'Espagne ... d'abord, par leur intelligence du platonisme renaissant. leur admiration de cette noble philosophie encore aujourd'hui vivante après vingt-deux siècles, et qui n'a perdu au contact du Christianisme que la partie périssable de toute œuvre humaine.'—Ibid. p. 455.

[2] 'Après les Thérèse, les Jean de la Croix, qui écrivent avec une sincérité naïve l'histoire de leur âme, viennent les docteurs qui enseignent ce qui se passe dans l'âme d'autrui : la poétique après les poèmes.'—Ibid. p. 424.

Chapter the Eleventh.

How can such joy as this want words to speak?
And yet what words can speak such joy as this?
Far from the world, that might their quiet break,
Here the glad souls the Face of Beauty kiss,

Their eyes on Him, Whose graces manifold
The more they do behold, the more they would behold.

GILES FLETCHER.

REMAINED five years after its foundation,' Teresa writes in her 'Book of the Foundations,' 'in the house of St. Joseph, Avila; and I believe, so far as I can see at present, that they were the most tranquil years of my life, the calm and rest of which my soul often misses. During that time certain young persons entered it as religious, whose years were not many, but whom the world, as it seemed, had already made its own, if we might judge of them by their outward manners and dress. Our Lord very quickly set them free from these vanities, drew them into His own house, and endowed them with a perfection so great as to make me very much ashamed of myself. I took my delight in souls so pure and holy, whose only anxiety was to praise and serve our Lord. His Majesty sent us everything we

had need of without our asking for it; and whenever we were in want, which was very rarely, their joy was then the greater. I used to praise our Lord at the sight of virtues so high, especially for the disregard of everything but His service. I, who was Prioress there, do not remember that I ever had any thoughts about our necessities, for I was persuaded that our Lord would never fail those who had no other care but that of pleasing Him. And if now and then there was not sufficient food for us all, on my saying that what we had was for those who wanted it most, not one of them would think that she was in need; and so it remained till God sent enough for all.'[1]

The rule, she says herself, was 'somewhat severe;' but she also tells us in her 'Life' of 'the joy and cheerfulness, and the few troubles,' they had at St. Joseph's, as well as the 'better health than usual of them all.' Their number was limited to thirteen. 'This is the perpetual aim of those who are here,' she writes, 'to be alone with Him alone. . . . If anyone thinks the rule hard, let her lay the fault on her want of the true spirit, and not on the rule of the house, seeing that delicate persons, and those not saints,—because they have the true spirit,—can bear it all with so much sweetness.'[2]

During these years of quiet she finished her 'Life,' which had been begun in 1561 by desire of F. Pedro Ibañez. The first thirty-two chapters had probably been written in the house of Doña Luisa de la Cerda; and her Dominican confessor at Toledo, F. Garcia, desired her to add to it the account of the foundation of St. Joseph's. Alvarez was sent from Avila to Medina del Campo in 1566, and Ibañez (who had so greatly assisted the foundation of St.

---

[1] *Fondaciones*, c. i. 1, 2.   [2] *Vida*, c. xxxvii. 31.

Joseph's), Fra Garcia, and Dominico Bañes appear to have been Teresa's confessors, even before the departure of Alvarez. Bañes was her principal director, for she says in her seventh 'Relation' that he was the person with whom she had the most frequent communications. Zöckler remarks that she was more and more led to choose her confessors in the two Orders, the Dominican and Jesuit, which almost alone at that time devoted themselves to learned theological research, and to the theoretical and practical study of mysticism; and that the position of mediatrix between these two Orders which she as well as her teaching gradually occupied, is one of the most interesting, and hitherto least noticed, aspects of 'the profoundly rich and many-sided work of this saint,' especially at a time when the sparks of bitter theological jealousies were already lit, which in Spain were soon to be kindled into a fierce flame.[1]

'Do you, my daughters,' she writes, 'go always for direction to learned men, for thereby shall you find the way of perfection in discretion and truth. It is very necessary for prioresses, if they would execute their office well, to have learned men for their confessors—if not, they will do many foolish things, thinking them to be saintly; and, moreover, they must contrive that their nuns go to confession to learned men.'[2]

She wrote the following letter to Ibañez on sending him the completed 'Life':—

'I.H.S.

'The Holy Spirit be ever with you, my father. Amen. It would not be anything improper if I were to magnify my

[1] *Zeitschrift für Lutherische Theologie*, 1865, p. 92.
[2] *Fondaciones*, c. xix. 1.

labour in writing this, to oblige you to be very careful to recommend me to our Lord; for indeed I may well do so, considering what I have gone through in giving this account of myself, and in retracing my manifold wretchedness. But still I can say with truth that I felt it more difficult to speak of the graces which I have received from our Lord than to speak of my offences against His Majesty. You, my father, commanded me to write at length: that is what I have done, on condition that you will do what you promised— namely, destroy everything in it that has the appearance of being wrong. I had not yet read it through after I had written it when your reverence sent for it. Some things in it may not be very clearly explained, and there may be some repetitions; for the time I could give to it was so short, that I could not stop to see what I was writing. I entreat your reverence to correct it, and have it copied if it is to be sent on to the Father Master, Avila,[1] for perhaps someone may recognise the handwriting. I wish very much you would order it so that he might see it, for I began to write it with a view to that. I shall be greatly comforted if he shall think I am on a safe road, now that, so far as it concerns me, there is nothing more to be done.

'Your reverence will do in all things that which to you shall seem good; and you will look upon yourself as under an obligation to take care of one who trusts her soul to your keeping. I will pray for the soul of your reverence to our Lord so long as I live. You will, therefore, be diligent in His service, in order that you may be able to help me; for your reverence will see, by what I have written, how profitable it is to give oneself, as your reverence has begun to do, wholly unto Him Who gives Himself to us so utterly without measure.

[1] Juan D'Avilla, 'the Apostle of Andalusia.'

'Blessed be His Majesty for ever! I hope of His mercy we shall see one another one day, when we, your reverence and myself, shall see more clearly the great mercies He has shown us, and when we shall praise Him for ever and ever. Amen.'

In 1564 she wrote the 'Way of Perfection,' for the instruction of her sisters, by desire of F. Domingo Bañes, the learned Dominican who, before he had ever seen her, had undertaken her defence before the town council of Avila.[1] Her other works are the 'Book of the Foundations,' begun in 1573 by order of F. Ripaldo, her confessor at Salamanca; the 'Interior Castle,' or 'Mansions of the Soul,' begun, in obedience to Velasquez, Bishop of Osma, at Toledo on Trinity Sunday 1577, and finished at Avila on St. Andrew's Eve the same year; an 'Exposition of the Canticles,' of which only a fragment which had been copied remains, as the work was burned by order of a priest; her 'Manner of Visiting Monasteries of Nuns,' written by desire of Fra Jerome Gratian; and her celebrated 'Constitutions,' translated into English for the first time by Mr. Lewis.[2] Besides these seven works she wrote seventeen short but fervent 'Exclamations of the Soul to God,' after communion in 1579. 'Never,' says Villeflore, 'did love express itself with such strength and enthusiasm as in this work.'

[1] 'Ces écrits de Ste. Thérèse mettent son âme à nu, et jusqu'à sa dernière heure, car depuis 1561 . . . elle ne dépose la plume que pour travailler et prier : le repos, non de l'oisiveté, mais du loisir lui a toujours manqué. Elle écrit, mais par ordre : ses confesseurs et directeurs l'exigent, dans le principe par défiance, pour la mieux connaître et la mieux juger, plus tard par admiration, et pour que rien ne soit perdu de la doctrine.'—*Les Mystiques Espagnols*, p. 326.

[2] Appended to his translation of the *Foundations*, Burns & Oates, 1871.

Her works were first collected and edited by Luis de Leon,[1] and were published at Salamanca, six years after her death. The manuscript of her 'Life' was kept by Philip II. at the Escurial in a silver casket, of which he always carried the key himself. Her letters, chiefly written during the last twenty years of her life, fill four thick quarto volumes,[2] in the last Spanish edition published at Madrid in 1793. Ticknor, who writes somewhat coldly of her genius, says that her letters, 'by the purity, beauty, and womanly grace of their style, may fairly claim a distinguished place in the epistolary literature of her country.'[3] Although written chiefly on serious subjects, they are full of vivacity, and of a *piquante* though gentle playfulness.[4] 'Her conversation fascinated,' say all her biographers. It is easy to believe it, judging from her letters. 'You make me laugh, my reverend father,' she wrote to F. Ambrose Mariano, 'when you say that you know the character of that young lady by only looking at her; we women are not so easy to know. A certain person has confessed a woman for years, and then

---

[1] 'She has seen God face to face, and she now shows Him to you,' he wrote in his Introduction.

[2] They contain 342 letters, and 87 fragments of letters.

[3] *History of Spanish Literature*, vol. iii. p. 169: 'Aucun ouvrage de Ste. Thérèse n'a été écrit en vue du public et dans une préoccupation mondaine; tous portent par conséquent le cachet du naturel et de la simplicité; il semble toutefois que ses lettres révèlent sous une forme plus vive et plus spontanée encore certains côtés d'une nature pleine d'un charme délicat.'

[4] 'Les ouvrages si recherchés, si estimés, si authentiquement approuvés pendant sa vie, seront toujours un des plus riches trésors de l'Eglise. Quelle longue chaîne ne formerions-nous pas, si nous rassemblions tous les témoignages honorables qui leur ont été rendus par les théologiens les plus célèbres et les auteurs les moins suspects?'—M. Emery, *L'Esprit de Ste. Thérèse*, Preface xv.

has been quite surprised to perceive one day that he did not know her at all.'

During her troubles with the Inquisition the Bishop of Osma, and F. Gratian, the Provincial of the Order, fearing that the teaching on prayer contained in her 'Life,' which was then under examination, would be lost for ever, begged her to reproduce it in a separate treatise. The result was the 'Interior Castle,' said to be her completest work, and the one which gives the exactest notion of her mysticism, and perhaps of Spanish mysticism. Written five years before her death, she gives us in it the fruit of her long experience of the inner life; and it is touching to trace in its form a lingering remembrance in the aged saint of the chivalrous tales which had charmed the Castilian girl. The thought which runs through it is of a fortress, a stronghold to be taken, and the country-woman of the Cid sees the soul, as an undaunted knight, set out to achieve the enterprise. This Castle contains seven *moradas*, or mansions, representing seven conditions of the soul—indeed, the Castle *is* the soul itself. With the instinctive perception which was so keen in her, she meets at once the objection, so often made in these days, to such self-analysis, and which neither Juan D'Avilla nor Luis de Granada seems to have perceived. 'I seem to write an absurdity,' she says, 'for if this Castle is the soul, it is clear that it cannot enter it, since the soul is nothing else than this Castle; one does not enter there where one is already.' But she is not daunted by this difficulty; the old Platonic maxim, 'Know thyself,' might have been the motto of the mystics. 'There are a thousand ways of entering into oneself,' she writes: 'certain souls keep in the outskirts of the Castle, without penetrating the interior, or suspecting that it contains so rich an abode; such are souls attached to exterior things, accustomed to live with the reptiles and wild beasts—that is to say, under the tyranny of passions and vices; and, without that, well-meaning souls, who are blinded by worldly occupations, and are incapable of entering into themselves and knowing themselves.'

Accordingly, she describes the soul as entering the Castle when it gives itself to prayer, and enduring various states of interior conflict and spiritual dryness, with intervals of sweetness, in its passage through the three first *moradas*. The fourth corresponds with the prayer of Quiet described in her 'Life.' In this 'mansion' she teaches that Quiet or recollection, in which the soul remains inactive and without sentiments of God, is to be shunned, since in all supernatural prayer the soul is active and vigorous, and has lively sentiments of God,—a remarkable pre-condemnation of the fanaticism of the Quietists. The fifth mansion is the 'prayer of union,' described in her 'Life;' and the sixth and seventh are 'rapture.' In the sixth mansion she says that the soul, though in rapture, still suffers; but in the seventh it is in continual beatitude, 'enjoying an habitual jubilation and feast.'[1]

To know oneself, and to pass from that knowledge to the knowledge of God, such is the teaching of the 'Interior Castle.'

There are but scanty remains of St. Teresa's poetry. The most celebrated is her famous 'Glosa,' of which each verse ends with the *refrain*, 'Que muero porque no muero.'

---

[1] 'On a dit qu'Ignace de Loyola avait été seul capable de s'analyser froidement, logiquement, dans cet état d'extase qui est l'opposé de l'état réfléchi. Cela est au moins aussi vrai de Ste. Thérèse; à cet égard, ses écrits pouvaient être mis à côté des *Exercices Spirituels*.'—*Les Mystiques Espagnols*, p. 360.

But her poetry possesses an especial interest, if it be true that 'psalms and hymns are the voice of the religious emotions, the religious affections, it may be the religious passions;' if they 'carry to the highest point whatever there is in a religion; and mark the level to which, in idea and faith, in aspiration and hope, it can rise.' 'The heart of a religion,' it has been beautifully said, 'passes into its poetry; all its joy, its tenderness and sweetness, if it has any, its deepest sighs, its longings and reachings after the eternal and the unseen,—whatever is most pathetic in its sorrow, or boldest in its convictions.' And indeed the last lines of the 'Glosa' are like a very sigh of love embodied in words:—

        O mi Dios, quando será,
        Quando yo diga de vera:
        Que muero porque no muero?

They must not be called the expression of weak feminine fancies. 'Till I shall come, till I appear before Him, I cease not to weep,' wrote St. Augustine, 'and these tears are sweet to me as food. With this thirst, with which I am consumed, with which I am ardently carried towards the fountain of my love, whilst my joy is delayed, I continually burn more and more vehemently. In the prosperity of the world, no less than in its adversity, I pour forth tears of this ardent desire, which never languishes or abates. When it is well with me as to this world, it is ill with me till I appear before the face of my God.'[1]

Such ardent love had indeed become the abiding habit of her mind. 'Ever since I saw the great beauty of our Lord,' she writes in the latter part of her 'Life,' 'I never saw anyone who in comparison with Him seemed even

[1] In Ps. xlii.

endurable, or that could occupy my thoughts ; for if I but turn mine eyes inwardly for a moment to the contemplation of the image which I have within me, I find myself so free, that from that instant everything I see is loathsome in comparison with the excellences and graces of which I had a vision in our Lord.'[1] She mentions that while she was at

[1] *Vida*, c. xxxvii. 5. Probably no English writer, at least for the last three hundred years, has expressed feelings so akin to St. Teresa's, on the subject of Contemplation, as Richard Baxter. 'Thou needest not look on Heaven through a multiplying glass,' he writes in his instructions for Meditation : 'open but one casement, that Love may look in ; give it but a glimpse of the back parts of God, and thou wilt find thyself presently in another world ; do but speak out, and Love can hear ; do but reveal these things, and Love can see : it's the brutish love of the world that is blind ; Divine Love is exceeding quick-sighted. Let thy Faith, as it were, take thy heart by the hand. . . . Let Faith lead thy heart into the presence of God, and draw as near as possibly thou canst, and say to it, Behold, the Ancient of dayes, the Lord Jehovah, whose name is I Am ! . . . Here, oh, here is an object now worthy of thy love ; here shouldst thou even put out thy soul in love, here thou maist be sure thou canst not love too much. . . . Thus do thou expatiate in the Praises of God, and open his excellencies to thine own heart, till thou feel the life begin to stir, and the fire in thy breast begin to kindle : as gazing upon the dusty beauty of flesh doth kindle the fire of carnal love, so this gazing on the glory and goodness of the Lord will kindle this Spiritual love in thy soul. Bruising will make the spices odoriferous, and rubbing the Pomander will bring forth the sweetness : Act therefore thy soul upon this delightful object ; toss these cogitations frequently in thy heart, rub over all thy affections with them, as you will do your cold hands till they begin to warm. What though thy heart be rock and flint ! this often striking may bring forth the fire ; but if yet thou feelest not thy love to work, lead thy heart further and shew it yet more ; shew it the Son of the living God, whose name is Wonderful, Counsellor, the Mighty God, the Everlasting Father, the Prince of Peace. Shew it the King of Saints on the throne of His glory, Who is the first and the last, Who is and was and is to come. . . . Thus whet the desires of thy soul by these meditations, till thy soul long (as David's for the water of Beth-

Toledo, one day when she was suffering from her heart, Doña Luisa de la Cerda brought out her jewels, 'particularly a diamond, which she valued very much. She thought this might amuse me; but I laughed to myself, and was very sorry to see what men made much of, for I thought of what our Lord had laid up for us.'[1]

'I believe I have never known real pain,' she writes, 'since I resolved to serve my Lord and my Consoler with all my strength; for though He would leave me to suffer a little, yet He would console me in such a way that I am doing nothing when I long for troubles. And it seems to me there is nothing worth living for but this, and suffering is what I most heartily pray to God for. I say to Him sometimes, with my whole heart, "O Lord, either to die or to suffer! I ask of Thee nothing else for myself." It is a comfort to me to hear the clock strike, because I seem to have come a little nearer to the vision of God, in that another hour of my life has passed away.'[2]

She had learned now to take the dryness and distractions, which used to torment her, cheerfully and even gaily, if one may use the word. 'It is only just now it happened to me,' she wrote while at St. Joseph's, 'to be for eight days in a

lehem), and say "Oh that one would give me to drink of the wells of Salvation;" and till thou canst say as he (Ps. cxix. 174), "I have longed for Thy Salvation, O Lord;" and as the Mother and Brethren of Christ, when they could not come at Him because of the press, sent to Him, saying, Thy Mother and Thy Brethren stand without desiring to see Thee, send thou up the same message; tell Him thou standest here without, desiring to see Him, He will own thee even in these near relations; for He hath said, They that hear His word, and do it, are His mother and brethren.'—Baxter's *Saints' Everlasting Rest*, sect. v. and vii., 11th edition, 1677.

[1] *Vida*, c. xxxviii. 5.   [2] Ibid. c. xl. 27.

state wherein it seemed that I did not, and could not, confess my obligations to God, or remember His mercies; . . . not that I had any bad thoughts; only I was so incapable of good thoughts, that I was laughing at myself, and even rejoicing to see how mean a soul can be if God is not always working in it. . . . Our Lord said to me once, consoling me, that I was not to distress myself,—this He said most lovingly,—because in this life we could not continue in the same state. At one time I should be fervent, at another not; now disquieted, and again at peace, and tempted; but I must hope in Him, and fear not.'[1]

Her soul was in peace. The fear of death, which had greatly troubled her, was removed. 'Now,' she says, 'it seems to me that death is a very light thing for one who serves God, because the soul is in a moment delivered thereby out of its prison, and at rest.' She perceives, with her clear sense, the true use of rapture, as 'a great help to recognise our true home, and to see that we are pilgrims here; it is a great thing to see what is going on there, and to know where we have to live; for if a person has to go and settle in another country, it is a great help to him, in undergoing the fatigues of his journey, that he has discovered it to be a country where he may live in the most perfect peace.'[2]

But she values such an exceptional condition chiefly for its fruits, saying that 'it seems to purify the soul in a wonderful way, and destroy, as it were utterly, altogether the strength of our sensual nature. It is a grand flame of fire, which seems to burn up and annihilate all the desires of this life.'[3] It came when she least thought of or expected

---

[1] *Vida*, c. xxxvii. 11, and xi. 23.   [2] Ibid. c. xxxviii. 7.
[3] Ibid. 23.

it, and she was still distressed at times, fearing illusions, and suffering in speaking of it to her spiritual guide. 'I thought he would laugh at me,' she writes, 'and say, Oh, what a St. Paul!—she sees the things of heaven; or a St. Jerome. And because these glorious saints had had such visions, I was so much the more afraid, and did nothing but cry; for I did not think it possible for me to see what they saw. . . . I have said it before, I think, and I still say now and then to my confessor, that it requires greater courage to receive these graces than to endure the heaviest trials.'[1]

She had little toleration for imaginary raptures: one whole chapter (the sixth) of her 'Foundations' is taken up with a discourse on spiritual delusions, and with warnings to prioresses on this subject. The next two chapters are on the proper treatment of 'melancholy nuns' (whom she desires may be allowed to eat fish but rarely, and not to fast so much as others), and on fancied revelations and visions. Nothing can be stronger or more full of common sense than these words of one who knew well what the true 'vision' and its effects were. She says that such delusions are generally the result of weakness from excessive austerities; and that she 'sees no good in this bodily weakness,' that 'it would be far better to spend the time in some good work than to be thus dreaming so long.' She advises prioresses to 'apply themselves with all diligence possible to the banishing of these protracted fits of dreaminess, and to assign to those subject to them duties in the house, for the purpose of taking their attention away from themselves.'

The true trance or rapture, she explains, lasts but a moment, though leaving such fruits and effects behind as cause it to be unmistakeable; but she entreats any of her sisters,

[1] *Vida*, c. xxxviii. 2, and xxxix. 30.

if she find her imagination occupied with a mystery of the Passion, or the glory of heaven, or any other matter of the kind, for days together, so as to make her unable to rouse herself from dwelling on it, to try by all means to 'distract herself as well as she can; if not, the time will come when she will learn the harm she has done to herself, and that it is the result either of great bodily weakness, or of the imagination, which is very much worse.' She compares it to madness, since in both states the 'reason is not under control;' and since 'the soul is endowed with a capacity for the fruition of God Himself, it ought not to remain the captive of any one subject of spiritual contemplation.'

'Whatever masters us in such a way as to make us feel that our reason is not free,' Teresa writes, 'should be looked on as suspicious, and that we shall never in that way attain to liberty of spirit; one of the characteristics of which is the finding God in all things, and the being able to think of Him in the midst of them.'[1] She gives instances of nuns fancying they should die unless allowed daily communion;[2]

[1] *Fondaciones*, c. vi. 17.
[2] She went to the convent where this occurred, having heard from the Prioress, she writes, that 'the longings of one of them had become so vehement as to make it necessary for her to communicate early in the morning to enable her, as she thought, to live; and they were not persons who would feign, or tell a lie, for anything in the world. . . . I saw at once what the matter was; . . . nevertheless I kept silence till I arrived at the monastery. . . . I began to speak to the two nuns, gave them many reasons, in my opinion, sufficient to make them see that it was a mere fancy their thinking they should die if they did not communicate. They were so wedded to their notion that nothing moved them, or could move them, in the way of reasoning with them. I saw that was useless, and told them I too had these desires and yet would abstain from communion, that they might believe they were not to communicate except when all did—that we would all three die together.

and says that such seeming love of God, 'if it stirs our feelings in such a way as to end in some offence against Him, or into troubling the peace of the loving soul that it cannot listen to reason, is plainly self-seeking only;' and that if there should be any trouble, or anger, or impatience with spiritual superiors, 'the desire for communion is a plain temptation.'

Such was the result of St. Teresa's long and deep experience, and she must have had many opportunities of watching the cases she describes during her five years of retirement at St. Joseph's. She was forty-seven when she went there; the most active part of her life did not, therefore, begin until she was fifty-two, when her judgment and spiritual life were 'mature and mellow :' the many foundations which made her famous in Spain (fifteen for men and seventeen for

... I showed great severity, for the more I saw they were not submissive under obedience, because they thought they could not keep it, the more clearly I saw it was a temptation. They spent that day in great distress, the next in somewhat less; and thus it went on lessening, so that ... they bore it all exceedingly well. Shortly afterwards both they and the whole community saw it was a temptation, and what a blessing it was to have it remedied in time.'—*Fondaciones*, c. vi. 13, 14.

St. Teresa was consulted in the case of a Cistercian nun, brought to such a state by fasting and austerities, that every time she communicated she 'fell down at once to the ground and there remained eight or nine hours, thinking it was a trance: all the nuns thought the same.' Teresa told her confessor, who was a 'very great friend' of hers, that this was but loss of time, 'that it could not possibly be a trance, and that it was only weakness;' she advised him to forbid the fasting and austerities, and 'make her take some distraction. She, being an obedient nun, did so,' Teresa says, 'and soon after recovering her strength, thought no more of her trance: and if it had been a real trance there would have been no help for it until God wished it should cease ; because the vehemence of the spirit is so great that we have not strength enough to withstand it.'—Ibid. 16.

women) were therefore all accomplished (with the exception of St. Joseph's) during the last fifteen years of her life. She describes herself how a certain restlessness grew upon her. 'Still, as time went on,' she wrote, 'my desires to do something for the good of some soul or other grew more and more; and very often I looked on myself as on one who, having great treasures in her keeping, wished all to have the benefit of it, but whose hands were restrained from distributing it.'[1] She had always, she tells us, had 'more devotion, more tenderness and envy' when reading in the lives of saints how they converted souls, than in reading of all the pains of martyrdom they underwent, for she thought our Lord 'prizes one soul which of His mercy we have gained for Him by our prayer and labour more than all the service we may render Him.' So it seemed to her that the graces He had given her during those years were very great, and that they were wasted in her; and, grieving for this, she felt her soul 'in bonds.'

She had indeed been gathering up wealth during the five years she had served God with fastings and prayers night and day; the time had come when she was to scatter it abroad, and as before the foundation of St. Joseph's, the fire of zeal needed but a spark to set it in a blaze. She had been at the Reformed Convent a little more than four years when Fra Alonso Maldonado, a Franciscan friar, came to see her, 'having the same desires that I had,' she writes, 'for the good of souls. He had just returned from the Indies. He began by telling me of the many millions of souls there perishing through the want of instruction. . . . I was so distressed because so many souls were perishing that I could not contain myself. I went to one of the

[1] *Fondaciones*, c. ii. 5.

hermitages, weeping much, and cried unto our Lord, beseeching Him to show me, when the devil was carrying so many away, how I might do something to gain a soul for His service, and how I might do something by prayer now that I could do nothing else. I envied very much those who for the love of our Lord could employ themselves in this work for souls, though they might suffer a thousand deaths.'[1] Maldonado preached a sermon to the community, exhorting them to intercede for these perishing souls, and went his way; but the effect of his words did not pass away. Teresa was troubled, having sense enough to see that, for such missionary work amongst her countrymen as she longed for, it would be necessary to have houses of Reformed Carmelite friars as well as nuns, and not seeing how this was to be accomplished. A short sketch of the condition of the Carmelite Order is necessary, in order to understand the work which occupied the remaining years of her life.

[1] *Fondaciones,* c. i. 6.

Chapter the Twelfth.

1567.

La lor concordia e i lor lieti sembianti,
Amore e maraviglia e dolce sguardo
Facean esser cagion de' pensier santi;
Tanto che il venerabile Bernardo
Si scalzò prima, e dietro a tanta pace
Corse, e correndo gli parv' esser tardo.

PARADISO, c. xi.

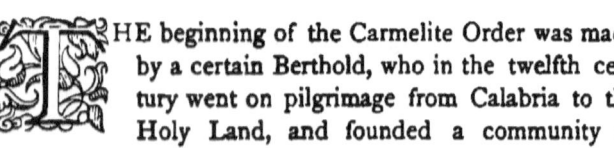HE beginning of the Carmelite Order was made by a certain Berthold, who in the twelfth century went on pilgrimage from Calabria to the Holy Land, and founded a community of hermits on Mount Carmel, upon the spot marked by tradition as the dwelling-place of the Prophet Elijah. Many pilgrims and others joined it during the Crusades; and Brocard, who succeeded Berthold as Superior, sought from the Church recognition and rule for the Order. This was given by his Ordinary, Albert, Patriarch of Jerusalem, in 1209. The Rule consisted of sixteen articles, and prescribed obedience to Superiors, the dwelling in separate cells, the erection of a common oratory, and the observance of fixed devotions, of poverty, labour, and at certain times

fasting and silence. It was confirmed by Pope Honorius III. in 1224. After the truce made by the Emperor Frederick II. had expired, the hermits of Mount Carmel retired from Palestine, and established themselves, in 1238, in Cyprus, soon after in Sicily, in 1240 in England, and in the south of France in 1244. The Order rapidly increased, and the first general Chapter was held at Aylesford in 1245, where an Englishman, Simon Stock, was chosen General of the Order. It flourished under his rule, spreading in France and Germany; but in 1247 the Rule was modified by Innocent IV., and brought into greater resemblance to that of the Mendicant Orders, the prevailing form of monastic life. The Carmelites changed their striped habit, supposed to resemble the mantle of Elijah,[1] for that of the Dominicans, taking, however, black for the habit, and white for the mantle, the reverse of the Dominicans. The Carmelite scapular, worn by people in the world, rivalled the Dominican Rosary in the privileges attached to its use.

The fourteenth and fifteenth centuries were unfavourable to the prosperity of the Order, which suffered severely from divisions and corruptions in the Church; and a reform was attempted by Thomas Connectus, a zealous but fanatical friar. Three reformed monasteries were founded by him before he was burnt at Rome as a heretic in 1433. One of them, notwithstanding the fate of the reformer, preserved its distinctive constitution, which was ratified by Eugenius III.; and the 'Congregation of Mantua,' as it was called,

[1] The Carmelite mantle was originally striped in white and dark brown, from which they were called in France 'les Barrés' (hence the old Rue des Barrés and Porte des Barrés at Paris). The Carmelites maintained that the mantle of Elias was white, but was blackened by the fire when he cast it to Elisha, the parts in the folds preserving their original whiteness.

became independent of the rest of the Order. Eugenius III. had granted, in 1431 or 1432, a greater mitigation of the Rule than had been given by Innocent IV., with the view of uniting all Carmelites under this milder constitution; and a still further dispensation from fasting was given by Pius II. in 1459.

It was under this mitigated Rule that Teresa found herself when she entered the convent of the Incarnation; her experience of its effects is not unlike that of Angélique Arnauld at Port Royal. She was not the first to feel the need for further reforms; they had been attempted, and in great measure carried out, by the Venerable John Soreth, General of the Order in 1462, in spite of bitterest opposition. In Cologne the monks had shut the door in his face; and finally, in a monastery at Nantes, poisoned mulberries were given to him. He escaped with difficulty to Angers, where he died from the effects of the poison.

But if Teresa's Rule far surpassed, in excellence and stability, all former reformations of the Order, Soreth had unconsciously prepared the way for it by being the first to establish Carmelite convents for women. Of these he founded five, watching over them carefully, and always visiting them himself. For once, the introduction of women became an element of strength and perfection, not of weakness and disorder. It was reserved for a woman to accomplish that wide-spread and thorough reform, which in its effects and permanence[1] has scarcely a parallel in the history of religious Orders; and it has therefore seemed worth while to dwell longer on the character and spiritual history of one who could exercise so immense and lasting an influence

[1] The Rule and Constitutions of St. Teresa are still kept, 'fully and entirely,' by the Discalced Carmelites.

than on the story of her latter years of active work, which has often been told.

In 1600, eighteen years after Teresa's death, the Discalced Carmelites, who already had a General of their own, were divided into two congregations—that of Spain, including Houses in Mexico and Brazil, and of Italy, or 'of the Prophet Elias,' the latter comprising all Teresian houses except those in Spain and her South American possessions. The Spaniards were so jealous of St. Teresa's Reform leaving Spain, that Philip II. actually ordered his ambassador at Rome to prevent discalced nuns from settling in the Madonna della Scala, which had been offered them by Clement VIII. The end of the dispute was the formation of the two Teresian congregations; the Spanish priding itself on keeping the rule of its beloved foundress in more exact strictness and purity than the Italian. The Reformed Carmelites are still divided into two congregations; the Italian Congregation having a 'General,' the Spanish one a 'Procurator-General,' both Superiors resident at Rome. The Congregation of Mantua was under the authority of the General of the Calced Carmelites, but had, at first, a Superior of its own, entitled 'Præpositus-Generalis,' and subsequently 'Vicarius-Generalis,' who, by leave of Pope Eugene IV., 1433, was elected by the members of the Congregation solely. The 'Dictionnaire des Ordres Réligieux' (p. 710) mentions that some convents of this Congregation were in existence in 1847. The General of the Italian Congregation, in little more than a hundred years, ruled twenty-three provinces, in France, Italy, Germany, Poland, Flanders, and Persia, besides numerous missions.[1]

[1] See Herzog's *Real Encyklopädie*, Art. *Karmeliter*, and Helyot's *Histoire des Ordres Monastiques*. Paris, 1714.

In this time of prosperity the old jealousy of other Orders revived, and the Carmelites especially insisted on their claim to a higher antiquity than any other Order. 'Some writers,' says Alban Butler, 'have endeavoured to prove that from Elias, and his successors the sons of the prophets, an uninterrupted succession of hermits had inhabited Mount Carmel, down to the time of Christ and His Apostles; and that, having embraced early the Christian faith, they continued their succession to the twelfth or thirteenth century, when having obtained this Rule they introduced their Order into Europe. The learned Papebroke, a continuator of the 'Acta Sanctorum' commenced by Bollandus, treated this claim to so high an antiquity as chimerical.'[1]

This was the beginning of a fierce controversy between the Flemish Carmelites and the Bollandists, directed by the former personally against Father Papebroke, upon whom (on the appearance of the three volumes of the 'Acta' for March) the bitterest invectives were poured. The anger of the Carmelites was intensified when one of the folios for April appeared, containing the life of Albert, Patriarch of Jerusalem, without any change in the writer's views as to the pretensions of the Order. The General of the Carmelites at Rome persuaded Papebroke to let him see a forthcoming folio for May, containing the life of St. Angelus, a Carmelite; and finding in it no retractation of the supposed error, he actually prevailed on the General of the Jesuits to order Papebroke to omit the Life from the volume. Several copies had, however, been printed, and the controversy made everyone eager to read the Life in question; so that all, even Carmelites, declared they would not take the folios for May if it were omitted. Papebroke made his own peace with his

[1] *Life of B. Albert, Patriarch of Jerusalem*, note.

General; but in 1690 the Carmelites, seeing that all attacks and libels were useless in making him retract, carried the affair to Rome, denouncing the fourteen folios of the 'Acta' which had appeared as full of errors.

Innocent XII. referred the matter to the Congregation of the Index, but meanwhile the Flemish Carmelites, thinking they had most credit in Spain, denounced the books to the Spanish Inquisition. The result was that they gained for the fourteen Bollandist folios the honour of being condemned by the Inquisition. A decree was passed, dated Nov. 14, 1695, condemning them all as 'containing several erroneous and heretical propositions, perilous to the faith, scandalous, impious, offending pious ears, schismatical, seditious, audacious, presumptuous, offensive to several Roman Pontiffs, the Holy Seat, Sacred Congregation of Rites, the Breviary, the Roman Martyrology—despising the excellence of some saints and many writers, little respectful to many holy fathers and very learned authors; and because they contained propositions offensive to the religious state, several Orders, especially that of the Carmelites, and many writers of different nations, principally of Spain,' &c.[1]

The decree fell like a thunderbolt on Father Papebroke and his coadjutors. They were comforted by finding their cause taken up by all the learned in Europe, by the Emperor Leopold I., and by many princes and prelates. The Jesuits requested of the Grand Inquisitor of Spain that they might be heard in their own defence, and the work examined anew; and on Aug. 3, 1696, a decree was passed permitting Papebroke, Jeanningh, and Baert 'to reply to the censures passed on their work!' and ordering a copy of the propositions which had been condemned to be given to

[1] See Helyot.

them. This forced Father Papebroke to reply to them article by article. The end was a decree of Innocent XII., in 1698, that, in order to avoid the scandal caused by the dispute, silence (perpetual, and under pain of excommunication) was imposed as to the question of the Primitive Institution of the Carmelite Order by Elias and Eliseus.

St. Teresa's Rule was simply a return to the original constitutions of the Order, as slightly modified by Innocent III. eight or nine years after the hermits had left Palestine, not with the aim of mitigating the Rule of Albert, but of adapting that which had been written for a company of Eastern hermits to the requirements of a European convent.[1] 'We keep the Rule of our Lady of Carmel,' she says, 'not the Rule of the Mitigation, but as it was settled by Fr. Hugo, Cardinal of Santa Sabina, and given in the year 1248, in the fifth year of the pontificate of Innocent IV., Pope. . . . And now, though the Rule be somewhat severe,—for we never eat flesh except in cases of necessity, fast eight months in the year, and practise some other austerities besides, according to the primitive rule,—yet the sisters think it light on many points, and so they have other observances, which we have thought necessary for the more perfect keeping of it.'[2]

---

[1] On the Carmelite Rule, see *Expositio Analogica Regulæ Carmelitanæ*; with the commentaries of John Sosethius on the Carmelite Rule, by Leon de St. Jean. Paris, 1625, in 4to.

[2] *Vida*, c. xxxvi. 27, 28. Teresa had intended that the nuns of her Reform should be barefooted; but finding it was made a reproach against her, she ordered that they should have 'sandals of hemp, and, for decency, stockings, but of frieze or hempen cloth.' Other austerities, instituted by Peter of Alcantara amongst the barefooted Franciscans, she lessened, causing them to be used seldomer, as three times a week instead of daily, and all such practices were strictly forbidden unless by rule or special permission.

St. Teresa and her sisters rose, according to their rule, at five in summer, and six in winter, continuing in prayer for an hour; after which the office was said, lauds, prime, tierce, sext, and nones, followed by mass, with slight differences on holy days. Mass was to be said in summer at eight, in winter at nine, after which all went to their duties in the house. 'If obedience employs you in outward things,' Teresa wrote, 'know that even if you are in the kitchen our Lord moves amidst the pots and the pans, helping us both within and without.'[1] Shortly before dinner, which was probably at twelve, a signal was made for 'examen of conscience,' and each one, wherever she might be, was to 'kneel down and make her examen briefly.'

Vespers were at two, followed by an hour of spiritual reading; Compline at six in summer, and at five in winter. After Compline silence was strictly kept until after Prime on the following day. Matins (for the following day) were to be said at nine, and were preceded by an hour of mental prayer: during this hour the sisters were allowed to read a spiritual book if they had not strength to spend it all in meditation. When matins were ended, a quarter of an hour was given to 'examen of conscience touching the spending of the day;' after which Teresa caused one of the sisters to read in Spanish the mystery on which the meditation was to be made the next day.[2]

'She would not have people give themselves to prayer,' Ribera says, 'before first attentively weighing how such a matter was to be begun. For this cause every night, after the office for matins had been said, she ordered that

[1] *Fondaciones*, c. v. 8.
[2] This was altered afterwards, as it was found better to read it just before the meditation to which it related.

something should be read in the choir of which next morning the meditation was to be made. She herself, in the first years of her mental prayer, did not attempt it without reading something which treated of the Lord's Passion, or other subjects relating to it, by which reading she was wont both to recollect her mind, to move her will, and excite affections. She said that by the words in the Gospel, which Jesus Christ spoke with His mouth, she was wont to recollect and move her soul more than by best composed books.'[1]

It is impossible to doubt the immense significance of the impetus given by Teresa to Reformation in a certain direction in Spain, occupying as it did the ground which might have been gained, at least for a time, by Lutheranism. 'In Spain as elsewhere,' M. Rousselot writes, 'the Catholic faith struggled against Protestantism, but nowhere did it triumph more quickly and surely. This success ought not to be imputed to the Holy Office, which was rather fitted to compromise it. The great mystics of the time at least contributed to it, by reproducing, in the most powerful form for acting on the heart, all that is purest, sweetest, and most poetical in Catholicism. St. Teresa and the Inquisition! The mind can scarcely bring them together or associate them in any common action, however limited; and yet it is this very contrast which the history of Spain has given us. It was in the classic country of the Inquisition that a teaching like that of the nun of Avila was ardently embraced and valued. The Inquisition might repress and destroy; it ruled by severity and terror; but a religion wholly imbued with the love of God and the love of men, which went straight to what lies deepest in human nature, was surely more powerful to defend primitive faith. . . . The Carmelite

[1] *Ribera*, l. iv. c. iv. 78.

Order seemed to her eminently fit to spread abroad the blessings of a religion of self-sacrifice and love, and at the same time to restore new splendour to the Church, for if she does not fear its stability, neither does she conceal from herself that primitive purity is corrupted. To serve the Church by means of the monastic Orders had been the thought of the Middle Ages; to reform her by the reform of these same Orders, and in general of the clergy, had been for long, and was still in the sixteenth century, the dream of many earnest souls. St. Teresa was of the number.'[1]

While she was thus musing, but seeing no way to carry her longings into effect, the General of the Carmelites, who always resided at Rome, came for the first time to Castile. His name was Fra Giovanni Battista Rossi. He had been elected General in 1564 without a single dissentient voice, and was sent to Spain by St. Pius V. (the last Pope canonized) at the earnest request of Philip II. His attempts at reform so angered the friars that they poisoned the King's mind against him. But at Avila he was to find the germ of a greater reformation than he could himself accomplish.

[1] *Les Mystiques Espagnols*, pp. 317 and 443. 'Le mysticisme devenant actif, poursuivant une œuvre de dévouement, se traduisant par l'amour du prochain comme par l'amour de Dieu, combattant l'hérésie luthérienne par l'amour et la prière, essayant de retremper la foi aux sources vives de la charité, se résumant, pour ainsi dire, en une femme, et se formulant par sa bouche, n'est-ce pas une œuvre en rapport avec l'esprit du Carmel.'—Ibid. p. 315. 'Her soul was restless,' writes Johannes a Jesu Maria, 'impatient of such great disaster, and her sex weighed upon her. She would fain make her way into the camp of the heretics, and bind them again into the covenant of the Church. But she was a woman, what should she now do? Whither should she turn? Hear a new thing. She certainly attained to this,—that she directed the reformation of ancient Carmel to the conversion of heretics with a most opportune and truly theological design.'—*Oratio*, iv. p. 498.

Teresa was alarmed and perplexed when she heard he was coming, because her new convent had, by the Brief from Rome, been withdrawn from his jurisdiction and placed under that of the Bishop of Avila, while yet she herself remained, by her first vows, subject to the General of her Order. 'I was afraid of two things,' she says : 'one was that the General might be angry with me—and he had reason to be so, not knowing how matters had come to pass ; the other, that he might send me back to the monastery of the Incarnation.'[1]

When he came to Avila, she did not shrink from the difficulty, but 'contrived he should come to St. Joseph's,' the Bishop permitting it. There she told him her whole story ; and he was greatly pleased, and only vexed with the Provincial, whose objections and vacillations concerning the foundation of St. Joseph's had caused it to be placed under the Bishop. He told Teresa that she was individually still his subject, and that he would willingly receive her again into the Order,—an offer which she joyfully accepted, for it had always been a pain to her to have made any divisions. Moreover, he fully sympathised with her wish to found more convents, though at first, at least, he only thought of their being for women. 'He consoled me greatly,' Teresa wrote, 'and assured me that he would not order me away. It cheered him to see our way of life, a picture, however imperfect, of the commencement of our Order. . . . He being well pleased that a work thus begun should be carried on, gave me the fullest authority in writing to found more monasteries, and denounced penalties against the Provincial who should stay my hand. I did not ask for this, only he understood by my manner of prayer that I had great

---

[1] *Fondaciones*, c. ii. 1.

longings to help any soul whatever to draw nearer unto God.'[1]

The Bishop of Avila, Don Alvaro de Mendoza, also obtained the General's consent for the foundation in his diocese of Discalced Friars, but great opposition was made, and, in order not to disturb the province, he 'refrained for the time.'

Teresa's influence, however, soon prevailed. Considering, 'after some days had passed by, if there were to be monasteries for nuns, how necessary it would be to have friars under the same rule,' she wrote to the General, urging the matter upon him. His answer was a license to found two monasteries of friars in Castile; she was not to found any in Andalusia, where the friars were very bitter against reformation. She was greatly comforted by receiving this license. 'Yet,' she says, 'my anxiety grew the more, because there was not a single friar in the province that I knew of who would undertake the task. . . . Neither had I a house to offer—not even the means to have one. There was I, a poor bare-footed nun, without any help whatever except in our Lord, having nothing but the license of the General and my good desires, and with no means whatever of carrying them into effect.'[2]

---

[1] *Fondaciones*, c. ii. 2. 'And indeed that spirit of Teresa, born for great things, did not stop here, as though she should be content with rules which might be useful merely for perfecting their own souls within the sacred cloister. But with outstretched arms of Divine charity she embraced the whole world, so that what the most illustrious founders of the two Orders of Ecclesiastical warfare—Dominic and Francis—accomplished, that Teresa also attained by her plan, intended to promote the salvation of others, more gloriously than can be expressed.'—*Oratio in Nat. S. Teresiæ*, vii. p. 510.

[2] *Fondaciones*, c. ii. 6.

In this perplexity she determined to go to Medina del Campo, where her old friend and confessor, Balthasar Alvarez, was now rector of the Jesuits. A young person, for whom there was no room at St. Joseph's, hearing that another house was to be founded, asked to be received into it: she had a very little money, only enough for the hire of a house and to help the expenses of the journey. With no further assistance Teresa left Avila on August 13, 1567, having lived at St. Joseph's eleven days less than five years. She took with her two nuns from St. Joseph's, four from the Incarnation, and Julian of Avila, the chaplain of St. Joseph's. He was the son of a merchant at Avila—his sister, Mary of St. Joseph, was one of the first four novices of the reform— and he became the faithful friend and companion of Teresa in her manifold journeys and labours. He had gone to Medina in July to confer with Father Alvarez, and had then, probably, taken the house.

'There was a stir in the city as soon as it was known,' Teresa wrote. 'Some said I was mad; others waited for the end of this folly. The Bishop—so he told me afterwards —thought it a very great folly, though he did not say so at the time; he would not trouble me or give me pain, because of his great affection for me. My friends told me so fast enough, but I made light of it all.'[1]

The house which had been taken was in such a ruinous condition that they could not go there at once, and slept for the first night at Arevalo, arriving at Medina on the eve of 'Lady-Day in August.' Teresa was greatly encouraged by finding Fra Domingo Bañes, her director, in the place. 'It was a great joy to me to see him,' she says, 'for under his direction I thought everything would prosper. . . . To him

[1] *Fondaciones*, c. iii. 3.

it did not seem that what I was going to do was so difficult as it seemed to everybody else.'[1]

Fra Antonio de Heredia, Prior of the Carmelite monastery of St. Anne's, took Teresa and her companions to the house which had been chosen: they went there on foot. 'It was a great mercy of our Lord,' she says, 'that we were met by no one, for they were, at that hour, shutting in the bulls that were to run the next day.' It was midnight of August 14 when they arrived. They had been told that there was a porch which could, with hangings, be made into a church, and immediately set about preparing it for divine service; but the roof was broken, the walls ruinous, and they had nothing but a few hangings, 'and they were little better than none, considering the length of the porch.' The night was now far spent, and Teresa was in distress, thinking 'it would never do to put an altar there.' However, the steward of the lady to whom the house belonged, and who had been charged to help them, produced some pieces of tapestry, and a piece of blue damask. Then they did not know what to do for nails; 'and it was not a time for buying any, so a search along the walls was begun,' and with some trouble enough were found. 'Some began to hang the tapestry,' Teresa writes, 'and we nuns to clean the floor; we made such haste that the altar was ready, and the little bell hung, by daybreak, when mass was said at once.'[2]

Great, however, was their distress next morning when they perceived the ruinous condition of the porch, without protection from the street, lest any irreverence should be committed 'in times so full of peril because of those Lutherans.' In the evening F. Alvarez came to see them, and Teresa entreated him to find a hired house into which

[1] *Fondaciones*, c. iii. 6.   [2] Ibid. 9.

they could go until their own was repaired. Meanwhile she left men to watch in the chapel; 'but I was afraid,' she says, 'they might fall asleep; and so I used to rise in the night to look on through the window, which I could easily do in the moonlight.'¹ After eight days a merchant lent them the upper part of his house, with a 'very large hall in it, decorated with gilding,' which they used as a church; and Doña Elena de Quiroga, niece to the Archbishop of Toledo, said she would help them at once to begin their permanent chapel. She and her daughter afterwards entered the Order. 'Others gave us abundant alms in the way of food,' Teresa says, 'but it was this lady who helped me most.'²

Their own house was finished in about two months, so that they 'were able to remain in it quietly for some years;' and the nuns grew 'in reputation with the people, who conceived a great affection for them.'³

Still, Teresa was always thinking of her plan for monasteries of reformed friars, who should preach the Gospel to the poor, and at last determined 'to discuss the matter, in the utmost secresy,' with the Carmelite Prior at Medina, Fra Antonio de Heredia. 'He rejoiced exceedingly when he heard the matter,' she says, 'and promised me to be himself the first. I took that for a pleasantry, and said so to him: though he was a good and recollected friar, thoughtful and fond of his cell, and learned beside, yet, for the beginning of a work like this, he did not seem to me to possess the requisite courage or the strength to bear the severity of the rule, for he was of a delicate constitution, and not inured to austerities. He insisted on it, and assured me that our Lord had for some time been calling him to a stricter life;

¹ *Fondaciones*, c. iii. 12.   ² Ibid. 13.   ³ Ibid. 17.

that he had made up his mind to go to the Carthusians, and that they had promised to receive him.'[1]

Teresa was not, however, satisfied, and asked him to 'wait awhile and try himself in the observances of those things he would have to promise to do.' This he did for a year, bearing all well, and 'made such great progress,' she says, 'that I gave thanks to our Lord for it, for it seemed to me that His Majesty was preparing him for the change.'[2]

Shortly afterwards she met the man whose name was to be for ever associated with hers, and who was to do and suffer so much in the cause of her Reform. 'A father, still young, who was studying in Salamanca, came to Medina. There was another with him as his companion, who told me great things of the life of that father, who was John of the Cross. I gave thanks to our Lord. I spoke to the friar, with whom I was greatly pleased, and learnt from him that he too wished to become a Carthusian. I spoke to him of my purpose, and pressed him to wait till our Lord gave us a monastery; and of the great good it would do, if he led a higher life, to continue in the same Order, and how much greater the service he would render to our Lord.'[3] He promised to devote himself to her Reform on condition she made no long delay. Still, she says, 'I was not satisfied with the Prior,[4] and so I waited for some time, and also for want of a place to make a beginning in.'[5]

[1] *Fondaciones*, c. iii. 15.   [2] Ibid.   [3] Ibid. 16.
[4] Antonio de Heredia.   [5] *Fondaciones*, c. iii. 16.

Chapter the Thirteenth.
1567, 1568.

Holy Virgins, Martyrs bold,
Lilies those of dazzling white,
Roses these with red hues dight,
In the garden of the Lord ;—
With a pensive ear she heard,
With a spirit inly wrought,
Marvelling in secret thought,
How the holiest and most pure
Most were given to endure ;
How it still was theirs to drain
Deepest cups of mortal pain.
ARCHBISHOP OF DUBLIN.

WHILE Teresa was at Medina she was earnestly entreated by Doña Leonora de Mascareñas, a noble and devout lady,[1] to go to Alcala, where a Reformed Carmelite convent had been established by Maria de Jesu, the nun whom she had met at Toledo, and who had first told her of the primitive Rule. Maria had not, apparently, carried out her scheme with as much discretion as her friend ; the severity was found to be more than the nuns could bear, and the convent needed to be set in order by some wise hand.

[1] She had offered to intercede for Ignatius Loyola when imprisoned at Alcala, and tormented by the Inquisition.

Teresa set out for Alcala, in November 1567, with Doña Maria de Mendoza, sister to the Bishop of Avila, and passed through Madrid, where she lodged, first in the palace of Doña Leonora de Mascareñas, and afterwards in a convent of Clares, of which Joanna, sister to St. Francis Borgia, was Abbess. The greatest ladies in Madrid thronged to see Teresa, some asking questions about spiritual matters, others proposing doubts to be solved, and some begging her to predict the future. 'But having received and returned their salutations, with greatest courtesy, she is said to have exclaimed, passing over these questions, "What beautiful streets there are in Madrid!" and to have soon, with commonplace words, so disappointed the expectations of feminine curiosity, that some, doubtless the least discerning, began to think she might be a good enough nun, but certainly could not be a saint, since she talked of such things.'[1] The nuns of St. Clare had more discernment. Teresa remained with them for a fortnight, at the request of the Princess Joanna, sister to Philip II., who conceived a warm friendship for her; and the nuns 'gave great thanks to God, because He had shown them a saint such as all could imitate; who indeed ate, and slept, and talked like others, and did not make use of affectations or artifices: they said that this was truly the Spirit of the Lord, since it is truthful and candid; such as Jesus Himself, when He lived on earth, was wont to exhibit.'[2]

Maria de Jesu joyfully welcomed Teresa on her arrival at Alcala, and desired nothing more than to follow her advice; and Teresa gave her, for the regulation of her convent, the constitutions observed at Avila and Medina.

Meanwhile Doña Luisa de la Cerda, her friend at Toledo,

---

[1] A.SS. § xxv. 456.   [2] Ibid. 457.

was urgent that a convent should be founded at Malagon, which belonged to her. Teresa objected, because the town was so small that it could not support the convent by alms, so that an endowment would be necessary. 'I laid the matter before learned men and my confessor (Bañes). They told me I was in the wrong, for the holy council[1] authorized the possession of revenues; that I ought not, because of any opinion I held on the subject, to give up the foundation of a house wherein our Lord might be so well served.' She therefore yielded, accepting the foundation and 'a sufficient endowment,' for she was determined that her houses should be either 'altogether poor, or possess enough, so that the nuns should never be forced to beg of anybody for that which might be necessary for them.'

This convent of Malagon, her third foundation, was opened on Palm Sunday 1568, the parishioners coming out in procession to meet the nuns, who went first with them to church, where a sermon was preached.

The next foundation was at Valladolid. Don Bernardino de Mendoza, brother of the Bishop of Avila, and of her friend Doña Maria, a young man living rather a worldly life, had offered her, five or six months before, 'a large and fine garden, within which was a considerable vineyard,' about a quarter of a league from Valladolid. He died suddenly about two months afterwards, and this made Teresa very anxious to carry out his wishes. She went to Valladolid, but 'fell into great distress' when she saw the place, though it 'was pleasant to behold, because the garden was so charming; it could not fail to be unwholesome, for it was close to the river.'

Julian of Avila was with her and John of the Cross, who,

[1] Of Trent.

she says, 'was learning our way of living.' They set about repairs, and took possession of the new convent on August 15, 1568. But nearly all the nuns soon fell ill; and Doña Maria de Mendoza came to the help of her dead brother's foundation, giving them another house, 'worth much more,' to which they went 'in a grand procession,' Teresa says, 'on the feast of St. Blasius (February 3, 1569), with much devotion on the part of the people.'[1]

'To this house came one in her early youth,' Teresa wrote, 'who showed us what the world is by despising it.' The story of her family is somewhat like that of St. Bernard and his brothers. She was the daughter of a widow, Doña Maria de Acuña, who had been married to the President of Castile. They had three daughters and one son. One of the daughters became a Dominican nun; another 'refused marriage and lived a most edifying life with her mother;' and the son, who was heir to large possessions, set his mind so strongly on a life entirely devoted to God, that nothing could move him from his purpose, and his mother joyfully consented that he should thus dedicate himself. 'O Lord,' Teresa writes, 'what a grand grace is that which Thou givest those to whom Thou givest such mothers—mothers who love their children so truly as to wish them to find their inherited dignities, entailed estates, and wealth in that blessedness which will never end! . . . Parents, at the cost of their own poor children, are resolved to maintain their vanity, and boldly withdraw from God the souls He is drawing to Himself, and from those souls so great a blessing; for, though it be not one that is to last for ever, it is one to which God calls them. . . . What were Thy possessions? Only toil, and sorrow, and insult. . . . Thine armorial bearings are five wounds:

[1] *Fondaciones*, c. x. 7.

... it is not ease, nor comfort, nor honour, nor riches that will obtain for us what He purchased by so much blood.'[1]

When Don Antonio de Padilla, the young son of Maria de Acuña, had thus given himself to a life of missionary toil, his eldest sister, Doña Luisa, became heir to his estates. But she, determined not to marry, 'esteemed them as lightly as her brother had done,' and renounced them in favour of the youngest sister, Casilda, who was ten or eleven years of age. Her family immediately took the extraordinary step of betrothing her to her uncle, a brother of her own father, obtaining 'a dispensation from the Sovereign Pontiff.'

Casilda became attached to her betrothed, but, after about two months, 'having spent the day, to her own great joy, with her bridegroom, whom she loved with an affection beyond her years, she fell into a profound sorrow, thinking how the day was ended, and that every other day must be ended in the same way. . . . That very joy which she received from the joy she had in perishable things became hateful to her. Then arose a sadness so great as to be more than she could hide from her bridegroom.'[2] He was obliged to leave her and take a journey at this time, and 'she felt it deeply, because she loved him so much. But our Lord revealed to her then the source of her suffering,' Teresa writes, ' that the soul was yearning after that which never ends.' She feared that 'if she gave herself more to the things of the world she might forget to strive after that which is eternal;' and greatly desired to be released from her engagement of marriage, saying, in answer to her sister's remonstrances, 'Why, then, did you renounce that state for yourself?'

[1] *Fondaciones*, c. x. 9, 11.   [2] Ibid. 14.

About this time she went with her grandmother, the mother of her bridegroom, to see the habit taken by a nun in the new convent. She was greatly pleased with it, and was troubled in mind at finding that prayer was no longer a pleasure to her. Her mother used to take her children with her into her oratory at certain hours, from the time they were seven years old, and teach them how to meditate on the Passion of our Lord. 'She has told me herself,' Teresa wrote, 'that she used to offer up her children to God. . . . I think at times how they will thank their mother when they see themselves in the fruition of everlasting bliss, and that it was she who helped them.'[1]

Casilda came one day to the monastery with her mother and sister, and once inside 'no one could thrust her out.' She cried and implored to be left there, and it was necessary to send for her confessor and Fra Dominic Bañes, who promised to help her to return another time; but as she was not twelve years old, the Prioress thought there should be a longer trial of her vocation. Her childish devices to escape showed plenty of strong will. One day she asked leave from her grandmother to go out with her governess, and passing the convent in her carriage, got down to ask for a glass of water at the wicket; then, as the door was opened to take in some fagots which she had caused her servants to bring as an alms, she hurried inside, weeping, and entreating the Prioress not to send her away. Her kindred in vain tried to shake her resolve, and at length procured an order from the King to remove her from the convent. She lived at home till she was twelve years old; when going one day to church, she sent her governess on a message while her mother was in the confessional, and immediately 'put her clogs in her sleeves,

[1] *Fondaciones*, c. xi. 2.

and taking up her dress, ran in all haste towards the monastery, which was a good way off.' She was permitted to take the habit there. Her story is a vivid little picture of Spanish family life at that time; but the wilfulness of her conduct is not noticed by Teresa. That this self-will was not entirely cured may be inferred from the fact that in 1581 she left the monastery, and entered another Order, becoming a Franciscan nun at Burgos, and dying Abbess of the house in 1610, 'sorry, however, that she had ever left the house of Carmel.'

A far more beautiful picture is drawn by St. Teresa of Beatrix Oñez, another nun in this convent, and related to Casilda. Of her she writes that 'her spirit filled all with amazement, seeing what great things our Lord was working in her,' and that she was 'always cheerful and modest—a certain sign of the inward gladness of her heart. There was no gloom in her silence, for though a very great observer of silence, she was so in such a way that nobody could call it singular. . . . She never complained of anything, never of any of her sisters; never by word or look did she hurt the feelings of anybody in all the duties she had to do. . . . Her outward and inward tranquillity in all circumstances was marvellous: it had its source in her ever thinking of eternity, and of the end for which God has made us. The praise of God was ever in her mouth, and she was always making thanksgivings; in a word, she was always in prayer. As to obedience, she never failed in that, but did whatever she was commanded to do readily, perfectly, and with joy.'[1]

One only thing she desired,—to suffer with Christ; and, on Holy Cross Day, 'while hearing a sermon, this desire to suffer so grew upon her that, the sermon over, she threw herself, weeping abundantly, on her bed; and on being

[1] *Fondaciones*, c. xii. 1, 2.

asked what so distressed her, begged her sisters to pray to God to send her much suffering, and she would then be happy.'[1]

'It is very common for souls given to prayer to wish for sufferings when they have none,' Teresa writes, 'but it is not common for many, when they have them, to bear them and be glad.' The calm joy of Beatrix Oñez endured, although an abscess formed, 'which caused the most frightful suffering, and required for its endurance all the courage with which our Lord had filled her soul.' She said to the Prioress, who was comforting her, and encouraging her to bear so much suffering, 'that she had no pain, and that she would not change places with any of her sisters who were strongest in health. She kept her eyes so fixed on our Lord, for Whom she was suffering, that she kept her secret to herself as much as she could, in order that those who were about her might not see how much she had to bear; and so, unless when the pain was sharp, she hardly complained at all.'

'When the time was come when our Lord was pleased to take her out of this life, her sufferings grew, and she laboured under so many diseases at once that the mere sight of her contentment under them drew the nuns often to visit her, because it made them praise our Lord.'[2] The chaplain of the convent had a great wish to be present at her death, looking upon her as a saint; and so, as she was in full possession of her understanding, 'they sent for him to absolve her and help her to die, if his services should be needed that night. A little before nine o'clock, when all the sisters were with her, and he himself also, all her sufferings ceased, about a quarter of an hour before she died.'[3]

> The wasting pain might not endure,
> 'Twas calm e'er life had flown.

---

[1] *Fondaciones*, c. xii. 4. [2] Ibid. 5, 9. [3] Ibid.

'She then in great peace lifted up her eyes; there was a joyous expression in her face, which seemed to shine, while she herself was as if gazing at something that filled her with gladness, for she smiled twice. . . . In that joy, with her eyes directed to heaven, she drew her last breath, looking like an angel.'[1]

Doubtless the life and prayers of such as Beatrix were preparing the way for the work which lay near Teresa's heart,—the missionary work of preaching the Gospel to the poor, for which she saw that it would be necessary to have convents of the Reformed Order of men. She had already gathered round her four companies of holy women, whose lives were one continual prayer, and whose example was a witness for God in the land; and now the time had come to found houses from which preachers should go forth into the highways, who had given up every earthly joy except the joy of winning souls to Jesus.

Amongst these St. John of the Cross holds the first rank; equally remarkable for the depth of religious devotion which alone would have given him power, and for the peculiar gifts which made him a kind of link between the genius of Peter of Alcantara and that of St. Teresa, uniting the extreme asceticism of the former with that mystical experience and active energy in practical works which distinguish the latter. He was born at Fontiveros, a little village between Salamanca and Segovia, in 1542, and was therefore twenty-seven years younger than Teresa, who, even after he became her confessor, never ceased to be the directing influence of his life.[2] 'Je le vois devenir enfant,' says

---

[1] *Fondaciones*, c. xii. 11.
[2] 'Nul doute que, dans les épanchements de ces deux âmes, la profonde sagesse de l'une n'ait ralenti l'essor parfois trop large de

Fénélon, 'aux pieds de Thérèse sa mère. C'est elle qui le conduit comme par la main pour la réforme de l'Ordre, et il recueille dans son sein enflammé les paroles de la sagesse.'

His father, Gonzalez de Yepez, who belonged to an ancient and noble Castilian family, boasting purest Spanish blood, had married out of love Catarina Alvarez, a maiden of low birth, and had never regretted his choice, although spending his life in daily labour in her native village. On his death, while John, the youngest of three sons, was still a little child, Catarina removed to Medina del Campo, where a pious nobleman, named Alonzo Alvarez, who had devoted himself to the care of a hospital, became interested in the boy, made him his assistant in the care of the sick, and afterwards sent him to the Jesuits' College, with a view to his taking orders and becoming chaplain to the hospital. But this was not to be his vocation; about the time when he was to receive minor orders, he felt himself more and more impelled to enter the strictest religious Order that he could find. 'The words of Jesus to the rich young man,' says the Lutheran writer who has already been quoted, 'drew him with irresistible force, as they had drawn so many cloister-saints before him, along the onward path of entire renunciation of the world and apostolical poverty; and a divine voice, which he believed he had heard in prayer, already announced to him his calling to be the Reformer of an ancient Order.'[1]

The voice fell on no unwilling ear; he entered the Carmelite convent of St. Anne at Medina, and was sent to complete his education at Salamanca. But his brilliant successes at the University seemed to him to savour too

l'autre, et qu'il ne faille attribuer à Thérèse les correctifs que Jean de la Croix impose à ses hardiesses.'—*Les Mystiques Espagnols*, p. 404.

[1] Zöckler, *Zeitschrift für lutherische Theologie*, 1866.

much of mundane vanity, although he was specially distinguished for his deep knowledge of Holy Scripture; and the mitigated Carmelite monastery did not satisfy his aspirations. He obtained leave from his superiors to observe the ancient Rule in all its original strictness, and used still greater austerities than it prescribed, while continuing his studies with diligence, both in the works of the great Christian masters and of the ancients. It was while he was preparing for priest's orders that he first met St. Teresa, in the autumn of 1567. He was then twenty-five years old, Teresa fifty-two; and the young ascetic, full of genius as well as religious ardour, feeble in body but strong in spirit, at once arrested her attention. She had met a kindred spirit; a soul on fire with the love of God; the man who was to be the chief ornament of her Reform, and its almost martyr. To leave the world, and lose himself in God, was the one aspiration of his soul, the one aim of his teaching; and he may have been the most audacious of the mystics because he was the most detached.

Teresa never doubted for a moment of his fitness for the work of her Reform; she had tried and proved his prior, Fra Antonio de Heredia; but, she says, 'there was no need to try father John of the Cross.' A nobleman of Avila, Don Rafael Velasquez, to whom she had never spoken, found out that she wished to have a monastery of discalced friars, and offered her as a gift a house in a small hamlet on the road to Medina. She went to see it on her way from Avila to Valladolid in June 1568, accompanied by Antonia, one of the first four novices of the Reform, and by her faithful chaplain, Julian of Avila.

'We set out early in the morning,' she writes; 'but as we did not know the road we missed it, and the place being but little known, we could not hear much about it. We spent the whole day in great toil, for the sun was very strong: when we thought we were near the place we had to go as far again. I shall always remember that wearisome and winding road. We reached the house a little before nightfall, and the state it was in when we entered was such that we could not venture to pass the night there, because of the extreme absence of cleanliness, and of the crowd of harvest-men. It had a fair porch, two rooms, one beyond the other, and a garret, with a small kitchen. This was all the building that was to be our monastery. I thought that the porch might be made into a church, the garret into a choir, which would do well, and the friars could sleep in the room. The nun who was with me, though much better than I am, and very much given to penance, could not bear that I should think of having a monastery there, and said to me, "Certainly, mother, there is nobody, however great his spirituality, who can bear this; do not speak of it."'[1]

However, when they reached Medina she told Fra Antonio of it, saying that if he had courage to remain there, God would be sure to help him, and that to begin was everything. She added, with her usual sharp common sense, that the meanness of the beginning would greatly prevent difficulties with the Provincial, for if they were settled in that little hamlet, no one would take any thought about them. Antonio answered 'that he would live not only there, but even in a pigsty.'

At Valladolid, where she went for the foundation of nuns already mentioned, she found the Provincial, 'an old man, very kind, and without guile,' and obtained his permission for her first foundation of friars. John of the Cross went to

[1] *Fondaciones*, c. xiii. 3.

the little house at Durvelo to prepare it, while Fra Antonio busied himself in providing necessaries for housekeeping. 'It was little enough,' Teresa says; 'he had provided only hour-glasses, of which he had five, and that amused me much. He said he was not going without provision for keeping regular hours. I believe he had not even wherewithal to sleep on.'[1]

John of the Cross had already been living for two months at Durvelo, the first friar of the Reform of St. Teresa, when he was joined by Fra Antonio, who had resigned his priorate of St. Anne's, at Medina; and on the first or second Sunday in Advent 1568 the first mass was said in the little porch, which had been made into a church. Teresa came to see them in the following Lent, on her way to Toledo. 'I arrived one morning,' she writes; 'Fra Antonio de Jesu was sweeping the door of the church with a joyful countenance, which he ever preserves. I said to him, "What is this, father?—what has become of your dignity?" He replied in these words, showing the great joy he was in: "I execrate the time wherein I had any."' She went over their poor little home, and says that two friends of hers, merchants, who had come with her from Medina, 'did nothing but cry,' seeing the tokens of poverty and self-renunciation. 'The choir was the garret, which was lofty in the centre, so that they could say the office in it, but they had to stoop very low to enter it and hear mass. In the two corners of it next the church they had two little hermitages filled with hay, for the place was very cold, in which they must either lie down or sit; the roof almost touched their heads. There were two little openings into the church, and two stones for pillows. . . .' They used to go out to preach in many places around where

[1] *Fondaciones*, c. xiv. 2.

the people needed instruction,' going 'a league and a half and two leagues barefooted to preach—for at that time they wore no sandals, which they were afterwards ordered to wear—and that in the cold, when the snow was deep; and when they had preached and heard confession, came home very late to their meal in the monastery. All this was as nothing because of their joy. Of food they had enough, for the people of the neighbourhood around furnished them with more than they had need of, and some noblemen who lived near came to confession, and offered them better houses and sites.'[1]

Amongst these was Don Luis of Toledo, a relative of the Duke of Alva; he persuaded the friars to remove to Mancera, where he had built a church, and where he now built a small monastery for them. The Provincial of the Order honoured the removal with his presence, bringing the discalced friars in procession from Durvelo to Mancera, and saying the first mass in the new monastery. This was on St. Barnabas' Day 1570. Teresa says that she 'could not give thanks enough to our Lord' in her excessive joy, hearing from a nobleman and his wife, 'who could not speak enough of their holiness,' of the good they were doing in the villages. She begged the fathers earnestly, however, 'not to be so severe with themselves in certain penances which they carried very far,' fearing 'lest Satan might be seeking how to kill them' before her desires for their usefulness could be realised. 'They, however,' she says, 'having gifts I had not, made light of my advice to give up their practices; and so I came away in the greatest consolation, . . . for I saw clearly that this was a much greater grace on His part than was that which He gave me in founding the houses of nuns.'[2]

[1] *Fondaciones*, c. xiv. 6, 7.   [2] Ibid. 11.

Chapter the Fourteenth.

1569—1573.

*Generat virgo filias
Mentis materna conscias,
Christi sponsas et socias,
Corruptionis nescias.*

. . . . .

*Construuntur cænobia,
Vasta per orbis spatia
Crescit sororum copia,
Claret matris notitia.*

MONE, HYMN. LATIN. iii. 869.

THE next foundation of St. Teresa, at Toledo, was not accomplished without many difficulties, through which she steered her course with much prudence. A merchant of Toledo, Martin Ramirez by name, had wished to found a convent of her Order there; but, dying before he could arrange it, left all in the hands of his brother Alonzo, of whom Teresa speaks as 'a most discreet man, fearing God, given to alms-deeds, and accessible to reason.' He wrote to her, bidding her hasten to Toledo if she accepted the foundation, the patronage of which he had transferred to his son-in-law, Diego Ortiz. To the latter Teresa wrote from Valladolid on January 9, 1569:—

'May the Holy Spirit be always in your soul, and impart to you His holy love and fear. Amen.

'F. Doctor Paul Hernandez has written to me concerning the favour and kindness of which you think me worthy—namely, that a house is about to be prepared by you for this sacred Order; . . . from which I hope that much honour may redound to the Highest Majesty, and to you great gain of spiritual blessings. . . . The Lord has condescended to dispel my fear from me; and now I am working with what diligence I can in arranging this house suitably; and indeed I think that with the help of God it will be finished in a short time. But I promise you not to delay in the very least, but to come immediately to Toledo, even neglecting my health, if by chance the fever should have returned; for it is just that, while there is nothing that you neglect, I in my turn should contribute at least a very little trouble and labour; since indeed nothing else is to be sought after by us, than that we should suffer something,—by us I say, who, although undeserving, desire to imitate Him, Who spent His whole life in sorrows. Then, neither shall I derive this advantage alone from this matter; for F. Paul Hernandez has written to me, that you are a man whose friendship will be very profitable to me. I indeed owe it to the prayers of others that I have kept up thus far; wherefore I entreat you by God, not to forget me in your prayers. I have hope, unless God shall have otherwise ordained it, that it will come to pass that I shall go to you at the latest in the second week of Lent. For since I have to visit monasteries which have been founded (by God's help) in these last years, it is necessary I should remain in them for some days, although I will hasten as much as possible. But those days shall be as few as possible, both because you wish it, and also because these monasteries are already so well arranged and settled that I have scarcely anything to do there, except to admire and praise God our Lord. May His Supreme Right Hand lead you in all your ways, and give you life and salvation with that increase of grace which I desire for you.'

To Alonzo Ramirez she wrote on February 19 :—

' May the Holy Spirit be with you and reward you for the consolation which you have given me by your letter. The bearer of your letter came very seasonably to me, who truly was anxiously seeking some way of writing to you about my affairs, in which duty I indeed am grieved that want of skill on my part should be felt by you. But I request that you will not determine anything about buying the house till I shall have come. For I should wish that it should be most suitable for our purpose, if indeed you, and that happy one who is now rejoicing in the glory of heaven, have thought us worthy of such kindness. As to the license, with God's good help, I shall easily obtain the King's license, although not without some labour. For I know by experience how unwillingly the evil demon endures houses of this kind, and how much he rages against us on account of them. But since we have God, Who can do all things, that vile enemy is compelled to retreat with shame and ignominy. . . . Meanwhile, do you beware of thinking that God will require nothing else from you beyond that which you are now thinking of. Yes in truth, He will require many things more. For He is accustomed to pay this reward for good works— namely, by requiring that we should do greater works. Truly to give money is something small, and little laborious; but when both you and your son-in-law and all of us, as many as shall bestow labour upon this foundation, shall be overwhelmed with stones (which was near happening at

Avila while we built the convent of St. Joseph), then we shall be splendidly treated, and not merely no loss, yea rather much gain, will arise from thence to the monastery and to ourselves. For the rest, may God direct this matter in whatever way He knows will be best; but be not you anxious.'

In March 1569 she arrived in Toledo from Valladolid, having visited Avila and Durvelo (as has been mentioned) on the way. She also passed through Madrid, and her friendship with the Princess Joanna, sister to the King, became closer during this visit. She was persuaded to allow her to show some of her writings to Philip II. He earnestly desired to see and speak with her, but she had left Madrid before she was informed of the King's wishes.[1]

At Toledo she was joyfully received by her friend Doña Luisa de la Cerda; but the matter of the new foundation did not prosper, being hindered by the interference of Diego Ortiz, a son-in-law of Alonzo. 'They began by insisting on many things which I did not think it right to grant,' she says; moreover, the Governor of the city would not give permission for the foundation; and the Archbishop of Toledo (who had gone to England with Philip II., and had been confessor to Queen Mary) was at this time in the prisons of the Inquisition, suspected of heresy.

Teresa resolved to speak to the Governor herself, an expedient which seldom failed with her, and, going to a church near his house, sent to beg him to speak to her. She represented to him how hard it was that people living at their ease should wish 'to hinder the doing of those things which are for the service of our Lord;' and she obtained his consent to her wishes before she left him. 'I

---

[1] *Acta Sanct.* t. vii. Oct. § xxv. 457.

came away very happy,' she writes; 'I thought I had everything while I had nothing, for all the money I had may have been three or four ducats; with these I bought two pictures on canvas, because I had no picture whatever to set on the altar, two straw mattresses, and a blanket.'[1]

She had broken with Alonzo Ramirez, but a house was found for her by a poor man named Andrada, who had come one day, sent by a Franciscan friar, to offer to help her in any way he could. At the time, she says, 'I thanked him; and it amused me and my companions to look at the help the holy man had sent us, for the young man's appearance was not that of a person with whom the Carmelite nuns could converse.'[2] However, he now found her a house, and brought her the keys of it: she was satisfied with it; and, a pious merchant becoming surety for the rent, Andrada told her she might send in her furniture. 'I told him there was little to send,' she says, 'for we had nothing but two straw mattresses and a blanket. He must have been surprised. My companions were vexed at my saying it, and asked me how I could do it, for if he saw we were so poor he would not help us. . . . We were for some days with no other furniture but the two straw mattresses and the blanket; and on that first day we had not even a withered leaf to dress a pilchard with, when somebody, I know not who it was, moved by our Lord, laid a fagot in the church wherewith we helped ourselves. At night it was cold, and we felt it, though we covered ourselves with the blankets and our cloaks of serge, which we wear over all.'[3]

It seems strange that her rich and noble friend, Doña Louisa, should have permitted her to be in such necessity. Teresa says herself, 'I did not ask her for anything, for I

---

[1] *Fondaciones*, c. xv. 6.   [2] Ibid.   [3] Ibid. 9, 13.

hate to give trouble, and she perhaps never thought of it, for I owe her more than she could give us.' Their need did not last long, for Alonzo Ramirez, seeing the house begun, came to their help, and others provided for them, 'in greater abundance than we desired,' she says. . . . 'I was in pain when my poverty was ended, and so were my sisters; and when I saw them sorrowing I asked them what the matter was, and they answered, "What is the matter, mother? We do not seem to be poor any longer."'[1]

She had other difficulties to contend with, for the nobles of Toledo were indignant that a family 'neither great nor noble, though very good in its own place,' should be patron of a religious foundation, and especially that they should have the right of burial in the church, a point upon which the Ramirez family insisted much. 'A great personage wished to have the chancel,' but Teresa was firm in giving it to Alonzo, considering, she says, that to act otherwise 'would have been a wrong done to him who did us the charity with so much good will.'

It was but the beginning of her troubles with great people; she was becoming too remarkable not to attract their notice, and some of them seem to have thought that their patronage was sufficient to secure her assent to whatever they proposed. It was Whitsun Eve, 1569, when all was arranged for the house in Toledo; and she was 'worn out with looking after the workmen,' when word was brought to her that the Princess of Eboli desired to speak with her. 'That very morning,' she says, 'as we were at meals in the refectory, I felt a great joy in seeing that there was nothing more to do, and that on this feast I could for some time

[1] *Fondaciones*, c. xv. 14.

taste of the sweetness of our Lord.'[1] But for her henceforward there was to be no rest below; the chord of self, smitten by Love, had nearly 'passed in music out of sight,' and even highest and purest consolations were to be put aside for the sake of ceaseless practical toil for the souls of others.

She was unwilling to leave Toledo, 'because there was great danger in leaving a monastery so newly founded, and to which opposition had been made;' on the other hand, she much desired to have the good graces of Ruy Gomez, Prince of Eboli, 'whose influence over the King and all people was so great.' This she felt to be especially important for the newly begun reform of the friars, which she knew was in greater danger than that of the nuns, and the success of which lay nearest her heart, since they could preach to and teach the ignorant and the sinful. So, by the advice of her confessor, she left Toledo on Whitsun Monday, in a carriage the Princess had sent for her, accompanied by her niece, Isabel de Cepeda, and another nun. They went through Madrid, lodging with Doña Leonora de Mascareñas, 'formerly governess of the King, and a very great servant of our Lord.'

During her stay in Madrid she was told of a young hermit who greatly desired to see her, Fra Juan de la Miseria, who was living with his companions very much in the way prescribed by her Rule. 'To me, who had but two friars,' she says, 'came the thought that it would be a great thing if by any means it were so.' He was at this time living with another brother, Fra Mariano of St. Benedict, who became one of the foremost of St. Teresa's helpers and disciples among the discalced friars. He was Italian by birth, a doctor in canon law, and had been sent to the

[1] *Fondaciones*, c. xvii. 1.

Council of Trent on account of his ability and wisdom. He afterwards entered the Military Order of St. John of Jerusalem, and fought at the battle of St. Quentin, was for some time in the service of the Queen of Poland, at the head of her household, and was engaged in many difficult religious affairs in Germany and the Netherlands. Desiring a life of religious retirement, he put himself under the direction of the venerable hermit Mateo de la Fuente, and followed him into the desert in the Sierra Morena, called the Tardon, or Cardon, because wild artichokes[1] grew there.

He remained there until the decree of the Council of Trent, by which all hermits were to be brought under the discipline of the regular orders, when he wished to go to Rome to beg that he and his brethren might be left as they were. This was his object when he became acquainted with Teresa and with her Rule. He at once felt it would satisfy his desires, and told her 'he would think of it that very night.' The next day his mind was made up, although 'amazed at the change so suddenly wrought in himself, especially by a woman.' He told her that the Prince of Eboli had given him a good hermitage and place for making a settlement of hermits at Pastrana, the very place to which she was going; that he would give it to her Order, and take the habit himself. She was extremely glad, since of the two monasteries which she had received license from the General to found, only one had been begun, and she was, she tells us, 'more anxious for the foundation of the monastery of the friars than for that of the nuns.'

The foundation for men was made without difficulty; she had sent for more nuns to Medina, and a great preacher, Fra Baltasar, accompanied them, who himself joined the

[1] Cardos sylvestris.

Reformed Friars, and gave the habit to Fra Mariano and Fra Juan, neither of whom were then priests. Teresa prepared their habits and mantles; and the function took place in the private chapel of the Prince of Eboli, which was splendidly decked for the occasion. The Prince, with many fellow-courtiers, his household, and neighbours, assisted at the service; Fra Baltasar preached the sermon, 'which vehemently moved all hearers,' but especially a young man of noble birth, who afterwards became a discalced priest.

But Teresa had abundance of trouble about the foundation for women, through the waywardness of her patroness, the Princess of Eboli, who, she says, 'insisted on certain things unbecoming our Order; and so, rather than consent to them, I made up my mind to go away without making the foundation; but the Prince, Ruy Gomez, in his good nature, which is very great, listened to reason, and pacified his wife.'

She does not mention the great annoyance which the Princess at this time caused her, by insisting on seeing her 'Life,' of which she had by some means heard. For a long time Teresa refused to give it to her, but at last yielded to Ruy Gomez, who begged her to content his wife, on condition that no one else should see it. The Princess allowed her household to read it, and laughed at it herself, until it became a subject of gossip in the palace, many blaming Teresa severely, and comparing her to the fanatical Magdalene of the Cross; and in the end this outcry led to the book being examined by the Inquisition.

However, the convent was founded, and, Teresa says, 'was held in great esteem by the Prince and Princess; the latter was very careful to comfort and treat them well down to the death of the Prince, Ruy Gomez,[1] when the devil—or perhaps because our Lord permitted it, His Majesty knoweth why—sent the Princess here as a nun, in the tumult of grief for her husband's death.' When the Prioress at Pastrana heard she was coming, she exclaimed, 'The Princess a nun! I give up the monastery for lost.' And so it proved, for, with all their attempts to content her, the Princess soon grew weary of the convent, insisting on all kinds of relaxations in her favour which it was impossible to grant, so that, Teresa writes, 'she became displeased with the Prioress and with all the nuns; and even after she had laid aside the habit, and while living in her own house, they were still an offence to her. The poor nuns were living in such disquiet that I strove with all my might, imploring the superiors to remove them, that they might come to Segovia, where I was then founding a monastery. . . . Thither they came, leaving behind all that the Princess had given them, but bringing with them certain nuns whom the Princess had ordered them to admit without any dowry.'[2]

About this time Philip II. had prevailed on the Pope, St. Pius V., to order a new visitation of the Carmelites in Spain, having been disappointed with the result of the former one made by Father Rossi. The Pope consented, and appointed, as Visitor of Castile, Pedro Hernandez, Prior of the Dominicans at Talavera. He received the Pontifical Brief in March 1570, or earlier, and began his tour with the new convent of friars at Pastrana, arriving there in Lent on foot, with one companion, and one ass to carry his baggage, saying to those who wondered, that he who went to visit saints should not travel after a secular fashion. While he remained at Pastrana he lived in every way as

---

[1] In 1573.   [2] *Fondaciones*, c. xvii. 15.

if he were one of the discalced friars, observing all austerities of the Rule, and was filled with admiration for the character of their foundress, speaking of her to the King, on his arrival at Madrid, in terms of highest encomium, as also to the Apostolic Nuntio, Nicholas Ormaneto.[1]

The number of young men who flocked to the reformed convent at Pastrana was so large that it seemed desirable to found one at Alcala, where they could be educated in the schools of the University. Permission had only been given to Teresa for the foundation of two convents of friars; but Hernandez gladly granted faculties for the foundation at Alcala, which was begun in November 1570 by Balthasar de Jesus. St. John of the Cross, who had remained as Prior at Pastrano, joined him soon after, leaving Father Angelo de Gabriel in his place at Pastrana.

Teresa returned to Toledo after the two foundations at Pastrana had been made; but soon received a letter from Martino Gutierrez, rector of the Jesuits' College at Salamanca, telling her that a monastery of her Order would be most useful in that city. Having obtained leave from the Bishop of Salamanca, she hired a house, where some students were then living, taking great care that no one should know for what purpose it was taken. It is curious to find her still obliged to observe precautions of this kind. 'I took the very greatest care of that,' she writes; 'nothing was to be known till after taking possession. Then, with the license of the Bishop and the house secured, relying on the mercy of God—for there was no one there who could give me any help at all in supplying the many things that were necessary for the furnishing of that house—I set out for the place, taking with me only one nun, for greater secrecy. We

[1] He had accompanied Cardinal Pole when Legate to England.

arrived on the eve of All Saints, having travelled a great part of the night before in the excessive cold, and slept in one place, being myself very unwell.'[1]

Her incessant journeys were from this time to the end of her life one of her greatest trials; the fatigue and difficulty of travelling in Spain were doubtless greater in her day than now; besides which, they were more felt, in an age of little travel, by one whose life until she was nearly fifty had been so still and secluded, and whose health was feeble. 'It has happened to me from time to time,' she says herself, 'while occupied in these foundations, to find myself amidst such pains and sufferings as distressed me much, for it seemed to me, if I were even then in my cell, I could have done nothing but lie down on my bed and turn to our Lord, complaining to His Majesty, and asking Him how it was He would have me do what was beyond my power. His Majesty would then give me strength, not without suffering, however, and in the fervour and earnestness with which He filled me I seemed to have forgotten myself. So far as I remember at present I never refrained from making a foundation through fear of trouble, though I felt a great dislike to journeys, especially long ones; but when I had once started I thought nothing of them, looking to Him in Whose service they were undertaken.'[2]

She took possession of the house in Salamanca alone with her companion on All Saints' Eve 1570. It was very large and rambling, with many garrets; and her sister 'could not get the students out of her thoughts, thinking that, as they were so annoyed at having to quit the house, some of them might be still hiding in it.' 'We shut ourselves up in a room wherein the straw was placed, that being the first

---

[1] *Fondaciones*, c. xviii. 3.   [2] Ibid. 4.

thing I provided for the founding of the house, for with the straw we could not fail to have a bed. That night we slept on it, covered by two blankets that had been lent us. ... When my companion saw herself shut up in the room she seemed somewhat more at her ease about the students, though she did nothing but look about her, first on this side and then on the other.... I asked her why she was looking about, seeing that nobody could possibly come in. She replied, "Mother, I am thinking, if I were to die now, what you would do all alone." I thought it would be a very disagreeable thing if it happened. I answered her, "Sister, when that shall happen I will consider what I shall do; now let me go to sleep." As we had spent two nights without rest, sleep soon put an end to our fears. More nuns came on the following day, and then all our terrors were over.'[1]

There were many troubles later on about the house at Salamanca, but for three or four years they remained in the same house, 'almost unheeded;' and, before two months were over, Teresa was entreated by the steward of the Duke of Alba, and his wife, to found a convent at Alba de Tormes. Teresa Layz, wife to the Duke's steward, a lady of noble family, had ardently desired to have children, never asking anything else from God 'but children who when she was dead were to praise His Majesty,' and thinking it 'hard that all should end with her, and that when her time was come she should leave none behind to praise God.' Her prayer was not granted in the sense in which she made it; and she determined to found a monastery, being much impressed by a dream in which she saw a meadow covered with white flowers, and heard a venerable man, who seemed to her to

[1] *Fondaciones*, c. xix. 5.

be St. Andrew, say to her, 'These children are different from those whom thou desirest.'

'She was very anxious to find out what order it should belong to,' Teresa writes; 'her wish being that the nuns should be few, and the enclosure strict. In discussing the matter with two religious, of different orders, very good and learned men, she was recommended by both to do some other good work in preference, because nuns, for the most part, are discontented people. . . . As they insisted so much upon it that there was no good in founding a monastery . . . she resolved not to go on with her work, and said so to her husband.'[1]

They determined to marry a nephew of hers to a niece of her husband, Velasquez, and to give them a large portion of their property. But soon after this arrangement had been made, the nephew, who was 'very good and very young,' died; and Teresa Layz, in great sorrow, fearing to have been the occasion of his death by giving up her first purpose in order to enrich him, determined with her husband that nothing should prevent them from making a religious foundation. Hearing soon after of St. Teresa's Rule, they found it fulfilled in every way what they had been looking for, and found means to speak with her. At first there was the old difficulty of some endowment, but not a sufficient one. 'I have never been without the courage and the confidence necessary for founding monasteries without revenues,' Teresa wrote, 'for I was certain God would never fail them; but I have no heart for founding monasteries to be endowed, and that scantily; I think it better not to found them at all.'[2]

Velasquez and his wife, however, in the end 'assigned a

[1] *Fondaciones*, c. xx. 10.   [2] Ibid. c. xxi. 12.

sufficient endowment for the number of nuns,' and gave up their own house to them, 'going themselves to live in one that was in a wretched state.' The convent of Alba de Tormes, the tenth which Teresa had founded, was opened on St. Paul's Day, 1571.

After a short stay at Alba, Teresa returned to Salamanca, remaining for a few days before entering the convent as a guest with Count Monte Rey, by command of the Provincial. From Salamanca she went to Medina, where a dispute had arisen between one of the novices, Isabel of the Angels, and her family as to her property. Teresa took the part of Isabel, and the Provincial, Salazar, that of the family; he was so incensed at this opposition, and also at the election of Agnes de Jesus as Prioress instead of Teresa de Quesada, a nun of the old observance, that he commanded both Agnes and St. Teresa to leave the convent, himself installing Doña Teresa de Quesada, who had never accepted the reform, as Prioress. They obeyed, and retired to their first beloved foundation at Avila.[1]

Soon after, Pedro Hernandez, Visitor of the Carmelites in Castile, came to Avila, and then first made her acquaintance, having heard much of her from Domingo Bañes. He sent her back by his authority to Medina, which Teresa de Quesada had already left; and in October of the same year recalled her to Avila, where he appointed her Prioress of her first convent-home, the monastery of the Incarnation, hoping that she might effect a reform there, which was greatly needed.

No command could have been less welcome either to Teresa or to the nuns of the Incarnation. Following the Mitigated Rule, they had no desire to have the eminent foundress of the Reform as Prioress, although their revenues

[1] *Acta Sanct.* t. vii. Oct. § xxix. 540.

had been so wasted and mismanaged that the nuns used to ask leave to go to their own homes in order to get proper food.

Teresa went first to St. Joseph's on arriving at Avila, and there made a solemn renunciation of the Mitigated Rule, binding herself by vow strictly to observe the original Rule during her whole life. A fac-simile of the document in Spanish is given by the Bollandists: it is dated July 13, 1571.

The Provincial, Salazar, with some friars, brought her himself to the Incarnation, reading in the outer chapel the letters of authority by which Hernandez made her Prioress. The announcement was received with a storm of invective and outcry, which increased so much when some of the better disposed went to meet her with the processional cross, intoning, as was customary, the *Te Deum*, that Salazar and his companions were obliged to drag her by force within the enclosure. But her gentle influence soon prevailed both in overcoming opposition and restoring order in the convent. Calling her first chapter together, she made the following address: 'My ladies, mothers, and sisters, I am placed by God, through obedience, in this house to exercise this office, which I neither solicited nor deserved. This election was most grievous to me, both because it laid on me a burden which I am unfit to bear, and because the liberty of election, which you have hitherto enjoyed, was taken out of your hands, and a Prioress has been given to you to whom it would be a great thing if she could learn from the least amongst you the virtues which she possesses. I come hither for no other cause than to serve you, and to do you pleasure in all things, so far as I shall be able. I hope that the Lord will assist me in this matter; and in other things there is not one amongst you who may not teach and correct me. Therefore see to it, my ladies, after what manner I may be able to deserve well of you: for it behoves me to pour out my blood and life for you, and I will do it with a willing heart. I am a daughter of this house, and sister to you all. I know the character and the needs of most: therefore there is no need that you should be averse to one who in so many ways belongs to you. Do not fear my government so much. Although I have lived hitherto with the discalced nuns, and governed them, I know indeed, by the goodness of God, after what manner those who are not discalced ought to be governed. One thing I desire,—that we may all serve the Lord with sweetness, and that we strive to observe the few points of our rules and constitution, for the sake of God, to Whom we owe so much. I do not forget how great our weakness is: wherefore if in deeds we cannot attain the summit of perfection, let us at least attain to it in desire. For the Lord in His goodness will so strengthen us, that gradually our actions may correspond with our intention and desire.'[1]

Her gentle words soon bore fruit. A few days later some of those who had been most adverse to Teresa, said to her, 'You would do well, mother, if you kept the keys of the locutory yourself; and if you committed the offices of the house to so and so,' naming those most acceptable to Teresa. She answered, 'If it appears well to you, dearest mothers, let it be so—I agree to it.' 'In this way,' says her Bollandist biographer, 'the citadel which had hitherto been impregnable—i.e. the locutory—was not taken by force, but yielded itself quietly to her.'[2]

[1] *Acta Sanct.* t. vii. Oct. § xxix. 542.
[2] Ibid. § xxx. 547.

She dismissed the gentlemen who desired to speak with the sisters, sending them on some pious business, by which the good being edified and the bad disgusted, they ceased to frequent the convent. A few young men, however, more audacious, sought to gain repute by conquering the formidable Prioress; and one especially, furious at being denied access to a nun to whom he was attached, asked to see Teresa in the locutory, and loaded her with abuse. She listened to him quietly and patiently, but when he had made an end, spoke in her turn, with such severity and vivacity, telling him if he dared to disturb the quiet of a single nun, the royal authority should be put in force against him, that he hastened out of the locutory, 'silenced by the thunder of her words;' and reported to his companions that it was no jesting matter to have to do with Teresa, and that those who would amuse themselves must go elsewhere.

Meanwhile, 'gradually and imperceptibly, the nuns of the Incarnation, turning from worldly things, and devoting themselves anew to God, began so fervently to exercise themselves in prayer, and in both internal and external mortification, that soon no further difference existed between them and the discalced than that of dress. And they regarded their Prioress with such true feelings of love, that if it had depended on them, they would never have suffered themselves to be separated from her.'[1]

[1] *Acta Sanct.* t. vii. Oct. § xxx. 548. 'She displayed a masculine prudence, foreseeing all things, regulating all things seasonably. For she governed in such a manner, that she by no means compelled souls, but led them most gently whither she would; since by the gentleness of her manners, the grace of her actions, the charm of her conversation, she made herself so lovely to all, that she ruled first minds, then bodies, with most pleasant sway. Truly she studied the characters of all, and suited herself to all in a manner certainly wonderful, and displayed a

She sent to Pastrana for St. John of the Cross, who had returned thither from the new convent at Alcala, to set in order matters which had gone wrong through the excessive harshness of F. Angelo. John of the Cross arrived at Avila in May, 1572, and remained there for four years as confessor to the nuns, living in a little hut close to the convent, which has become famous through its connection with St. Teresa and with himself. The chapel, divided into inner and outer, still exists as in their time. The stalls for the nuns, in the inner chapel, are held in great veneration, since they have all been occupied by Teresa, and are never used by the nuns, who sit on a low form beneath them. The stalls themselves are ornamented with flowers, each nun having the care of a stall. In the outer chapel, on the Gospel side of the altar, is a wooden statue of St. Teresa, said to be well carved, placed in the stall which she occupied as prioress, and representing her as giving the signal for beginning the recitation of the office by laying her right hand on the book which she holds in her left. The stall has been so much hacked by devotees, anxious to carry away a piece of the wood, that the whole is now enclosed in a glass case; the Prioress of the Incarnation sitting on its right hand.[1]

The following letter was written to her friend Doña Maria de Mendoza, on March 7, 1572:—

May the grace of the Holy Spirit of Jesus be ever with you. Amen. I have thought of you much in this weather, and feared lest its excessive severity should injure your health; indeed, it seems to me that it has injured mine not

gravity combined with affability, so that she was equally loved and honoured by all; which is to be reckoned as a proof of the highest wisdom.'--Johannes a Jesu Maria, *Oratio*, vii. p. 509. Op. vol. iii.

[1] A.SS. § xxx. 543, 544.

a little. Praise be to God! since we shall see an eternity not having changes of times; may He indeed grant that we may so pass through temporal things, as to deserve some time to enjoy so great a blessing. . . . I think that I scarcely enjoyed good health for six weeks, and that at the beginning, since God saw, I think, that nothing could then be done without it. Now He Himself does everything, for I know not how to do anything but take care of my body. Especially for the last three weeks He has added to my quartan ague pain in the side and "angina." Even one of these ailments would suffice to cause my death if it pleased God; but He does not seem hitherto to will that I should obtain that blessing. A vein having been thrice cut, I got a little better: the quartan ague went away, but the fever did not leave me entirely. . . . I am weary of seeing myself so infirm, that I am unable to come out of my corner, except to mass. But the greatest pain is that of my back teeth, from which I have suffered now for six weeks. I enumerate all these things to you, lest you should be angry with me for not having written to you, and that you may see how liberally the Lord gives me those things which I always ask earnestly from Him. It certainly seemed to me impossible when I came here, that this weak and infirm nature of mine should be able to bear so many labours. For besides the ordinary business, which indeed is very great in these monasteries, I am troubled by most important matters which do not relate to this house; so that it is truly manifest that we can do all things in God, as St. Paul says. God grants to me that, enjoying so little health, I perform all.

'Sometimes I have laughed with myself, that I am left without a confessor, and so completely alone, that I have no one with whom I can have any communication for the sake of consolation to myself, otherwise than by sight. Although, as far as relates to the relief of the body, there has been no want of great affection and care towards me, and in this very place they have shown me much kindness. For the rest, this house gives me sufficient food, nor indeed had I felt the want of this. The bounty which the Lady Magdalene gave is almost expended, hitherto we had made our breakfast from it; to which also was added that which you and some other persons gave with so liberal a hand to very poor nuns. While I see these nuns of the Incarnation now so calm and good, it is distressing to me what they suffer. God is altogether to be praised, Who has so changed them, that those very ones who were most rebellious are now the most content and loving to me. In the present time of Lent they visit no one, whether woman or man; although, which has been very inconvenient to this house, they are suffering from great want. They bear all with great peace. Most truly there are here excellent hand-maidens of God, and all as it were make progress in improvement. . . . I am by the appointment of God affected with such a state of health, that I seem to have come here only to shrink from penance and take care of the body.'

Teresa remained at the Incarnation for nearly two years, which appear latterly to have been peaceful, and during which some of the highest graces she records were given to her. She was much occupied with correspondence concerning the increasing foundations of friars, and was ever mindful of her beloved convent of St. Joseph's, at Avila, caring for all its concerns as though she had been living there. Her reformed friars had been introduced into Andalusia, at the request of Francis Vargas, appointed Visitor of the Carmelites in Andalusia by St. Pius V., and five houses had been founded there: at Altomira, La Roda, Granada, Peñuela, and Seville. Teresa's Castilian prejudice against the Andalusians always continued, and the troubles which began there between the old Order and the Discalced seem in some degree to justify it.

In July 1573 she was sent by Hernandez to Salamanca, where the nuns were in great distress, on account of the unhealthiness of their house. She had evidently by this time become a great authority in all practical matters, especially the purchasing and arranging of houses. She was accompanied by her faithful Julian of Avila, and says herself, 'we looked at the house that we might be able to say what should be done to it, for experience has taught me much in these matters.'[1]

It was Michaelmas before they could move into a suitable house, which she had duly bought and secured; and the very next day, she says, 'came the nobleman, the owner of the house, so exceedingly out of temper that I did not know what to do with him, and Satan urged him so that he would not listen to reason: we, however, had fulfilled our bargain with him, but it was useless to tell him so. . . . I now resolved to give up the house; that did not please him, because he wanted to have the price of it at once.'[2]

She says that in none of the monasteries of the primitive rule had the nuns so much to suffer as at Salamanca; and after her death they were forced to leave the house, through the annoyance caused to them by the owner, Don Pedro de la Vanda. They settled outside one of the gates. The house is said to have been almost ruined by the Portuguese during the wars of succession.

[1] *Fondaciones*, c. xix. 7.   [2] Ibid. 2.

It was during her stay at Salamanca at this time that she began to write her 'Book of Foundations,' by the desire of Father Ripalda, her confessor at that place. 'I am now in Salamanca, in the year 1573,' she writes in the Prologue to the 'Foundations,' 'and my confessor, the master Ripalda, Father Rector of the Society, has ordered me to write. He, having seen the book containing the story of the first foundation,[1] thought it would be a service done to our Lord if I committed to writing the story of the other seven monasteries which, by the goodness of our Lord, have since that time been founded, and told at the same time how the monasteries of the Barefooted Fathers of the Primitive Rule began.' She says that at first she thought it a thing impossible, because of the many things she had to do—letters to write and matters to transact, from which she could not release herself; but that experience had shown her 'the great blessing it is for a soul never to withdraw from under obedience.' And so, considering that 'obedience gives strength,' she began to write, and finished at this time as far as the foundation of Alba, the last which had then been accomplished.

[1] In her *Life*.

Chapter the Fifteenth.

He who will fight the devil at his own weapon, must not wonder if he finds him an over-match.

SOUTH.

PEDRO HERNANDEZ, the Apostolical Visitor, had said to Teresa that he did not wish her at present to make any more foundations; but, while in Salamanca, she tells us that she wrote to him saying, 'he was aware the Most Reverend the Father-General had commanded me never to fail to make foundations wherever an opportunity occurred; that the Bishop and city of Segovia had consented to admit a monastery of our Order, which I would found if he would order me; that I was informing him of the fact for the satisfaction of my conscience, and whatever orders he might give I should be safe and contented.'[1] He gave her permission, and a noble lady of Segovia, Doña Anna de Ximena, took the house and provided all necessary both for the church and the nuns, taking the habit herself with her daughter; so that Teresa 'had but little trouble in the matter.' 'But,' she writes, 'that there might be no foundation made without some trouble, I was always unwell during the six months I was

[1] *Fondaciones*, c. xxi. 2.

there; besides, I had gone thither inwardly ill at ease, for my soul was in very great dryness and darkness; I had a fever upon me, and loathed my food, with many other bodily ailments, which for three months oppressed me sorely.'[1]

There was still opposition to her foundations; though possessing the sanction of the Bishop, she says she 'would not enter but in secret the night before.' She had only verbal permission from the Bishop, who was absent in Madrid, on business as President of Castile, not thinking it necessary to have it in writing; but, she writes, 'I made a mistake, for the Vicar-General, when he heard that a monastery had been founded, came at once in great wrath, refused to allow mass to be said any more, and sought to imprison him who said it, a bare-footed friar,[2] who had come with the father Julian of Avila, and another servant of God who had travelled with us, Antonio Gaytan. The latter was a nobleman, "once very worldly," but who now was only "intent on serving our Lord more and more."' He travelled much with Teresa, devoting himself to helping her in every way; so that, she adds, 'even among the servants who were with us, there was not one who served us in our necessities as he did. He is a man of much prayer, and God has given him such graces that what is annoying to others he accepts with joy and makes light of; all the troubles he has had in these foundations he regarded as nothing, whereby it seems clear that God called him and Father Julian of Avila to the work: Father Julian, however, has been with me ever since the first monastery was founded. Our Lord must have been pleased, for the sake of such companions, to prosper all my undertakings. Their conver-

[1] *Fondaciones*, c. xxi. 3.   [2] St. John of the Cross.

sation on the journey was about God, for the instruction of those who travelled with us and who met us on the road.'[1]

The monastery of Segovia was opened on March 19, 1574. The Vicar-General 'would not quit the church without leaving a constable at the door: however, the nuns remained there until they had bought a house, and with it, too, many lawsuits.' Teresa says, 'We had had one already with the Franciscan friars for another which we bought close by; about another house we had to go to law with the friars of the Order for the Ransom of Captives, and with the Chapter, which had a rent-charge on it. O Jesus, what it is to have to contend against many minds!'[2]

The matter was only finally arranged a few days before Teresa's priorate of three years at the Incarnation expired. She returned there, and was re-elected; but did not accept the office, and retired to her own St. Joseph's, where she was chosen Prioress.

Before leaving Salamanca for Segovia she had received letters from a lady in the town of Veas, the parish priest, and other persons, asking her to go there and found a monastery. Hernandez sent her word, on seeing the letters, that he did not wish her to give pain to the writers by refusing, but that she need not trouble herself, since Veas was under the jurisdiction of a military order, the Knights of St. James, and that he knew they would not consent. The foundress of the proposed convent was Doña Catalina Godinez, the daughter of noble parents. Until the age of fourteen, Teresa says, 'she was very far from giving up the world; on the contrary, she thought so much of herself that she looked upon every offer of marriage which her father brought to her as not fitting for her. One day, in an inner

---

[1] *Fondaciones*, c. xxi. 4.   [2] Ibid. 7.

room' beyond that in which her father was, who had not yet risen, she happened to read on a crucifix that was there the title on the upper part of the cross ; when in a moment, as she was reading it, our Lord changed her heart. She had been thinking of an offer of marriage made to her, which was an exceedingly good one, and saying to herself, " How little satisfies my father, provided I marry an eldest son ! while I intend that my family shall have its beginning in me." She had no wish to be married, for she thought it a meanness to be subject to any one ; neither did she know whence her pride arose. Our Lord knew how to cure it, blessed be His compassion ! Accordingly, while she was reading the title a light seemed to have entered her soul, as the sun enters a dark room, whereby she saw the truth. In that light she fixed her eyes on our Lord nailed to the cross, shedding His blood, and thought of the ill-treatment He received and of His great humility, and then how differently she was demeaning herself in her pride.'[1]

From this time she devoted herself to prayer and to good works ; but after a few years was laid low by a terrible illness, which lasted for seventeen years. After her parents' death she earnestly desired to found a monastery, and sent the letters mentioned to Teresa ; but when the answer came ' she was so ill that her confessor told her she must be quiet, for if she were in the monastery they would send her away ; it was therefore very unlikely they would receive her in her present state. She was very much distressed at this, and turning to our Lord in great earnestness, said, ' O my Lord and my God, I know by faith that Thou canst do all things ; then, O Life of my soul, either take away from me these desires or give to me the means of carrying them into effect.'[2]

[1] *Fondaciones,* c. xxii. 4, 6.   [2] Ibid. 22.

She recovered; and having spent four years previously in trying to get a license for the proposed convent from the Knights of St. James, she now went to Madrid to treat about it·herself; but after remaining there for three months, her request was in the end refused. She then presented her petition to Philip II., who seems at least to have had the merit of admiring St. Teresa; for 'when he saw it related to the barefooted nuns of Carmel, he ordered it to be granted forthwith.' The convent was founded on St. Matthias' Day 1575, the people coming to meet the new nuns 'in procession with solemn rejoicings. There was great joy everywhere,' Teresa says,—'even the little children showed it to be a work pleasing to our Lord.'[1] Doña Catalina, with her younger sister, received the habit the same day. The former wished to be only a lay-sister, and there was no persuading her otherwise, Teresa says, 'till I wrote to her, giving her many reasons, and finding fault with her for having a will of her own instead of yielding to the Father Provincial. I told her that this was not the way to increase her merit, with much beside, treating her somewhat sharply. But it is her greatest joy to be thus spoken to; and in this way she was won over, very much against her will.'[2]

While Teresa remained at Veas she first saw one who was henceforth to be most closely connected with her Reform, taking a larger part in its practical working than anyone else, and exercising an influence over herself which is almost surprising, considering that he scarcely possessed the original genius of St. John of the Cross, and was infinitely inferior to Teresa in mental and spiritual gifts. Probably his decision in practical matters, and power of administration, had an especial attraction for one side of her character.

[1] *Fondaciones*, c. xxii. 19.   [2] Ibid. 24.

Jerome Gratian of the Mother of God, as he was called in the Carmelite Order, was son to Diego Gratian, secretary to Charles V. and Philip II. Educated by the Jesuits, he hesitated for some time between their Society and the Reformed Carmelites, fearing the austerity of the latter; but having occasion to go to the convent at Pastrana to arrange with the Prioress, Isabel de San Domingo, concerning the reception of a nun, he also visited the monastery of friars in the same town, and beholding ' so much devotion and good-will in the service of our Lord,' he determined to cast in his lot with them. The Prioress had apparently been impressed by him, for when he spoke to her she told him to pray that he might enter the Order himself. 'She saw how pleasing was his address,' Teresa says; 'and it is so much so, that for the most part those who converse with him come to love him; it is a grace from our Lord, and he is extremely beloved therefore by all his subjects, both friars and nuns; for, though he overlooks no fault—herein he is very exact regarding the prosperity of the Order—he does it all with such winning sweetness that no one is able to complain of him.'[1]

He was professed in March 1573; and his talents for governing must at once have made an impression, since Fra Francisco de Vargas, Apostolical Visitor of the Carmelites in Andalusia, delegated his authority to him, making him Visitor of Andalusia, although not thirty years old at this time. Vargas had written, in May 1573, to Fra Mariano, begging him to come to Andalusia, and bring with him from Pastrana some friars who had never belonged to the Mitigated Order, as he judged them most fit to introduce the Reform into his province. Mariano accepted the invitation, and chose

[1] *Fondaciones*, c. xxiii. 7.

Gratian as his companion. But he knew well that Hernandez, Visitor of Castile, and therefore his Superior for the time, would not permit them to leave Castile, being unwilling to lose them, and thinking the Reform not sufficiently established to spend itself in new foundations. Fra Mariano, therefore, had recourse to the stratagem of requesting the Provincial, Salazar, to give him leave to go to Seville on business, taking any monk he pleased with him; and having obtained this permission, he chose Jerome Gratian. They were detained in Toledo, where Antonio, Teresa's first friar, had been made prior of a Mitigated monastery, by a command from the General of the Order that Fra Mariano should take orders. After Ember Week in September they proceeded to Granada, and were cordially received by Vargas, who, having been himself elected Provincial of the Dominicans, committed to Gratian all the authority he had received from the Pope over the Andalusian Carmelites.

Meanwhile Salazar, vexed at losing Gratian, and through a subterfuge, sent orders both to him and Mariano to return instantly. They replied that, being in Andalusia, they were now under the authority of Vargas, and must obey him. Their journey was the beginning of the quarrel between the old Order and the Discalced which so troubled the latter years of Teresa's life: the former were naturally offended with Vargas for delegating his authority to a young friar of the Reform, thus placing a discalced monk over the Mitigated convents. Gratian seems to have behaved with remarkable prudence in his difficult circumstances, restoring to the old monks the convent of San Juan del Puerto at Granada, which Vargas had caused them to give up to the Reformed Friars, and going himself with some companions to a Mitigated convent at Seville. Here for some time he lived in brotherly concord with the old monks; but the latter soon began to complain of the Reformers, and to stir up domestic strife,—a strife which was to spread through Spain. They said the times did not need these Reformers; that they were casting odium on the old Mitigated Rule; that it was intolerable to introduce these Castilian novelties into Andalusia, &c.

Gratian left the convent and retired with his brethren to a little hermitage at hand. He was not left in peace: reproaches and complaints against him filled the city, so that Vargas, coming at this time to Seville as Visitor of the Dominicans, wrote the following letter to Philip II. to invoke his protection for the discalced:—

'Our most Holy Father, at the instant request of your Majesty, commanded me to visit the Carmelite Fathers in this province of Andalusia. Having exercised this office, which greatly concerns the honour of God and of your Majesty, with all the diligence I could for four years, I arrived at this conclusion—namely, that the only means by which this reformation could be effected, was to bring in discalced fathers from those who live at Pastrana. Therefore, at my invitation, F. Mariano, F. Jerome Gratian, and other fathers came to this city of Seville, who by their life and doctrine are of much edification to the citizens, although persecutions are not lacking to them from the Mitigated Fathers. I consider it right to inform your Majesty of the affair, so that, as often as occasion offers, you may show favour to these good men: by which both the holy work begun by them may receive increase, and others may be moved to amendment of life: how greatly this is needed I wrote lately to the Nuncio of His Holiness. Juan de Padilla, the bearer of this letter, will explain the whole matter, on whom

your Majesty will bestow that confidence of which you have
already found him worthy. May the Lord God preserve both
you and your most Serene Consort and offspring. From
this city of Seville, March 15, 1574, the most humble subject
and servant of your Majesty has written, F. Francisco de
Vargas, of the Order of Preachers.'[1]

Pius V. died in 1572, and the General of the Carmelites,
F. Rossi, the same who had first given license to St. Teresa
to found two convents of Reformed Friars, now obtained
letters, in August 1574, from the new Pope, Gregory XIII.,
recalling the powers granted to Hernandez and Vargas as
Visitors of the Carmelites. Rossi was apparently moved
by the representations of the Mitigated Friars, who were
alarmed by the rapid progress of the Reform. He did
not use this brief immediately, knowing that the King
favoured the Reform; and the matter coming to the
ears of the Nuncio at Madrid, Nicholas Ormaneto, he
restored to Vargas his powers as Visitor, formally associating
Gratian with him in the office, and explaining the affair to
the Pope's satisfaction. Ormaneto had been the friend of
St. Charles Borromeo, assisting him in all his work of reformation at Milan, and greatly favoured St. Teresa's Reform.
By his desire, Gratian left Seville for Madrid after Easter
1575, and on his way went to Veas, where his meeting with
Teresa took place.

There he first became her confessor, and a great confidence was established between them; he 'told her much
about his soul,' and gave her a treatise which he had written,
and which, she says,[2] 'filled me with great devotion.' 'I

[1] *A. SS.* t. vii. Oct. § xxxii. 587.
[2] 'Ce traité fut suivi de plusieurs autres . . . qui relèvent directement
de la doctrine de Ste. Thérèse. Il les place sous sa protection . . . elle

am not able to refrain from speaking of one who has rendered such great services in the renewal of the primitive rule; for, though he was not the first to make a beginning, he came in due time, for I should have been occasionally sorry that the Reform had been begun, if my trust in the mercy of God had not been so great. I am speaking of the houses of the friars, for those of the nuns have, by the goodness of God, prospered even until now, and those of the friars have not failed; but they had in them an element of rapid decline because, not forming a province by themselves, they were governed by the fathers of the Mitigated Rule. Those who could have governed them had no authority such as Fra Antonio de Jesus, who was the first to make a beginning; nor had they any constitutions given them by the Most Reverend the Father-General. In every house they did as they pleased. Before the constitution was given them, and before they had a settled government of their own, there was trouble enough, some of them being for this, and others for that. I was often in great distress about them.'[1]

Such being the state of things, it is easy to imagine the joy with which the founders of the Reform welcomed Gratian, possessing as he did ability for practical affairs, and authority as 'Commissary Apostolic' to 'rule and govern both the friars and the nuns of the barefooted Carmelites.' Teresa's personal influence had hitherto been sufficient to govern the latter, and they had willingly accepted her celebrated Con-

<small>est son guide, mais c'est à peine s'il la suit aussi loin qu'elle pouvait le mener. Se bornant à reproduire sa pensée avec une nuance visible de réserve . . . écho fidèle, mais affaibli de Ste. Thérèse, sans vues originales, sans autre soin que de faciliter aux fidèles les abords de la spiritualité, à quelle distance n'est-il pas de Jean de la Croix.'—*Les Mystiques Espagnols*, p. 410.</small>

[1] *Fondaciones*, c. xxiii. 12, 13.

stitutions: these were now given to the friars, adapted to their use. She says that she had been longing to see Gratian, because of the good accounts she had had of him; 'but I rejoiced still more,' she adds, 'when I had begun to converse with him, for he pleased me so much that I did not think that they who had spoken so highly of him really knew him at all.'[1]

He told her what she had not known before, that Veas was in Andalusia, and that she was therefore now under his authority, which he immediately used by commanding her to make a foundation at Seville. 'I had always resolutely refrained,' she writes, 'for certain reasons from making any foundations in Andalusia, and if I had known when I went thither that Veas was in the province of Andalusia, I should not have gone at all.'[2] She set out for Seville in May 1575, hastening because of the heat, from which she suffered so much that she fell ill with a violent fever. The Saint never has a good word for Andalusia or Andalusians, and writes to her sisters, 'You must remember that the heat there is not like that of Castile, being much more oppressive.'

She arrived with her companions at Cordova on Whitsun-Eve, hurrying on so as to arrive early, and hear mass 'unseen by anybody.' They had been directed to a certain church for this purpose, but on arriving found it full of people, for a sermon was to be preached. 'When I saw it all,' Teresa writes, 'I was greatly distressed, and thought it would have been better for us to have gone on without hearing mass than be in the midst of so much confusion. Father Julian of Avila did not think so, and as he was a theologian we had all of us to yield to his opinion. . . . We alighted close to the church; though nobody could see our faces, for we always wore our large veils, it was enough to disturb

[1] *Fondaciones*, c. xxiv. 1. [2] Ibid. 2.

everybody to see us in them, and in our white mantles of coarse cloth which we wear, and in our sandals of hemp: so it happened. The surprise, indeed, was great for me and for everybody: as for myself, it must have taken away my fever altogether. . . . I tell you, my daughters, that these were some of the worst moments I ever passed, though you may perhaps think nothing of it, for the people were in confusion, as if bulls had broken in among them.'[1]

Fra Mariano, who was still at Seville, and had hired a house for the nuns, seems to have been given to effecting his purposes by guile. He had contrived, as we have seen, to bring Jerome Gratian with him to Andalusia, against the wishes of his own Visitor, Hernandez; and now he had concealed from Teresa the fact that no permission had been obtained from the Archbishop of Seville for the new foundation, since he did not approve of convents without endowments. He was favourable to the Reform, and 'had,' Teresa says, 'occasionally written to myself, showing me great affection.' Nevertheless, she adds, 'Father Mariano would never let me write to the Archbishop; but he won him over by degrees himself, and by the help of letters of the Father-Commissary[2] from Madrid. . . . It pleased God at last that he came to see us, when I spoke to him of the harm he was doing us. In the end he told me to do what I liked and as I liked, and from that time forth was gracious and kind to us on every occasion that offered.'[3]

'No one would suppose,' she continues, 'that in a city so rich as Seville, and among a people so wealthy, I should have had less help in making a foundation than in any other place wherein I had been. . . . I do not know whether it

---

[1] *Fondaciones*, c. xxiv. 8.   [2] Fra Jerome Gratian.
[3] *Fondaciones*, c. xxiv. 9, 12, 14.

be that part of the earth where I have heard people say the
devils, by the permission of God, have more power to tempt
us. . . . As to those who had spoken so much to the father,
the Apostolic Visitor,[1] about entering the Order, and who
had asked him to bring the nuns to Seville, they must have
seen later that our life was too austere, and that they could not
bear it. One only came to us, of whom I shall speak later.'[2]

Teresa seems almost to have agreed with the Castilian
proverb, *Jesus y cruzes y pedradas en los Andaluzes*; thus
accusing them of greeting strangers by throwing stones at
them, making the sign of the cross, and calling upon the
Holy Name, as though to defend themselves against devils.
'Certainly,' she says, 'I did not know myself, though I
did not lose my ordinary trust in our Lord.' Just at this
time her brother, Lorenzo de Cepeda, arrived from the
Indies, where he had been living for thirty-four years, and,
distressed at the troubles of his sister—whose most devoted
lay disciple he became—purchased a good house in Seville,
and settled her and her companions there. Teresa wished
to take possession quietly, but 'the Archbishop ordered
the clergy and certain confraternities to join the procession, and the streets to be decorated.' A certain priest at
Seville, Garcia Alvarez, who had taken the discalced nuns
under his protection, adorned their cloister and church, and,
Teresa writes, 'arranged many devices. Among these was a
fountain of orange-flower water, which we had neither wished
for nor had anything to do with: it was afterwards a great
joy to us. It was a comfort to us to witness such solemn
preparations for our feast, so much decoration of the streets,
the music, and the minstrelsy. . . . The Archbishop carried
the most holy Sacrament. You see here, my children, the

---

[1] Either Vargas or Gratian.   [2] *Fondaciones*, c. xxv. 1, 2.

poor Carmelites honoured of all, who shortly before seemed as if they could not get a drop of water, though there was plenty in the river. The people came in crowds.'[1] She does not mention that, on kneeling to request the Archbishop's blessing, he, in the presence of all the people, begged her to bless him.

This was on June 3, 1576, and on New Year's Day of that year the twelfth convent of discalced nuns had been founded at Caravaca, by Anne of St. Albert, whom Teresa sent from Seville for that purpose, being unable to go herself. It was the first nuns' convent which she had not founded in person, and it was not accomplished without her writing to the King on the subject, as Caravaca was under the jurisdiction of the Knights. Philip 'gave orders for the issuing of the license,' on receiving Teresa's letter; 'for when he heard of our way of living in these monasteries,' she writes, 'and of our observance of the primitive rule, he helped us in everything.'[2]

The convent at Caravaca was founded by three young ladies, 'children of the greatest persons in that town:' two of them took the habit; the third was, Teresa says, 'much given to melancholy,' a great fault in her eyes, and one against which she warns her nuns at great length, saying that 'we often lay the blame of our imperfections and caprices' on 'low spirits.' Her concluding words on this subject are striking and beautiful:—

'May His Majesty pour down His grace abundantly on us, for then nothing will hinder us from advancing ever more and more in His service.... I implore you in His Name, my sisters and my daughters, to pray to our Lord for this; and let everyone of those who shall hereafter enter look on herself as

[1] *Fondaciones,* c. xxv. 11.   [2] Ibid. xxvii. 5.

if the primitive rule of the Order of the Virgin our Lady had its beginning in her, and never in any way consent to any mitigation of it. Consider that the door is opened for very great laxity by very little things, and that the world may come in before you are aware of it. Remember that what you possess in peace has been wrought in poverty and toil; and if you look deeply into it, you will see that most of these houses were generally founded, not by man, but by the mighty hand of God, and that His Majesty is most ready to carry on the work He has begun if we do not hinder Him. Where do you think a poor woman like myself, under obedience, without a farthing in the world, or any one to help her, found the means to do so great a work? My brother, who helped in the foundation of Seville, had some means, courage, and good dispositions wherewith to help us, but he was then in the Indies.

'Behold, my daughters, behold the hand of God: He did not honour me in this because of my illustrious birth; in whatever light you may look upon it, you will find it to be His work. It is not right we should in any way impair it, even were it to cost us our life, our good name, and our peace; still less when we have all these together, for life is to live in such a way as not to be afraid of death, or of anything which may happen while it lasts, in the possession of that continual joyfulness which you now have all of you, and of this prosperity that never can be greater, consisting in the utter absence of the fear of poverty, or rather in the desire of it. Then, is there anything with which you can compare the peace wherein you live, whether inward or outward? It is in your power to live and die in it as you saw those die who have died in these houses. Then if you always pray God to further this work, having no confidence in yourselves

—if you put your trust in Him, and are courageous—seeing that His Majesty loves it, He will not withhold His mercy.

'Have no fear that you will ever be in want of anything. Never fail to receive those who come to be nuns merely because they are without worldly goods, if they are virtuous, when you are satisfied with their good desires and their abilities, and they come not simply for a place to live in, but rather to serve God in greater perfection ; for God, on the other hand, will give you that twofold which you should have had with them. . . . I can assure you that my joy was not so great when I received those that brought much with them as it was when I received those who came for God's sake alone ; on the contrary, I had fears about the former, while those who were poor cheered my spirit, and gave me so much pleasure as to make me weep for joy : that is the truth.'[1]

Teresa adopted about this time her little namesake, the youngest daughter of her brother Lorenzo, who henceforth became her greatest earthly joy. She left Seville for Malagon, and from thence went to Toledo, where she ended the second part of her 'Book of Foundations.' 'I finish to-day,' she writes, 'the Vigil of St. Eugenius, November 14, 1576, in the monastery of St. Joseph, Toledo, where I am staying by the order of the Commissary Apostolic, Fra Jerome Gratian of the Mother of God, whom we now have as the Superior of the barefooted Carmelites, men and women, of the Primitive Rule, being at the same time Visitor of those who keep the Rule of the Mitigation in Andalusia.'[2] The authority given to Gratian as Provincial of the Discalced was the first separation made between the old Order and the Reformed, and troubles which were to fall heavily upon Teresa and her best friends had already begun.

[1] *Fondaciones*, c. xxvii. 9, 10, 11.   [2] Ibid. 23.

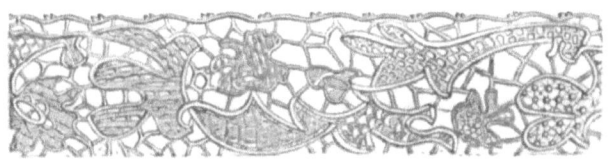

Chapter the Sixteenth.

1575—1577.

*A perfect woman, nobly planned
To form, to counsel, to command;
The reason firm, the temperate will,
Endurance, foresight, strength, and skill.*
                              WORDSWORTH.

HE General of the Carmelite Order, Father Rossi, published the letters which he had obtained from Gregory XIII. at a General Chapter of the Order, held at Piacenza May 22, 1575; and a decree was passed severely censuring the Discalced Friars as rebels to their lawful superiors, and ordering the suppression of their houses in Andalusia.[1] Tostado, a Portuguese monk of high character, was appointed to carry out this decree. Serious charges had also been made against Teresa. 'Before I came away from Seville,' she wrote, 'there was brought to me from the General Chapter, which I think ought to have highly considered the increase of the Order, a decree, made by the deputies assembled, enjoining me not only to make no more foundations, but also, on no account whatever, to leave the

---

[1] *Acta Sanct.* t. vii. Oct. § xxxvi. pp. 634-638.

house I should choose to dwell in, which was something like sending me to prison, for there are no nuns whom the Provincial may not, when necessary for the good of the Order, send from one place to another—I mean, from one monastery to another. And the most grievous thing was this: our Father-General was displeased with me, certainly not with reason, but on account of the reports of persons who had given way to passion; and this it was that had given me pain. At the same time two other and very grave charges were brought against me, but they were not true.'[1]

'When the foundation in Seville had been made, no other foundations were made for more than four years: the reason was that great persecutions of the friars and nuns arose all at once, so that the Order was on the brink of ruin. . . . The friars suffered much, especially the foremost among them, from the false accusations brought against them, and the opposition made to them by nearly all the fathers of the Mitigation. The Most Reverend our Father-General, though a most saintly man, and though he had given authority for the foundation of all the monasteries except the first—that of St. Joseph in Avila, made by authority of the Pope—was so influenced by the fathers of the Mitigation that he would allow no more friars of the Primitive Observance: nevertheless he was always friendly to the monasteries of the nuns.

'Now, because I had helped herein, he was made to show his displeasure against me, and that was the greatest trouble I had to bear while making these foundations, and I had to bear many; for to give up helping in the furtherance of this work, which I saw clearly was for the service of our Lord and the advancement of our Order, men of the highest

---

[1] *Fondaciones*, c. xxvii. 18. One was 'lo ultimo que de una mujer se puede decir,' 'the last thing to be said of any woman.'

learning, to whom I confessed, and by whom I was advised, would not allow me; and, then, to go against what I saw was the will of my superior was a very death, for, beside my obligation as his subject, I had a most tender affection for him, and it was justly due to him. The truth is, I wished to please him herein, but I could not, because I was under Visitors whom I was bound to obey.'[1]

Her letter to the General, Rossi, in the early part of 1576, trying to appease any displeasure on his part, is so long, that the less important parts are here omitted:—

'Jesus. The grace of the Holy Spirit be ever with you. Amen. Since I came to this city of Seville, I have written to you three or four times.... In these letters I told you that three convents had been founded this year—at Veas, Caravaca, and here. You have in them eminent handmaidens of God, subject to you. The two first have revenues, but this third one has none.... For the rest, as I am certain that some of my letters have reached you, I omit to repeat in detail the things which I have related. Further, I told you how greatly the real words of these discalced fathers (I mean Gratian and Mariano) differ from the reports made of them. They are truly your sons, and, in all that touches the root of the matter, I am bold to say that none of those who most profess themselves your sons can snatch from them this praise. But since they made me a mediatrix, in the hope of recovering your favour (for they did not dare to write to you themselves), I entreated you for them as earnestly as I could, and do so now again. For the love of our Lord, grant them pardon, grant somewhat to my intercession. I have no reason for wishing the truth concealed from you; moreover, I think I could not be silent without

[1] *Fondaciones*, c. xxviii. 1, 2.

offence against God, and against you, a father most dear to me; and even if that reserve did not offend God, still it would seem to me untruthful and malicious. When we shall stand before the Lord, you will see how much you owe to your true daughter, Teresa of Jesus. . . . I have before told you of the office which the Nuncio had bestowed upon F. Gratian, whom he summoned to himself. You must know further that at the same time he ordered him to visit the discalced friars and nuns in the province of Andalusia. I know also most certainly, whatever others may say, that Gratian did all that he could to refuse this visitation in Andalusia, and that his brother, the King's secretary, agreed with him in wishing him to be rid of an office which could only bring him great worries. As the thing was done, if those fathers[1] would have believed me, all might have been managed without any quarrel, as it ought to be between brothers. . . . I have always been used, as we say, to make a virtue of necessity; for which reason I could have wished that, when they prepared for resistance, they had considered who would gain by it. On the other hand, I do not greatly wonder that they are wearied by so many visitations and novelties, which for our sins we have seen the last few years.[2] . . . But now, as the Visitor belongs to our own Order, it will not seem so great a reflection on us; and I also hope that if you will take care they understand that Gratian is in favour with you, all will go well. He writes to you, ardently desiring this favour from you, and wishing for nothing but to give you pleasure and be your obedient son. . . . I pray and beseech of you to answer him kindly, to overlook past

[1] The Mitigated friars.
[2] She is evidently alluding to the conduct, as Visitor, of Vargas, who was a Dominican.

faults, and to receive him again as your son and subject, as he most truly is. And, indeed, it is the same with that poor Mariano, only that sometimes he does not understand himself; whence I should not wonder if he had written to you far differently from what was in his mind. . . .

'But consider, I entreat of you, that it is the part of children to err, and of fathers to overlook and forget their faults. Again I beseech of you, by the love of our Lord, to consider for how many reasons it behoves you to grant me this favour. You do not perhaps understand them far off as I do here. Although it be true that we poor women are not fit to give advice, yet occasionally we hit the mark. It seems to me that no evil could follow, but rather much good, if you would receive into favour those who, if present, would most gladly cast themselves at your feet (nor does God Himself refuse to pardon); and if thus it might be known to all how acceptable it is to you that reform should be effected by your own son, whom on this account you joyfully forgive.

'If there were many to whom this office of reformation could be committed, I might feel otherwise; but since, as it appears, none is so signally gifted as this father (which I know for certain you would say yourself, if you saw the man), why do you not show yourself delighted to have such a one subject to you? Then all the world would know that this reformation (if indeed it should prosper) was your work, and accomplished through your counsel and orders. . . .

'I have just heard the decree by which the General Chapter has forbidden me to leave my abode. . . . I assure you, in all sincerity, that as far as I know myself, it would have been a great joy and happiness to me if you yourself had sent this command to me by letter, whence I should have perceived that you enjoined it out of compassion for the great labours which I (equal only to bear small things) have undergone in these foundations ; and so should have counted repose granted to me by you not punishment, but a reward. And even now, though the mandate has reached me in quite another way, still I rejoice that at length for a little time I am permitted to rest. . . .

'No one ever understood here that the power could be taken from superiors by decrees of the Council or the Pope's Brief, of sending nuns anywhere, for useful purposes, or affairs of the Order, which may frequently arise. . . . And although I had your Letters Patent, I went nowhere to found houses (and it is clear that I could not go about for any other purpose) without the written command or permission of my superior. Yet F. Angelo[1] has fastened on me the charge of apostasy, and has traduced me as one excommunicate : may God forgive him. He would have done much better if he had turned his wrath against Valdemoro, who being Prior of Avila, drove the discalced fathers[2] from the convent of the Incarnation, not without great offence of the people, and cruelly afflicted and troubled the nuns of that convent, who were living most holily to the glory of God. . . .

'May God bring a remedy for all these evils, and preserve you to us for many years. . . . I commend myself to those reverend fathers, your companions, that they be mindful of me in their prayers. Your subjects and daughters here entreat you to grant them your blessing, and I ask the same for myself. From Seville,' etc.

---

[1] Salazar, the provincial of the Carmelites.
[2] John of the Cross and Germano. They were brought back by order of the Nuncio, Ormaneto, but after his death were cruelly persecuted. See p. 290.

It is not surprising that the General of an Order should have found the authority of occasional Visitors embarrassing, especially when they belonged to another Order. Rossi had proved in many ways his sincere desire for reformation throughout the Order, though he did not wish it to be effected by forcing the rule of the discalced upon the old friars. Hernandez had carried out his mission in Castile in accordance with these views; but Vargas seems to have been far from exercising the same prudence in attempting a reform in Andalusia. His letter to the King shows that his only hope of a real religious revival in the Order lay with the discalced friars; but the subterfuge by which Mariano contrived to bring Gratian into Andalusia was a bad beginning. It is severely blamed by the Bollandists, as is likewise the imprudence of many acts of Vargas, especially the delegation of his powers to Gratian, by which all the old Carmelites in the province were placed under the authority of a discalced friar, only a few months professed, and not thirty years old.

It was not unnatural that Rossi should have requested from the Pope the recall of powers which were thus used, nor yet that the Nuncio Ormaneto, being on the spot, and seeing the practical good effected by the Reform, should use *his* powers to confirm Gratian's authority. This he did at Madrid in August 1575, making all smooth with the Pope, and with the full approval of the King, to whom Teresa had written the following letter on July 19, 1575:—

'Jesus. The grace of the Holy Spirit be ever with your Majesty. In commending fervently to the Lord the affairs of this sacred Order of the B. V. M., and pondering how needful it is that this work, begun by God, should not fail, nothing seemed to me so efficacious a remedy for our troubles as that your Majesty should rightly understand all that pertains to the establishment of this work I have lived for forty years in this Order, and, reviewing all things, I clearly perceive that, unless the Discalced soon have a Provincial of their own, great injury will arise, nor will it be possible for the Reform to last. Therefore, because the power of accomplishing this lies with your Majesty, whom I perceive to be given by the Blessed Virgin as a protector of our Order, I have taken upon myself humbly to request the same from your Majesty for the love of God, and of His glorious Mother. Therefore let your Majesty command that this thing be done, for the evil demon leaves no stone unturned to prevent it. . . . Our matters would turn out admirably, if in these beginnings of our work that office[1] were asked for the Discalced father who is called F. Jerome Gratian, a man for some time known to me, young, but endowed with such gifts . . . that I believe him born for promoting this Order. May our Lord so direct matters that your Majesty may deign to grant my petition, which concerns His service. For the favour which you showed me, when you granted me license to found the convent of Caravaca, I kiss your Majesty's hands many times. For the love of God I entreat you to forgive my boldness; I know indeed that it has been too great, yet I think I shall not be importunate, since God hears the cry of the poor, and you are in His place. May God grant your Majesty such quiet and length of days as I continually ask of Him for you and as Christian matters require. I have written July 19. The unworthy servant and subject of your Majesty,   'TERESA DE JESUS.'

Gratian accomplished his visitation in Castile without opposition; but, on arriving at Seville in November, and

---

[1] Provincial of the Reform.

reading the Nuncio's letter in the Mitigated convent, such a tempest arose that news was brought to Teresa that the monks had taken arms, closed the doors, and killed Gratian. She could scarcely command her voice to recite the office, and tells us in her ninth 'Relation' that she was 'utterly disturbed, so that she could not even pray.' She was braver when herself attacked. Some foolish accusations made against her at this time by a novice whom she had rejected were taken up by the Inquisition; and Gratian, going to visit her one day, found the street filled with horses, mules, and officials of the Holy Office, and the priest who had informed against her waiting in a corner of the street, to see the nuns carried to prison. Gratian was filled with alarm, but found his friend calm and joyful. The Inquisitors were satisfied with their search, severely blaming her accusers, and desired her to write an account of her way of prayer and interior life, and submit it to Rodrigo Alvarez, a Jesuit. Her eighth 'Relation' was written on this occasion.

In a letter to her brother Lorenzo, written some time later, she says, 'I have received good news of my writings. The Grand Inquisitor read them himself, a thing unheard of hitherto; it seems that they had been spoken of with praise. He said himself to Doña Luisa[1] that he had found nothing in them which was matter for the Inquisition, and that they contained nothing bad, but rather much that was good. Also, out of his great kindness to the Discalced, he asked why I had not yet founded a monastery at Madrid. He is the same who not long ago was made Archbishop of Toledo.[2] He is most favourable to our work, as Luisa writes to me, who has friendly relations with him, and seems, I know not where, to have conversed with him.'[3]

[1] De la Cerda. [2] Gaspar de Quiroga. [3] *Acta Sanct.* xl. 751.

The next move against the Discalced was in a Chapter held at Moraleja, May 12, 1576, by the Provincial Salazar, to which he invited none of the Reformed, except the three Priors of Mancera, Pastrana, and Alcala, accounting the other houses to have been founded without authority. The Nuncio advised the three friars to go to the Chapter, but not consent to anything against their Rules. Before they arrived it had been decreed that the Discalced were to have no separate houses, but were to be dispersed among the old convents. They were to be called Contemplatives, the Mitigated friars, Observantists, and were to live together, each observing their own Rule. Against this decree, which would soon have extinguished the Reform, Juan de Jesus, Prior of Mancera, protested, declaring that the Discalced would alter nothing except by command of Gratian, the Nuncio, and King.

Some provocation had evidently been given to the old friars, for Teresa's letters from Toledo at this time show how anxiously she tried to soften the severity of Mariano and Antonio de Jesus (her first friar) towards them.

In September Gratian, as Visitor by the Nuncio's authority, held a counter-Chapter at Almodovar, where separate officers were chosen for the Reform, thus taking the first step towards severing it from the Mitigated Order. A decree was also passed that the same rule should be observed in all reformed monasteries, and Juan de Jesus was appointed to enforce it. Teresa earnestly desired that some of her friars should be sent to Rome, to obtain from the Pope and General of the Carmelites a distinct constitution of their own. She writes to Gratian at Almodovar: 'Those who return from the Chapter praise you greatly; nor can I but give thanks to God that all has gone so well there. For this no small praise is due to you. All comes from the hand of

God; and perhaps, as you indeed rightly say, much has been done by prayers. I am greatly rejoiced by this most excellent and useful decree in the matter of pushing forward a common observance in our houses. I have urged F. Roca[1] to promote manual labour diligently, for it is of great importance amongst us; and as he told me that nothing had been done about it in the Chapter, I said I would write to you: besides, it is prescribed by those constitutions and rules, the observance of which he has been appointed to enforce. . . . He also told me at length that you were considering how, by any means, we might obtain through our Father-General our constitution into a separate province. It would be indeed an intolerable strife if we were to carry this out in opposition to our Superior. If money is wanted for this work, God will give it. It might be committed to the members of our Order who are going to Rome. I beg of you, for God's sake, do not let them delay; and do not count their journey a small or unimportant thing, for it is really the chief point in the whole matter. . . . If nothing can be done with the General, then let them go to the Supreme Pontiff. . . . Indeed, since I see that *Methusaleh*[2] is so favourable to us, I know not why we delay, for we are plainly gaining nothing here, and permitting an excellent opportunity to slip through our fingers.'[3]

This was the most burdened period of Teresa's life, for 'not only nuns, but also men of the Reformed Order, although there were many amongst them conspicuous for prudence, knowledge and virtue, had recourse to her as

[1] Juan de Jesus.
[2] The Nuncio Ormaneto. Teresa uses feigned names at this time for those she writes of, lest her letters should fall into the hands of enemies. [3] *Acta Sanct.* § xxxix. 713.

their mother and foundress. She received numerous letters from all parts; and carried on business with magnates and the principal men amongst both secular and regular clergy, knowing that, as it were, the shade and protection of many were necessary for her Reformation, as for a tender and delicate plant: hence she sought to conciliate and preserve good-will by every means in her power. To so many and such various labours was added another work, undertaken out of obedience to her confessors and charity towards her sisters—viz. writings concerning religion and heavenly doctrine, and these expressed in that style which the whole Church admires.'[1] Her health suffered much, and she complains at this time, in letters to her brother Lorenzo, that she was hindered in mental prayer by bodily weakness, and expresses fears that for the rest of her life she would not be equal to much work.

The temporal necessities of her sisters were also an anxiety to her at this time, for the Reform being unpopular, necessary supplies fell off; and at Veas absolute want was so

[1] *Acta Sanct.* t. vii. Oct. § xxxix. 723. 'Pour se faire une juste idée de cette portion de la vie de Ste. Thérèse, il faudrait la replacer dans le milieu où s'est déployée son activité, parmi ses compagnes, aidée de quelques-unes, dirigeant les autres, veillant sur toutes, les contenant par son exemple, ses écrits, ses lettres; parmi ses coadjuteurs, les amis dévoués à son œuvre, les théologiens de tout ordre, de tout rang, moines, prêtres séculiers, docteurs, évêques, inquisiteurs; éclairée par ceux-ci, protégée par ceux-là, suspecte à plusieurs . . . car elle a conquis sa sainteté, elle n'y est pas arrivée de plain-pied. Il faudrait enfin la montrer travaillant sans relâche, pendant vingt ans, au triomphe de son entreprise, sans cesse sur les routes, courant d'une ville à l'autre . . . surmontant tous les obstacles, dégoûts, pauvreté, dédains, persécutions, à force de courage, de foi et de sacrifices; vie militante, humble, dévouée, vraiment sainte.'
—*Les Mystiques Espagnols*, p. 319.

great that Gratian, visiting the convent at the end of 1576, took counsel with the Prioress, Anna de Jesus, as to the expediency of removing it to Granada. Teresa, on being consulted, wrote thus to the Prioress: 'This fear lest we should be left destitute of necessary things seems to me a sign of little faith in God; if indeed there is not the smallest animal to whom His Most High Majesty does not supply food. Cast all your care and anxiety, my daughters, upon the most gracious Jesu; I answer for it that He will never leave you nor forsake you. Especially, since it is only a short time since the convent was founded there, it does not seem expedient that it should be so quickly withdrawn from thence. Wait for some years. Then, if God does not bring a remedy for your wants, it will be a sign that a change will be pleasing to Him.'[1]

Velasquez, a canon at Toledo, and afterwards Bishop of Osma, became at this time Teresa's spiritual guide, and was ever after one of her warmest friends and admirers, promising to come to her from whatever distance whenever she should need him, and fulfilling his promise, to her great help and comfort. 'He made me feel safe,' she says, speaking of him after he was a Bishop, 'by means of passages from the Holy Scripture, which is a way that has most effect upon me when I am certain that he who speaks understands it, and is also of good life.' She thought it necessary now to beg of Gratian not to eat in the refectory of the Mitigated Friars when he went to Seville, desiring the Prioress of her convent to provide his meals for him, though strongly cautioning her against any extension of this liberty. 'Although,' she writes, 'all things are pure at this time, I know what will happen in future if even now caution is not observed.'

[1] *Acta Sanct.* § xl. 737.

In June 1577 the Nuncio Ormaneto died. This was the greatest blow to the Reform. 'Another came,' Teresa writes, 'whom God seemed to have sent for the purpose of trying us by sufferings. He was in some way related to the Pope, and must have been a great servant of God, but he began by favouring very much the friars of the Mitigation. The information he received from them convinced him that it was not right to go on with what we had begun, and so he began to carry out his purpose with the very greatest severity,—censuring, imprisoning, and banishing those who he thought might be able to withstand him.'[1]

[1] *Fondaciones*, c. xxviii. 3.

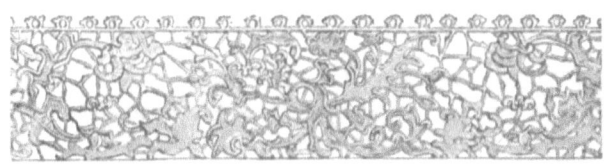

Chapter the Seventeenth.

1577—1581.

> *You were used
> To say, Extremity was the trier of spirits;
> That common chances common men could bear;
> That, when the sea was calm, all boats alike
> Show'd mastership in floating; Fortune's blows,
> When most struck home, being gentle wounded, crave
> A noble cunning.*   CORIOLANUS.

THE new Nuncio, Philip Sega, Bishop of Ripa Transona, required Gratian immediately to resign the office of Visitor of the Carmelites, bestowed upon him by Ormaneto; the King, however, persuaded him to refuse. Tostado meanwhile began actively to carry out the decrees of the General Chapter against the Discalced, now that the Nuncio who had protected them was dead. Great was the confusion in Andalusia—some obeying Tostado, and others Gratian.

In July 1577 Teresa was sent to Avila by Velasquez to arrange the transfer of her first house of St. Joseph's from the jurisdiction of the Bishop to that of the Order. 'I found the Bishop was of a very different mind,' she says, 'and would not at all consent to the change; but when I told him some of the reasons I had ... as he has a most sound understanding, and as God helped him, his thoughts led him to other reasons more weighty than those I had given him, and he resolved to make the change. . . . It was necessary to have the consent of the nuns. To some the change was very disagreeable; but, as they loved me much, they yielded to the reasons I gave them, especially this—that when the Bishop, to whom the Order owed so much, and whom I loved, was gone, they could not have me any longer among them.'[1]

While she was at Avila the nuns of the Incarnation elected her as Prioress. Tostado, in great anger, sent Fra Juan Gutierrez, the Provincial, to the convent, who ordered that another election should take place, threatening with heavy censures and excommunications those who should vote for St. Teresa. She describes the scene in a letter to the Prioress of Seville:—

'As though they had not attended to those threats, fifty-five nuns elected me. As the Provincial received the vote of each one, he declared her excommunicate and accursed; and tearing the paper violently, threw it into the fire. It is now fifty days since the excommunicated nuns have been prevented from hearing mass, or from entering the choir, even when no office is being sung. But what is more wonderful, the day after that annulled election the Provincial recalled them, that they might vote again. When they answered that the election being made they could not repeat it, he again anathematized them; and having assembled the other nuns, who were forty-four in number, he made another Prioress, and sent the document of the election to Tostado, that he might confirm it.

[1] *Fondaciones*, c. xxxi. 48. The Bishop of Avila was about to be removed to Palencia, and Teresa seems to have thought that his successor would be unfavourable to her.

'But although the new Prioress has been confirmed by him, the first nuns, persisting in their conviction, say that they will only obey her as Vice-Prioress. Learned men say that they are not excommunicated, but that these friars are guilty of disobeying the Council,[1] which decreed that a Prioress should be elected by the plurality of votes. Meanwhile the nuns sent word to Tostado that they would have me as Superior. He refused to suffer it, nor would he permit anything but that they might receive me into the convent of the Incarnation for the purpose of religious retirement. What will happen I know not. For the rest, to sum up, everyone is dismayed and offended by this business: I indeed would willingly forgive whoever has sinned against me, if they would only leave me in peace. I do not at all covet to be in that Babylon; especially as I am now in weak health, and am always worse when I am in that house. May God grant that all may turn out for His greater glory, and deign to deliver me from that office.'[2]

She at length prevailed on the nuns to obey the Prioress approved by Tostado as her deputy; but the King himself had to interfere before they were released from excommunication. Writing on December 10 to the Prioress at Seville, Teresa says, Tostado 'sent F. Ferdinand Maldonado for the purpose, who absolved them with so much worry that it would take me too long to write it in detail, and left them more saddened and desolate than before, on account of their choosing me to be over them, and not the one whom those fathers wished. Two discalced friars, sent to the convent by the late Nuncio and Commissary Apostolic, were taken from them and carried off like criminals. May they be delivered out of the hands of those fathers! I had rather

[1] Of Trent. [2] *Acta Sanct.* § xli. 772, 773.

see them amongst the Moors. The day they were taken, they are said to have been twice beaten, and treated in the worst manner possible. Maldonado, Prior of Toledo, took John of the Cross away with him to Tostado; while F. Germano, who, they say, was spitting blood, was carried to Moraleya, to the convent of St. Paul, by the Prior of Avila, who, on his return, told the nuns who were on his side that he had given that traitor excellent punishment for his crimes. This occurrence was, and is, more painful to those maidens than any of their misfortunes, however great. Of your charity commend them to God, and also those holy men, who have now been eight days in captivity. The nuns testify that they were truly saintly, and that no one ever saw them act otherwise than as befitted apostolic men.'[1]

Teresa might well wish that her friends were rather in the hands of the Moors than of their Carmelite brethren. They were taken on the day of their capture to the convent of Mitigated Friars at Avila, and there beaten; on the next day, when they were brought into the sacristy to be questioned by Maldonado, John of the Cross managed to escape, and hastened to his abode, close to the Incarnation, where he destroyed some letters from St. Teresa, and other important papers, which might have brought her into trouble. He was quickly followed and recaptured, when Maldonado ordered that he and his companion should be still more severely beaten than on the previous day. He was then sent to Toledo and imprisoned in a cell ten feet long and six wide, fed on bread and water, and cruelly scourged, at first daily, afterwards three times in the week. He was denied light, fresh air, or even a change of garment for three

---

[1] *Acta Sanct.* § xli. 775. 'Jener eingefleischte Seraph,' Alzog calls St. John of the Cross.

months, although the only crime laid to his charge was his fidelity to the Reformed Rule, in spite of the decrees of the Chapter of Placentia.

Teresa wrote to the King on the day after his arrest, telling him the whole story with the utmost plainness, and evidently with confidence that he would be on her side. After the recital of their wrongs, she continues: 'On this account I entreat your Majesty, for the love of our Lord, to command them to be set at liberty; and to forbid these Mitigated friars to attack with such ferocity all the unfortunate Discalced. It may be that the latter gain much by silence and suffering, yet scandal is caused to the people. . . . If your Majesty does not bring a remedy to our misfortunes, I see not how our affairs can be saved from ruin.'

Philip II. would willingly have assisted her, but the Mitigated Carmelites had not exceeded their spiritual powers, and all their cruelty to St. John of the Cross was by way of recalling an erring brother through religious discipline. After he had been six months in prison at Toledo, the Prior was changed, and the new Superior lightened his sufferings in many ways, permitting him occasionally to take exercise in a hall outside his cell. On one of these occasions John observed a window, from which he thought it would be possible to escape, and, having managed to loosen the bolt of his door, he tore the covering of his bed into strips, and let himself down from the window at night, after he had been nine months in captivity. He made his way to the convent of discalced nuns at Toledo, who managed to conceal him, when he was sought for the next day, by sending him within the enclosure to hear the confession of a sick sister. At noon of the same day the treasurer of the Cathedral, Canon Gonzalez, took him in a closed carriage to his own house, concealed and nursed him, and, at length, managed to convey him to the Reformed Carmelite convent at Almodovar.

It was during these troubles that St. Teresa wrote her 'Interior Castle,' by desire of Gratian, who feared the loss of her writings, which were still in the hands of the Inquisition. It was written in less than six months, and was finished at Avila a few days before St. John of the Cross was imprisoned. Severe bodily suffering was added to her other troubles: her arm was broken on Christmas Eve of this year, 1577, from a fall downstairs as she was going into choir for Compline, and she endured great torture from its being set and re-set unskilfully. She said at the time to a Dominican friar: 'I doubt, my father, whether there is any human body now alive that has suffered such ills as this one of mine.'[1]

Tostado, whose enmity she chiefly feared, left Spain at the end of 1577, in consequence of the King's opposition; but his absence did not greatly better Teresa's affairs. The four men whom she was wont to call the four pillars of her Reformed Carmel were almost useless to her—Antonio de Jesus and John of the Cross being in prison, Gratian forbidden to exercise his office of Visitor, Mariano causing anxiety through his violence. The Nuncio, Sega, was strongly prejudiced against all these men except John of the Cross; and called Teresa herself 'a restless, gad-about woman, intractable and contumacious, an inventor of evil doctrines under pretence of piety, guilty of breaking enclosure, contrary to the decrees of Trent and the commands of her superiors, a despiser of the apostolic precept, which does not permit women to teach.'[2]

Still the King protected the Reform, and by a royal

[1] *Acta Sanct.* § xli. 786.   [2] Ibid. § xlii. 797.

edict of the Supreme Council declared that the Nuncio had no power to annul Gratian's office; and the latter was commanded, through the new Bishop of Avila, President of the Council, to continue his visitation. 'Gratian most humbly entreated,' Teresa wrote in a letter at this time, 'that such a burden should not be imposed upon him. But he (the Bishop) replied that this was the fixed and final will of God and the King, which no upright man would resist: he added that his own office of governing as Bishop was not so very pleasant; and so on. When Gratian begged that he might, therefore, go to the Nuncio, the President forbid it, but said he was to come to him, if there were need for it. Also Gratian received amplest letters from the King's Council, by which he could invoke the aid of the secular arm whenever it should be necessary. Besides, he always thought, as may be supposed, that the Nuncio had no regular authority in the Order; while the King took it ill that the latter had, without his knowledge, acted so hastily against Gratian. . . . The mind of Gratian was distracted by doubts; for if, neglecting the King's wishes, he should obey the Nuncio, it would be the worse for us, since we should lose the favour of the King, who hitherto had sustained us and interceded for us with the Holy Father: especially as it was, moreover, reported to us that the Nuncio had arranged we should be visited by that Tostado, who, as he was a Calceate, and sent by the General with power as his delegate, had certainly proposed to himself to destroy all our houses.'[1]

In this perplexity, and after many attempts to see the Nuncio at Madrid, Gratian went with Mariano to Pastrana, where Antonio de Jesus already was, having been released from prison. Sega insisted on unconditional obedience, in

[1] *A. SS.* § xlii. 798, 799.

spite of the royal decree, and sent two fathers of the Mitigation to Pastrana to receive their submission. There was a moment of hesitation; the Discalced fathers were divided in opinion, and Gratian retired to his cell to take counsel with a lay-brother, Benedict, eminent for holiness. By his advice he resolved to submit, partly on account of the popular tumults which would arise if the King's decree was put in force contrary to the orders of the Nuncio, partly on account of the respect due to the latter as representing the Sovereign Pontiff.

Sega was somewhat appeased at this submission, but, on the other hand, the King was much displeased; nor were the fathers received into favour by the Nuncio, who sent all three to different Mitigated convents, in a kind of captivity. There is a fragment of a letter from St. Teresa to Gratian at this time, which is as follows:—

'May the Holy Spirit be with you, and increase your courage and strength in sustaining this contest. There is hardly anyone at this time whom God permits to be attacked with so much fury by the devil and the world. May the Name of the Lord be blessed, Who willed that you should deserve such great rewards of virtue. Certainly, if we were not so soft by nature, we should easily perceive by the understanding what cause we have for gladness. It consoles me that you no longer consider yourself excommunicated; I indeed have never had even the slightest doubt on that subject.'[1]

'Everywhere this time was calamitous to Teresa's Reform. The King was cool to the Discalced, the Nuncio hostile, the General, Rossi, alienated from them; powerful adversaries threatened them on every occasion for injuring them; nor

Acta SS. § xlii. 804.

had their friends any power to help them. The convents were disturbed and divided by domestic discords, while some took the side of their opposers, and some thought it most glorious to endure with fortitude the utmost for their Rules; nor was there anyone who by his authority could unite divided minds in one opinion.'[1] In a letter of October 4, 1578, Teresa writes to F. Hernandez, S. J. : 'I have suffered so many and such various misfortunes since August in last year, that it would be a great comfort to me if I were permitted to see you, and to pour out into your bosom some part of my griefs (for I could not relate all). Just now we have arrived at the height of misery, as he who brings you this letter will inform you, a most trusty man, and, for his love to us, a partaker in our calamity. . . . Our whole safety or destruction is, after God, in the hands of the Nuncio; who, truly on account of our sins, has lent such faith to the accusations made against us by the Calceates, that I do not see how things are to turn out. As for me, I am called a gad-about, and restless ; because I founded monasteries I am said to have founded them without license of the Pope or the General : what crime can be worse, or more unworthy of a Christian? But those good people spread reports of other things horrible to relate and intolerable, both of me and of F. Gratian, who, alas! visited them. . . . I believe indeed that all this has fallen upon us because God wills that we should suffer much. And now there is not one who cares for the truth, or will even say one good word for me. . . . Alas, my father, in a cloudy season how few friends do we find ! . . . As I do not doubt that you have heard all this of us, and more, from the Nuncio, it would be a great thing if you, who are in some

[1] *Acta SS.* § xlii. 805.

degree an eye-witness, since you know my soul, would correct his misapprehension. . . . They say that this is a new Order—a novelty invented. Let them, therefore, read the primitive Rule, which we keep without mitigation, but with that rigour with which it was first given by the Sovereign Pontiff. Especially I beg and entreat of you to speak in my name to the father who is confessor to the Nuncio, and to make him acquainted with the whole truth ; so that he may exhort the Nuncio not to publish abroad the worst things, to my injury, without any previous examination.'[1]

Worse trials were at hand, through the rashness of her own friends. In their extremity the chief friars of the Reform, who had been released from confinement, determined to elect a Provincial of their own. In vain St. Teresa wrote to Gratian that she had consulted Daza and another, who both agreed that such an election would be unlawful without the consent of the General or of the Pope ; in vain she tried to effect a separation from the Calceates with the goodwill of all, and entreated her friars to await the return of two who were to be sent to Rome. Gratian, in despair, determined to try and carry out by his own strength what he had lost the hope of effecting by the help of others.

Fra Antonio, who had been elected Definitor at the first Chapter at Almodovar, called a second Chapter at the same place on October 9, 1578 ; and, in spite of the warnings and entreaties of St. John of the Cross, who had arrived there after his escape from Toledo, and of Fra Juan de Jesus, the Discalced friars elected a Provincial for themselves—Fra Antonio—and appointed two fathers as deputies to Rome.

Their excuse was that the Visitors appointed by Pius V., Hernandez and Vargas, had given permission to the Dis-

[1] *Acta SS.* § xlii. 805-809.

calced, when their office of visitors should cease, to elect a Provincial of their own. Fra Juan answered that Gratian had given up this power by his absolute submission to the Nuncio.

Nothing could exceed the indignation of the latter when he heard of the proceedings at Almodovar. He annulled them all; imprisoned Gratian, Mariano, and Antonio in separate monasteries; ordered Teresa to go to Toledo and confine herself to the convent there; and, she wrote, 'made a father of the Mitigation our Superior, who was to visit our monasteries of nuns and friars.' He was desired by this decree (October 16, 1578) to restore the Mitigated Rules; and it was an apparently final blow to Teresa's Reform. For a moment even her spirit sank, and her attendant, Anna,[1] says that the whole of that day she ate nothing. 'I considered myself as the cause of the whole tempest,' she wrote afterwards; 'and if they had thrown me into the sea with Jonas, the storm would have ceased.'[2]

Her courage soon returned. Yepes, who was at Toledo, says that when letters from Gratian arrived, announcing that all was over with the Reform, and when all lost heart and hope, 'the spirit of Teresa alone enjoyed serenity and greatest confidence; . . . rising above all tempests and clouds, and

[1] Anna de San Bartolomé, the first lay-sister of the Reform. Teresa had brought her from Avila, when she went there in 1576, on her way from Seville to Toledo, and Anna remained with her henceforth as her inseparable companion and attendant. After the death of Teresa she was sent to the Netherlands, and founded a house at Antwerp. There she received and instructed Miss Worsley, an Englishwoman, who became the first Superior of a House of English Teresians at Antwerp. In 1794 the French Revolution obliged them to take refuge at Llanherne in Cornwall.

[2] *Fondaciones*, c. xxviii. 4.

illuminated with celestial light, she seemed to see the near haven, the end of that perilous and tremendous storm; and soon she said to us these words : " We must suffer troubles but this Order will not perish."'

She wrote at once to the King, enclosing it to Fra Mariano, who was much in his favour, bidding him to fear nothing, and not to give way to weakness, or to say he could endure no longer, since 'we can do all things through Christ.' 'Be full of faith,' she added, 'for it is by faith that we can do great works for God.' Her letter to the King has not been preserved; but Philip seems to have withheld his help at this time, being angry with Gratian for his submission to Sega. To Fra Juan de Jesus Teresa wrote on March 25, 1579 :—

'Your letters were brought to me in this prison, where I am filled with joy in all tribulations which I endure for my God and my Order. One thing troubles me—that you sorrow too much on my account; I pray you, my son, to lay aside this care, and to exhort the rest to do the same. For indeed, if I were old Paul (though I be far from Paul's sanctity), I should not be ashamed to say that prisons, labours, persecutions, torments, ignominy, and reproach are gain to me, for the sake of my God and of my Order. Never did troubles befall me more easy to be borne than at this time. The Lord is wont in truth to visit the afflicted and the imprisoned with His special help and grace. I render infinite thanks to my God—and certainly it is just that we should all offer thanks—for the benefits which He has bestowed on me in this prison. Can there be anything, my son and father, more sweet, more joyous, more pleasant, than to suffer for our good God? This is the sure, this is the more certain way to God, since the Cross ought to be our joy and delight. Therefore, my father, let us seek the Cross, let us choose the Cross, let us embrace difficulties : for if they did not at some time befall us, it would be all over with the Discalced Order.

'You write to me that the Nuncio not only has forbidden Discalced convents to be founded in future, but also at the request of the Father-General has decreed that the convents already founded are to be destroyed; also that the said Nuncio is most incensed against me, and calls me a restless, gad-about woman ; lastly, that the whole world is in arms against me and my sons, and that they are hiding in steep places in the mountains, and in the most obscure houses, lest they should be found and taken captive by their enemies. That indeed is what I lament, what I feel, and what kills me, that for a sinner and a bad nun my sons suffer so many persecutions and troubles, deserted indeed by all, but not by God, Who, I am certain, will never forsake us, nor abandon those who so dearly love Him. . . .

' In the meanwhile, do you remain in the house of Maria de Mendoza until you hear further from me ; and let F. Mariano take one of these letters to the King, and the other to the Duchess of Pastrana ; take care not to go out of the house lest you should be apprehended : we shall soon see ourselves at liberty. I am well and in strong health, thanks be to God. . . . God make you a holy and perfect Discalced Carmelite.' [2]

Teresa had received much comfort and assistance at this time from the celebrated Nicholas Doria, who joined her Reform during its most troublous days, becoming a novice in 1577; and ' made such great progress in a short time,' she says, ' that it is clear our Lord chose him to help the Order; which he did, in these days of persecutions, which were so full of trouble, because the others who could have helped us were some of them in exile, others in prison. . . . He is very prudent, for when he was staying in the monastery of the Mitigation in Madrid, he was so reserved, as he had other affairs to transact, that they never discovered he was engaged in ours, and so allowed him to remain.'[1]

The Carmelite General, Rossi, had died in September 1578, just before the disastrous Chapter of Almodovar, and was sincerely mourned by Teresa, in spite of all he had made her endure. 'I cannot,' she wrote to Gratian, on October 15, 1578, 'remember without pain how much he innocently suffered on our account: if we had applied to him all would have gone well, . . . although you also would scarcely believe me about that.'

To add to her distress, the convent of Seville was in trouble, through slanders brought against the Prioress by the confessor, who was angry at her remonstrating about some imprudence on his part, and who did not scruple to make vilest accusations to the Inquisition against Teresa also. Teresa only laughed when she heard of the slanders against herself, and said, 'If they wish to tell lies, they at least tell them in such a way that nobody believes them.'[2] To the nuns at Seville she wrote:—

'Jesus. The grace of the Holy Spirit be with you, my sisters and daughters. Be sure that I never loved you so much as at this time, and you yourselves have never had so fair an occasion as now of serving the Lord; since indeed He bestows upon you an immense favour by making you able to feel His Cross for a little while, and a part of that desolation which He in far greater measure suffered on the Cross. O blessed day in which you came to that place

[1] *Fondaciones*, c. xxx. 5.   [2] *Acta SS.* § xlii. 817.

where such happy times awaited you! I almost envy you: and in very truth, when I heard of all these changes, which were fully related to me, when I heard it was proposed to drive you from the convent, and other news of that kind, I did not grieve, but rather I exulted inwardly with great joy; because you appear to me, without crossing the sea, to have gained, by the goodness of the Lord, the mine of eternal treasures; with which I hope that you will be so enriched in the same Lord that to us also who are here somewhat of your riches may be granted. . . . But if you are oppressed by great grief for these things, do not be anxious about it; for God wills that you should thence fully understand that you relied too much on yourselves when you were so desirous of suffering.

'Pray, then, pray, my daughters. Remember that God will not try you beyond what you can bear, and that He is with you in your tribulation. . . . Let humility shine forth amongst you; which virtue you must all exercise towards your new Superior, especially the Prioress who has been deposed from office. . . . Remember that God often wills to try whether our works agree with our vows and words. . . . If you will help each other, the good Jesus will help you; Who, although He sleep upon the sea, yet, when the tempest waxes fierce, by His might restrains the storm. He desires our prayers; and loves us so much that He is always intent on finding occasions for us to advance in goodness. May His Name be blessed for ever. Amen. Amen. Amen. . . . Try to be of good cheer; and consider how little it is, if the thing be rightly weighed, which we suffer for so good a God, and Who has suffered so much for us. Not as yet have you shed your blood for His sake. You are amongst your sisters, not at Algiers. What grieved me most in the report, drawn up by order of the Father Provincial, was that some things were written which I well know were false, because I was then present. For the love of our Lord, examine well whether any of you said those things through fear or confusion. For if only there be not sin against God, all the rest matters not; but I was oppressed with grief to find lies, and lies to the injury of others: however, they found no credit with me, for it is obvious to all with what purity and holiness F. Gratian behaved himself amongst us, and how greatly he helped us to go forward and increase in the fear of the Lord. Therefore, even though it were about trifles, it would be a grave fault to impute blame to him. Out of charity admonish those sisters, and rest in the most Holy Trinity, in Whose care I desire you may be.'

Through the exertions of Nicholas Doria, the matter was fully examined; Gratian was entirely cleared, to the satisfaction of the Nuncio and the Provincial; and the latter restored the accused Prioress with honour to her office.

Brighter days were at hand, and the end of the struggle must be briefly told. Don Luis de Mendoza, Count of Tendilla, took up the cause of the Reform, and spoke with such vehemence to the Nuncio that the latter complained of it to the King. Philip promised to reprimand him, but added: 'I know very well the enmity of the Mitigated Carmelites against the Discalced, and am full of suspicions concerning it, since it is entertained against men dedicated to an austere and perfect life.'[1] Sega was startled, and found also that his severity was displeasing to many prelates. The Count of Tendilla, while apologising for his vehemence, laid documents before the King proving the innocence of the Discalced friars. They were sent by Philip's orders to Sega,

[1] *Acta SS.* § xliii. 825.

who seems to have sincerely wished to do justice, and accepted four assessors to examine the cause. 'As soon as our Catholic King Don Philip knew what was going on,' Teresa writes, 'and learnt how the barefooted Carmelites lived and kept their rule, he took our cause into his own hands, and would have the Nuncio not to be the sole judge of it, but assigned four grave persons, three of whom were religious, to be his assistants, in order that justice might really be done us. One of these was the Father-Master Fra Pedro Hernandez, a man of most saintly life, very learned and able. He had been Apostolic Commissary and Visitor of the fathers of the Mitigation of the province of Castile, and we also of the Primitive Rule were subject to him. He knew well and truly how both the one and the other were living, for we all wished for nothing but the making known our way of life. Then, when I saw that the King had named him, I looked on the matter as settled, as, by the goodness of God, it is. . . . Though the noblemen of the realm and the Bishops who took great pains to put the truth before the Nuncio were many in number, yet it would all have been to little purpose if God had not made use of the King.'[1]

The Nuncio, on examining the matter, acknowledged his mistake, recalled his decree of October 16, 1578, which virtually crushed the Reform, and gave them Fra Angelo de Salazar, who had so long known Teresa, as their Provincial. Being in weak health, he made Gratian his delegate in Andalusia, and, though belonging himself to the Mitigation, was full of kindness to the Discalced, whose convents in Castile he visited himself.

The tempest was over, and the vessel of the Reform,

[1] *Fondaciones*, c. xxviii. 4, 5.

steered by the hand of a woman, had escaped into smooth water. But she plainly saw that nothing final could be accomplished until the end which she had aimed at throughout was reached,—the separation of her Reform from the Mitigation. By her advice Fra Juan de Jesus and the Prior of Pastrana were sent to Rome to try and obtain a pontifical Brief to that effect. They were obliged, even then, to travel disguised as cavaliers, for fear of the Mitigated friars. After many delays their mission was successful, and, by a Brief of Gregory XIII., dated June 22, 1580, the Discalced were severed from the Mitigation. A Chapter was summoned by the Pope's commissary at Alcala, February 1, 1581, when the severance was formally accomplished, and Gratian was elected Provincial of the separate Reform of St. Teresa.

'When I was in Palentia,' she writes, 'it pleased God to make a separation of the friars of the Mitigation from the friars of the Reform, each division to be a province by itself, which is all that we desired for our own peace and quietness. On the petition of Don Philip, our Catholic King, a most ample Brief was brought from Rome for the purpose, and his Majesty helped us in the end as he had in the beginning. A Chapter was held in Alcala, . . . the cost was borne by the King, and at his command the whole University helped the friars. The Chapter was held in great peace and concord in the college of St. Cyril of the barefooted Carmelites, which we possess there.'[1]

This was, she says, 'one of the greatest joys and pleasures that I could have in this life, for I had been for more than twenty-five years in trouble, persecution, and distress, too long to speak of; our Lord alone can know of them. Then to see the end of it all! No one, unless he knows the

[1] *Fondaciones*, c. xxix. 24.

trouble I underwent, can tell the joy that I had in my heart, and the desire I had that all the world should give thanks to our Lord.'[1]

Teresa wrote a long letter to Gratian before the opening of the Chapter, which exhibits strikingly her powers of administrating and governing, and the lead which she now took in all affairs of the Order. She says it is most important for the nuns that he should be elected Provincial; if he should not be chosen, she wishes for Nicholas Doria; John of the Cross she does not think has the gift of ruling, but would do well, since he would always follow Gratian's advice. She evidently desires to keep the convents of women under her own direction. 'Our matters,' she says, 'ought not to be communicated to the friars, nor did F. Pedro Hernandez ever communicate them; whatever he laid down in decrees had always been discussed between him and me, nor did he do anything unknown to me.' She goes into particulars which ought to be arranged in the Chapter, entreating that Superiors may be urged to provide good food, and to insist on scrupulous cleanliness of beds and of table linen, &c. If the nuns are to have shoes, she begs him not to say what they are to be made of, 'but simply say they may wear them, else their scruples would be endless.'

Nor must her gentle reproof, written earlier, to Gratian be omitted: 'I will tell you of a certain temptation which I have perceived, and still perceive, in *Eliseus*' (Gratian himself). 'He seems to me at times not to be sufficiently careful to speak the whole truth in every matter. Although I know it is in things of small moment, yet I could wish that he were much more accurate in this way. Out of love I wish

[1] *Fondaciones*, c. xxix. 25.

that you would persuade him to this in my name, for, where this carelessness exists, there entire perfection cannot be. You see in what things I interfere, as if no other cares were pressing on me.'[1]

St. Teresa's own account of the troubles of her Order, which is very slight, ends with these words : ' Now we are all in peace, friars of the Reform and friars of the Mitigation ; no one hinders us in the service of our Lord. Therefore, my brethren and sisters, make haste to serve His Majesty, Who has so abundantly heard our prayers. Let those who are now alive, who have seen these things with their own eyes, consider His graciousness unto us, and the troubles and disquiet from which He has delivered us; and let those who are to come after us, who will find everything easy, for the love of our Lord never allow any observance tending to perfection to fall into disuse. Let them never give men occasion to say of them what is said of some orders, "Their beginning was praiseworthy"—and we are beginning now—but let them strive to go on from good to better. Let them consider that the devil, by means of very slight relaxations, makes an opening by which very great ones may creep in. Let it never happen to them to say, "This is nothing—these are extremes." O my daughters, everything is important if it does not help us onward. . . . The fight, my sisters, will be but for a moment, and the issue is for ever. Let us leave alone those things which are nothing, and attend to those which bring us near to Him Who is our end, to serve and love Him more and more, for He will be for ever and ever. Amen. Amen.'[2]

[1] *A. SS.* § xliii. 2. 84.   [2] *Fondaciones,* c. xxix. 26.

Chapter the Eighteenth.

1580—1582.

*L' onda dal mar divisa
Bagna la valle e 'l monte,
Va passagiera,
In fiume—
Va prigioniera
In fonte—
Mormora sempre e geme,
Fin che non torna al mar;
Al mar dov' ella nacque,
Dove acquistò gli umori;
Dove da lunghi errori
Spera di riposar.*

THERE lived for a time at the court of Philip II. a lady whose story carries us back in imagination to annals of the earliest hermits, and seems to belong more rightfully to dim records of Eastern Thebaids than to European history in the sixteenth century. Her name was Doña Catalina de Cardona; she was descended from the royal house of Aragon, and for some time had been governess to Don Carlos and to his brother Don Juan, living most devoutly in the world, but always filled with the desire of retiring to some lonely place, where she could give herself entirely to prayer. Her spiritual advisers did not encourage her in this design. 'As the world is now so very discreet,' St. Teresa remarks, 'and the great works of God wrought in His saints, men and women, who served Him in the deserts, are almost forgotten, I am not surprised that they thought her desire foolish.'[1]

At length, having been encouraged by a Franciscan friar, she persuaded a hermit to take her to some lonely place and leave her there, never telling anyone where she was. He consented, and took her, clothed as a man, to a small cave near La Roda, gave her three loaves, and then left her. When the loaves were finished she lived on such herbs and roots as she could gather for three years, until she was found by a poor shepherd, who after that brought her bread and meal. Her life was one of utmost austerity in every way, so that it seems a wonder how she could have existed. Then she began to be talked about, and the people visited her in such crowds as were more than she could bear. 'She spoke to all,' Teresa writes, 'with great charity and love. As time went on the people thronged around her more and more, and he who could have speech of her thought much of it. She was so wearied herself that she said they were killing her. There came a day when the whole plain was full of carriages. . . . There was no help for it but they must raise her up on high that she might give them her blessing, and in that way get rid of them.'[2]

She had been intimate in the world with the Prince and Princess of Eboli, and, wishing to found a monastery of friars at La Roda, she went to Pastrana, hearing of the Carmelite friars who had lately made a foundation there; and was received with great honour by the Prince, who, with the

[1] *Fondaciones*, c. xxviii. 19.   [2] Ibid. 23.

Duke of Gandia, the successor of St. Francis Borgia, went out to meet her. She was greatly pleased with Teresa's friars, and took the habit herself, but without any intention of becoming a nun—indeed, she insisted on having the dress of a Carmelite lay-brother, so that, on going to Madrid to seek means for establishing her monastery, the Nuncio Ormaneto was scandalised by hearing that a Carmelite brother was driving about in carriages with ladies, giving his blessing to the people, for 'whenever she went abroad she could not avoid the crowd.' He caused Doña Catalina to be brought to him, and, after conversing with her, seems to have been satisfied.

She obtained means to found the monastery in Madrid, and the King procured the license for her : it was the sixth house of Reformed friars, and was opened at La Roda in April 1572, the church being built where her cave was; and another made for her on one side, where she lived during the remaining five years of her life, only leaving it once to go to Madrid, and beg from the King the life of Don Gonzalo, brother to the Archbishop of Toledo. It was granted to her, after it had been refused to everyone else, and she returned to her cave; where she was not left untroubled by the Inquisition, but they were satisfied with the report of the messenger sent to examine her.

During Doña Catalina's life, four young ladies who had gone to see her, impressed by her example, determined to live a secluded life of devotion, and, being joined by a widow lady with her four daughters, they sent to St. Teresa, entreating her to come and make a foundation in their town, Villanueva de la Jara. This was in 1576, during her troubles, and she was very unwilling to make this foundation, 'because,' she says, ' I considered it would be a very difficult thing to train in our way those who had been accustomed to live in their own.' Her confessor, Velasquez, bade her answer them kindly; but nothing was done until 1580, when, being in Malagon, she was persuaded by Fra Antonio, who had been staying at Doña Catalina's monastery of La Roda, and by Doctor Ervias, the parish priest of Villanueva, to go to the latter town. 'My dread of receiving these sisters was very great,' she writes; 'I thought they would be a faction banded together against the sisters whom I might take thither, as it usually happens.'[1]

Fra Antonio came to fetch her, and she, with the nuns whom she had chosen to begin the foundation, left Malagon on February 13, 1580. They halted at the monastery of La Roda, sending notice of their arrival to Villanueva, which was three leagues distant. 'The monastery,' she writes, 'stands in a desert and most pleasing solitude; and when we drew near, the friars came forth in great orderliness to receive their Prior. As they advanced barefooted in their coarse cloaks of serge they moved all to devotion; and I was melted at the sight exceedingly, for I thought I was living in the flourishing age of our holy fathers. On that plain they looked as white fragrant flowers, and so I believe they are in the eyes of God, for in my opinion He is most truly served there. . . . I was very sorry for the death of the saint by whom our Lord founded the house; I did not deserve to see her, though I desired it greatly.'[2]

St. Teresa and her companions were received with great joy at Villanueva. 'The whole municipality,' she says, 'and certain others, with Doctor Ervias, came forth to receive us. . . . When we were yet far away we heard the ringing of the bells, and on our entering the church they began the

[1] *Fondaciones*, c. xxviii. 12.   [2] Ibid. 17.

Foundation at Villanueva.

Te Deum, one verse sung by the choristers, the other played on the organ. . . . The procession moved on in great pomp; we, in our white mantles, and faces veiled, were in the middle, near the most holy Sacrament; and close to us our barefooted friars, who had come in great numbers from their monastery.'[1] From the church Teresa went to the house where the nine women had lived in solitude for nearly six years, 'stinting themselves in their food,' she says, ' that they might have the means of paying the messengers who came to me. . . . When we entered the house they were standing at the door within, each of them dressed as usual, . . . for they would never put on any religious dress, hoping for ours. . . . They received us with tears of great joy, and those tears were certainly not feigned. Their great virtue shone forth in their joy, in their humility, and in their obedience to the Prioress and to all those who came to make the foundation. They could not do enough to please them.'[2]

St. Teresa tells us how these devout women, having few outward helps, had 'directed themselves by means of the books of Fra Luis de Granada and Peter of Alcantara;' also of their difficulties in saying offices, their breviaries not agreeing, for the new Breviary of Pius V. having lately come into use, they had been given some old books by secular clergy who needed them no longer.

This was the thirteenth convent of Discalced nuns; and Don Alvaro de Mendoza, who had been so good a friend to Teresa when Bishop of Avila, was anxious that she should found a house in Palencia, of which he was now Bishop. Her late severe troubles, age, and sickness had somewhat impaired the energy of her spirit, and she felt only unwillingness for this new undertaking. She had gone from Villan-

[1] *Fondaciones*, c. xxviii. 31, 32.   [2] Ibid. 35.

ueva, in March 1580, to Valladolid, where her beloved niece, Maria de Ocampo, was Prioress, and, Teresa says, 'did all she could to help me, for she wished much for the foundation in Palencia; but she also had her fears when she saw me so lukewarm. Once let me draw near to the true fire . . . and it is done; and that will show it was generally not I who did anything in these foundations, but He only Who is Almighty.'[1] She was seriously ill at Valladolid, having had a stroke of paralysis, and says, 'though my strength had begun to come back, yet such was my weakness that I lost that confidence I usually had when I begin any of these foundations. I thought everything impossible. . . . One of the greatest trials and miseries of this life seems to me to be the absence of a grand spirit to keep the body under control; illnesses and grievous afflictions, though they are a trial, I think nothing of if the soul is strong, for it praises God, and sees that everything comes from His hand. But to be on the one hand suffering, and on the other doing nothing, is to be in a fearful state, especially for a soul that has had earnest desires never to rest inwardly or outwardly.'[2]

She had recourse to her old friend and confessor at Salamanca, Doctor Ripalda, who came at this time to Valladolid. 'He began by rousing my courage,' she says, 'and told me that my cowardice was the effect of old age; but I saw well enough it was not, for I am older to-day and I feel none of it.'[3] She went to Palencia on the Feast of the Innocents, 1580, and was most affectionately received by the Bishop, who took care that she should have all she needed. Also, she says, 'the joy shown by the people was so great and general as to make it very remarkable, for there

[1] *Fondaciones*, c. xxix. 5.   [2] Ibid. 3.   [3] Ibid. 4.

was no one who took it amiss. It was known that the Bishop wished it, and that was a help to us, for he is greatly beloved there; but the whole population is the best and noblest I have seen, and accordingly I rejoice more and more every day that I have made a foundation there.'[1]

When the house which she had taken was prepared for the nuns, 'the Bishop would have them go with great solemnity, and accordingly it was done one day within the octave of Corpus Christi. He came himself from Valladolid, and was attended by the Chapter, the religious Orders, and almost the whole population of the place, to the sound of music. . . . I should like to speak much in praise of the charity of the people of Palencia—of all together and of each in particular: the truth is, it seemed to me like that of the primitive Church—at least, it is not very common in the world now; they knew we had no revenue, and that they would have to find us food, and yet they not only did not forbid us to come to them, but declared our coming to be a very great grace which God gave them.'[2]

While Teresa was at Palencia she received a letter from her constant friend Velasquez, Bishop of Osma, who was then at Soria, saying that a noble lady, Doña Beatrice de Beaumont and Navarre, desired to make a foundation there, and begging her to come. She was glad to go, 'wishing,' she says, 'to make known to him certain matters relating to the state of my soul, and also to see him, because I have a great affection for him, the fruit of the great service he has done me.'[3] Personal affection for friends and kinsfolk never grew cold in her; in spite of some words of hers as to 'detachment' and indifference in these matters, she could

---

[1] *Fondaciones*, c. xxix. [2] Ibid. 21-23.
[3] Ibid. c. xxx. 2.

not carry them out in practice. She complains of herself
with great *naïveté*, speaking of the trial it was to her to leave
behind her daughters and sisters when going from one place
to another. 'That was not, I may tell you,' she wrote, 'the
least of my crosses, for I love them so much—especially
when I considered that I might never see them again, and
saw them sorrowing and weeping; for though they are
detached from everything else, God has not given them this
kind of detachment, perhaps that it might be a greater
anguish for me. Neither was I detached from them, though
I strove to the utmost of my power not to show it, and even
rebuked them; but it was of no use, for the love they have
for me is great and real, as may be clearly seen in many
ways.'[1] If she attempted to crush the warm affections of
her loving heart, she was certainly unsuccessful in the endea-
vour, and seems herself to acknowledge that 'it was of no
use.'

She had little trouble in the foundation at Soria, and much
joy in meeting her friend, who, she says, 'was at a window
of his house when we passed, and thence gave us his blessing.
It was a great comfort to me, for the blessing of a bishop
and a saint is a great thing. The lady, the foundress, was
waiting for us at the door of her own house, for it was there
the monastery was to be founded: we did not see how to
make our way in, because of the great crowd present. That
was nothing new, for wherever we go, so fond is the world
of novelties, the crowd is so great as to be a grave annoyance
were it not that we cover our faces with our veils; that
enables us to bear it.'[2] She caused the curtains which
covered her carriage to be raised when the Bishop gave his
blessing. A great procession of clergy and nobles on horse-

[1] *Fondaciones*, c. xxvii. 16. [2] Ibid. c. xxx. 7, 8.

back accompanied her, and many came into the house to greet her; she conversed courteously with all, but did not lift her veil until only ladies were left with her.[1]

Here also her friend and biographer, Father Francis Ribera, saw her for the last time. He was passing through Soria, on his return from Rome, where he had gone to attend the fourth general congregation of the Jesuits; and says that he had seen her the previous year at Valladolid on his way thither. 'Truly,' he continues, 'I the rather remember this visit at Soria, both because it was the last (for henceforth it did not fall to my lot to see her) and also because I greatly grieve that I was there four days and did not know until the last that Teresa was also tarrying there, which if I had known at the first, all that time I should have received abundant fruit and consolation from her holy conversation.'[2]

The house at Soria was formally opened on August 6, 1581. 'A father of the Society preached,' Teresa writes, 'the Bishop having gone to Burgo;[3] for he never loses a day or an hour, but is always at work, though he is not strong, and the sight of one of his eyes is gone.'[4] She left Soria on August 16, and arrived at Avila on the 23rd. There she found her most beloved home of St. Joseph's in a miserable state. 'Not only had the nuns, through the fault of their confessor,[5] fallen away from their first piety and fervour of religious observance, ... but also, as to temporal things, they almost needed alms, and were oppressed with debt. For these reasons, and compelled by hunger, as the saint playfully wrote not long after to the Prioress of Seville, they determined to elect Teresa Prioress, for which (Maria of Christ willingly resigning the priorate) they easily obtained

---

[1] *Ribera*, l. iii. c. v. annot. 9.   [2] Ibid. 82.   [3] Burgo de Osma.
[4] *Fondaciones*, c. xxx. 9.   [5] Julian of Avila.

permission from the Provincial Gratian, in spite of the saint's refusal on account of age and infirmities, to the great profit both of their temporal and spiritual affairs.'[1]

After she had been at Avila about two months St. John of the Cross arrived, bringing with him horses and all that was necessary for a journey to Granada, urging upon Teresa that she should go there herself, as the foundation offered her there would be the first in that part of Spain. But she was already preparing to go herself to Burgos, having been entreated to do so more than two years previously; so she sent Anna de Jesus with John of the Cross to found the house at Granada. Anna seems to have excelled all her nuns in ability and greatness of mind. After Teresa, she had been the great support of the Reform; yet it is to her that on this occasion Teresa wrote the severest letter of blame which is to be found in her correspondence. It is too long to transcribe. She reproves her with the greatest sharpness for four things especially: first, that she had taken too many nuns with her, and thus had incommoded her host at Granada; secondly, that she had chosen those nuns to go who she knew were fondest of her; thirdly, that she had not made Gratian and herself (Teresa) acquainted with all that was done; and fourthly, that after she had been elected Prioress by the nuns she took it ill that Gratian only styled her 'Superior.' 'I am entirely ignorant,' Teresa writes, 'who they are that have gone with you, for you have carefully concealed all about them from me and the Father-Provincial; nor did I think you would take so many; but I suspect they are those who are fondest of yourself. . . . What does it matter, my mother, whether the Father-Provincial calls you Superior, or Prioress, or Anna de Jesus? He

[1] *Acta Sanct.* xlviii. 940.

understands well, that unless you are over the others, you were not to be called by a higher appellation than those who were Prioresses as well as you. You have told that father so little about your affairs that you ought not to wonder if he does not know whether you have made an election or not. Truly it made me ashamed when I saw my discalced sisters give way to such follies; and not only think of them, but even speak of them, in which Mother Maria of Christ surpasses the others. . . . The said mother extols the greatness of your mind, as if that could not co-exist with humility. May God give to my discalced nuns humility, obedience, and subjection; for without those virtues all these other fine actions are nothing but the beginnings of great imperfections. . . . Consider, I beg of you, that you are laying the foundations of an Order in a new kingdom; therefore it is fitting that you and all the rest should not have the hearts of weak women, but of strong men.'[1]

Teresa spent New Year's Day, 1582, her last on earth, in her native city, and at her first foundation of St. Joseph. She left it on January 2, never to return. 'For although,' Ribera writes, 'the time drew near when Teresa was to pass to the more blessed and better life, in which she should enjoy perpetual life, the Lord did not grant her any relaxation in this life.'[2] Having been entreated to found a house at Burgos by certain fathers of the society, she begged her old friend, Bishop Alvaro de Mendoza, to ask license for her from the Archbishop of Burgos, at the time she was about the foundation at Palencia. It was apparently willingly granted, but the Archbishop added, Teresa writes, 'that he was influenced by his knowledge of Burgos in what he did; that I must come in with the consent of the town;

[1] *Acta Sanct.* § xlix. 952, 953.   [2] *Ribera*, l. iii. c. vi. 85.

in short, the conclusion was that I was to go and treat in the first place with the city ; . . . that he was present when the first monastery was founded in Avila, and remembered the great trouble and opposition I had to bear; that he wished in this way to guard against the same thing here. . . . To me there seemed a want of courage in the Archbishop, and I wrote to thank him for his friendship to me, saying that it would be worse if the city refused its consent than if we made the foundation without saying anything about it, because it would bring more trouble on his Grace. I think I saw beforehand how little we could rely on him if any opposition were made to my obtaining the license.'[1]

She therefore gave up the scheme, and returned, as has been related, to Avila, 'very far from thinking at the time,' she says, 'that I should have to return so soon.' The matter was taken up by a devout lady at Burgos, Doña Catalina de Tolosa, who so exerted herself that she obtained the permission of the council of the city, binding herself to give a house and to maintain it. She wrote pressing Teresa to come without delay, as other Orders were seeking for houses at Burgos; and in spite of the cold, which was very bad for her illness, she set out, accompanied by Gratian, 'partly,' she says, 'because he was then to be at leisure, . . . and partly that he might look after my health on the journey, because the weather was so severe and I so old and sickly, and because my life was thought to be of some importance. It was certainly a providence of God, for the roads were in such a state—deep under water—that it was highly necessary for him and his companions to go on before to see where we could pass, and to help to drag the carriages out of the mud.'[2]

[1] *Fondaciones*, c. xxxi. 5, 6.   [2] Ibid. 14.

At one place near Burgos, called the Floating Bridges, the travellers were in considerable danger, the waters having risen so high that they could not see the road, nor know where to go; and even Gratian, who made light of all annoyances, 'was then not without fear,' Teresa writes, 'for when I saw ourselves go into a world of water without a way or a boat, notwithstanding the encouragement of our Lord, I was not without fear myself: what, then, must my companions have felt? We were eight on the road; two were to return with me, five to remain in Burgos. . . . I was myself suffering from a very severe sore throat, which I caught on the road to Valladolid, nor had the fever left me; and as the pain therefrom was great, it hindered me from feeling much the incidents of the journey. I have that sore throat even now at the end of June.[1] . . . The nuns were all happy, for once the danger passed it was a pleasure to speak of it.'[2] Teresa had insisted on going first through the water; desiring the others, if she were drowned, to return.

They were hospitably received by the good Catalina de Tolosa; though the great fire, which had been lighted that they might dry themselves, made Teresa so ill that she could not sit up, and had to transact all business with those who came to see her the next day, through a grating with a curtain drawn over it, near which she lay.

'Early in the morning,' she says, 'the Father-Provincial went to his Grace to ask his blessing, for he thought that was all he had to do. He found him changed, and angry at my coming without his leave, as if he had never sent for me or meddled at all in the matter; and accordingly he spoke

[1] She died on October 4, so this must have been written about three months before her death.
[2] *Fondaciones*, c. xxxi. 16, 17.

to the Father-Provincial in great wrath against me. Then, admitting that he had sent for me, he said he meant I was to come alone to arrange the affair with him; but to come with so many nuns, God deliver us from the annoyance it gave him! To tell him that we had already arranged with the city, as he had asked us to do ; that there was nothing more to be done but to make the foundation, ... was all to no purpose whatever.'[1]

Gratian had asked her, before leaving Avila, whether she had the Archbishop's license in writing.' 'I answered him,' she says, 'that they had written to me from Burgos, saying that they had arranged with him, that the consent of the city had been asked and obtained, and that the Archbishop was satisfied with it.'[2] But now, for three weary months she had to learn her mistake. Nothing would persuade the Archbishop to allow her to begin her work, or to have divine service in the house she was in : first, it must not be until an endowment was made, and securities given for the purchase of a house ; then, when the sureties were found, he would not allow it until the house was actually found. Gratian had to go away, leaving directions, she says, 'that we were to find a house, in order that we might have one of our own ; and that was very difficult, for up to that time we had not found one for sale.'

At length a physician, Aguiar, found a house which was suitable, and bought it for her. 'The Archbishop,' Teresa writes, 'heard of it at once, and was very glad we had prospered so well; he thought it was due to his obstinacy, and he was right. . . . He came to see the house ; it pleased him much, and he was very gracious to us, but not gracious enough to give the license.'[3]

[1] *Fondaciones*, c. xxxi. 19. [2] Ibid. 13. [3] Ibid. 37.

All this time Catalina de Tolosa had worked incessantly for St. Teresa, 'as cheerfully,' the latter says, 'as if she had been the mother of everyone of us,' though suffering much from certain clergy, to whom she had promised to leave money after her death, and who now feared to see it diverted to other purposes; besides, 'it can never be told,' Teresa adds, 'what the shiftings of the Archbishop cost her, for it was a very great distress to her to think that the house might not be founded, and she was never weary of doing us good. The hospital was very far from her house, and yet she came to see us most readily nearly every day, and sent us all we had need of; then people never ceased from talking to her, and, if she had not been the courageous woman she is, that talking might have put an end to everything. . . . Oh, the distress of Catalina de Tolosa! that can never be told. She bore it all with a patience that amazed me,' Teresa writes. 'All the furniture we required for fitting up the house she gave us—beds and many things besides; . . . it seemed as if we were not to be in want of anything, though her own house might be so. Among those who were founders of our monasteries there are some who gave more of their substance, but there is not one who had the tenth part of the trouble it cost her. . . . It was a great sorrow to me to see her suffering, for though she for the most part kept it secret, yet there were times when she could not hide it, especially when they appealed to her conscience, which was so tender that, even among the great provocation which she received, I never heard a word from her by which God might be offended. They used to say to her that she was going to hell, and ask her how she could do what she was doing when she had children of her own. All she did was with the sanction of learned men; if she had wished to act otherwise,

I would not have consented for anything on earth to her doing what she might not do, if a thousand monasteries had been lost thereby; much more, then, would I not have consented for one. But, as the plan we were discussing was kept secret, I am not surprised that people thought the more about it. She answered everyone with so much prudence, —and she is very prudent—and bore it so gently, that it was plain that God was teaching her how to be able to please some, and endure others, and giving her courage to bear it all. How much greater is the courage of the servants of God when they have great things to do than is that of people of high descent if they are not His servants! She, however, was without flaw in her blood, for she is the child of a very noble house.'[1]

Teresa at length wrote to her friend the Bishop of Palencia, begging him to write again to the Archbishop, who was a great friend of his. He was very angry, and sent her a letter for the Archbishop, which was open, and 'of such a nature,' she says, 'that had we sent it on we should have ruined everything; . . . though it was most courteous, it contained some truths which, considering the temper of the Archbishop, were enough to make him angry—he was so already on account of certain messages the Bishop had sent him. They were very great friends—and he said to me that, as they who were enemies before were made friends at the death of our Lord, so on my account two friends had become enemies: I replied, that he might see by that what sort of person I was.'[2]

She wrote again to the Bishop, entreating him to write another and 'a very affectionate letter' to his friend. He did so, but told her that all he had done for her hitherto was

[1] *Fondaciones*, c. xxxi. 28, 38.   [2] Ibid. 39.

as nothing compared to his writing that letter. However, it had the desired effect: the Archbishop granted the license, and the house was formally opened on the next day, April 22, 1582. 'The Archbishop and the Bishop of Palencia remained very good friends,' Teresa says, 'for the Archbishop at once showed himself very gracious unto us, and gave the habit to a daughter of Catalina de Tolosa, and to another nun who soon came in; and until now people have never failed to provide for us.'[1]

[1] *Fondaciones*, c. xxxi. 45.

Chapter the Nineteenth.

Dulce sonat ex æthere vox,
Hyems transiit, occidit nox.
Surge, veni ; quid, sponsa, moraris ?
Veni, digna cælestibus aris ;
Imber abiit, mæstaque crux,
Lucet, io, perpetua Lux. BALDE.

E must turn to the accounts of others for the story of the last months of St. Teresa's life, and chiefly to the record left by the inseparable companion of her later years, the lay-sister Anna. But in the previous year the aged saint had made a last 'Relation' of her spiritual state, at the desire of Velasquez, Bishop of Osma, and the greater part of it is given here, both for its own beauty and as a fitting close to the story of that wonderful inner life which has been chiefly told in her own words. It was written from Palencia, in May 1581.

'Jesus.

'Oh, that·I could clearly explain to your Lordship the peace and quiet my soul has found! for it has so great a certainty of the fruition of God, that it seems to be as if already in possession, though the joy is withheld. I am as one to whom another has granted by deed a large revenue, into the enjoyment and use of which he is to come at a certain time, but until then has nothing but the right already given him to the revenue. In gratitude for this, my soul would abstain from the joy of it, because it has not deserved it; it wishes only to serve Him, even if in great suffering; and at times it thinks it would be very little if, till the end of the world, it had to serve Him Who had given it this right; for in truth it is in some measure no longer subject, as before, to the miseries of this world; though it suffers more, it seems as if only the habit were struck, for my soul is, as it were, in a fortress with authority, and therefore does not lose its peace. Still, this confidence does not remove from it its great fear of offending God, nor make it less careful to put away every hindrance to His service—yea rather, it is more careful than before. But it is so forgetful of its own interests as to seem, in some measure, to have lost itself, so forgetful of itself is it in this. Everything is directed to the honour of God, to the doing of His Will more and more, and the advancement of His Glory.

'Though this be so, yet in all that relates to health and the care of the body, it seems to me that I am more careful than I was, that I mortify myself less in my food, and do fewer penances: it is not so with the desires I had; they seem to be greater. All this is done that I may be the better able to serve God in other things, for I offer to Him very often, as a great sacrifice, the care I take of my body, and that wearies me much, and I try it sometimes in acts of mortification; but, after all, this cannot be done without losing health, and I must not neglect what my superiors command herein, and in the wish for health much self-love must also insinuate itself. . . .

'The imaginary visions have ceased, but the intellectual

vision of the Three Persons and of the Sacred Humanity seems ever present, and that, I believe, is a vision of a much higher kind ; and I understand now, so I think, that the visions I had came from God, because they prepared my soul for its present state ; they were given only because I was so wretched and so weak ; God led me by the way which He saw was necessary, but they are, in my opinion, of great worth when they come from God. . . . The acts and desires do not seem to be so vigorous as they used to be. . . . I seem to live only for eating and drinking, and avoiding pain in everything, and yet this gives me none, . . . because, so far as I can see, I am not under the sway of any strong attachment to any created thing, not even to all the bliss of Heaven, but only to the love of God ; and this does not grow less,—on the contrary, I believe it is growing, together with the longing that all men may serve Him. . . . I am at peace within ; and my likings and dislikings have so little power to take from me the Presence of the Three Persons, of which, while it continues, it is so impossible to doubt, that I seem clearly to know by experience what is recorded by St. John, that God will make His dwelling in the soul : and not only by grace, but because He will have the soul feel that Presence. . . . This is almost always the state I am in, except when my great infirmities oppress me. Sometimes God will have me suffer without any inward comfort ; but my will never swerves—not even in its first movements— from the will of God. This resignation to His will is so efficacious, that I desire neither life nor death, except for some moments, when I long to see God ; and then the Presence of the Three Persons becomes so distinct as to relieve the pain of the absence, and I wish to live—if such be His good pleasure—to serve Him still longer. And if

I might help, by my prayers, to make but one soul love Him more, and praise Him, and that only for a short time, I think that of more importance than to dwell in glory.

'The unworthy servant and daughter of your Lordship,
'TERESA DE JESUS.'

Before Teresa left Burgos, she was in great danger from an inundation of the river, on the banks of which the convent was built, and so situated that the overflowing waters separated them from the other inhabitants of the city, so that no one could get to them. 'Our mother's cell was so wretched,' says her faithful nurse, 'that one could see the stars through holes in the roof, and the walls let in the frost. She suffered much from the cold, which is excessive in those parts. The waters had already reached the first floor. . . . From the sixth hour in the morning to the middle of the night we remained saying Litanies, without rest or food, for the flood had carried away all our provision. . . . Our fright was so great that we did not even think of getting any food for our mother. Wherefore, when it was now late, she called me and said, "See if a little bread remains, my daughter, and give me, I beg of you, a mouthful, for my strength is failing me." I was filled with grief on hearing these words; and we called one of the strongest of the novices, who went into the water up to her waist, and drew out a loaf, with which our mother and the others were a little refreshed. We should all have perished with hunger, but certain men of the city swam to us, and breaking the doors, made a way for the water to flow out. Our mother's room shook, almost as if it were feeling the cold and rain, so I put one of the two coverlets that I had in my bed over her, and hung the other about her bed; but so that she should not perceive it, for she would not have allowed me to do so. When she fell asleep, I sat quietly near her, and when she called me feigned to rise from my bed, so that she said to me, "How can you come so quickly, my daughter?" While she was asleep I washed her clothes and her linen, which was a solace and pleasure to me, knowing how greatly my invalid cared for cleanliness and neatness; on which account I spent many sleepless nights, but most gladly for love and service towards her. . . . All that time I was as well in body and mind as if I had slept the whole night, and eaten plentifully; it seems the Lord so ordained it for the comfort of our holy mother, for if she had seen my care for her injure me, it would have incredibly afflicted her. Thus did the Lord grant this and other favours to me, a miserable sinner, on account of His servant and my dearest friend Teresa, whom I was not worthy to serve.'[1]

Teresa left Burgos in August 1582, with this tender nurse, and her favourite niece, Teresita, who was soon to make her profession at Avila. They went by Palencia to Valladolid, where new troubles awaited Teresa, on account of her brother Lorenzo's will, in which he had left all his wealth to the convent of Avila, in case his children should die without issue. Their friends disputed the will, and one of them came to the convent, and heaped reproaches on Teresa, telling her 'she was not what she seemed, and that there were many amongst secular people who set a better example of virtue than she did.' The Prioress took part against Teresa, and even expressed the wish that she should leave the convent. 'When we prepared to do so,' Anna writes, 'near the gate she took hold of my habit, and said, "Go, and return hither no more." These words wounded our mother most bitterly, since they were uttered by one of her

[1] *Acta Sanct.* § li.

own daughters, from whom she expected greater respect than from seculars, and yet by whom she saw seculars preferred to herself.'[1]

Nor did she meet greater kindness at Medina del Campo, on arriving there. For having admonished the Prioress at Medina concerning some small matter which was amiss, the latter took the reproof so ill, that Teresa was greatly grieved, seeing her daughters falling away from their former obedience, and determined to go to another convent. 'But that insubordination and insolence grieved our mother so sorely,' writes Anna, 'that she ate nothing that evening and remained awake all the night.'[2]

She was very anxious to go to Avila, where she was to give the veil to her niece, Teresita; but F. Antonio met her at Medina, having come at the urgent request of the Duchess of Alva, on purpose to take her with him to Alva. She was very unwilling to go; but as F. Antonio was deputy Provincial in Gratian's absence, she made a last sacrifice of her own wishes to obedience. 'Thither, therefore, she was carried in a litter, suffering great pains all the way, and very much sickness; insomuch that when she came to Peyñaranda, the next town, she felt such excessive torments, together with such an incredible decay of strength, that she quite swooned away.'[3] They had arrived at Medina on September 15, and left it the next day, without taking food, meaning, Anna says, to eat on the way.

'But,' she continues, 'when we had journeyed the whole day, we could find no food with which to restore her strength. When at night we had come to a poor village, not even there could they give us anything to eat except some dried figs.

[1] *Acta Sanct.* § lii. 1012.   [2] Ibid. 1013.
[3] *Ribera*, l. iii. c. vii.

So when our mother, fainting and burning with fever, said to me, "What have you, my daughter? I pray you to give me something, for I am exhausted," I gave four reals to buy two eggs. But when I found that even at that price nothing was to be bought, and that the money was brought back to me, I could not look without tears at the half-dying saint, nor can I find words to express the grief which I then felt : it seemed to me that my heart would break. I burst out crying, because I was so destitute that I had no means of giving relief or help to my dearest mother dying before my eyes. But she, bearing all with angelic patience, said to me, "Restrain your tears, my daughter, for even this has fallen out so by the will of God." The nearer the time approached when she was to depart from this life, the more the Lord tried her in all things ; and she took all, as she had always done, in a most saintly way.'[1]

'The next day,' Ribera writes, 'going to another town, they met with nothing but boiled herbs and onions, to make amends for the meanness of their dinner the day before. . . . The same night, being the Vigil of St. Matthew, she was brought to Alva. She was then so spent and sick that when they came in she was persuaded to go to bed, and take a little rest. Yet the next morning she got up, and both diligently visited the house above and below, and went to the church to hear mass ; where likewise, with great fervour of spirit and extraordinary devotion, she received the blessed Sacrament. After which she passed some days, being sometimes better, sometimes worse, as to her distemper, till the Feast of St. Michael the Archangel ; on which day, after hearing mass and communicating (which was now her daily practice), she took to her bed, and never rose out of it any more.

[1] *Acta Sanct.* § lii. 1014, 1015.

'Three days before her decease she spent a whole night almost in earnest prayer and devout supplications to God; and in the morning she called for F. Antonio to hear her confession.[1] . . . Some of the nuns heard F. Antonio speak to her, to entreat our Lord not to take her away so soon, but to leave her longer in this life, for the good of her children. To whom she replied that she seemed no further needful in this world. After which she began to give many wholesome advices and directions to her daughters; which, though she had never omitted, now, as being near her end, she uttered with great energy and power, and clearer expressions of love than she was wont. On the Vigil of St. Francis (October 3), at five in the evening, she asked for the most *Sacred Viaticum* of the body of our Lord; being by that time so weak and spent that she could not stir herself in her bed, nor turn from one side to another but by the help of her sisters. And whilst they were going for the blessed sacrament, joining her hands together, she said to the religious women that were about her: "I beseech you, for the Lord's sake, my most dear daughters and ladies, to observe the ordinances and constitutions of the Rule very exactly and entirely; and likewise I beg of you not to regard the ill example which this negligent nun hath given you; but whatever I have herein offended, I desire you would forgive me for it."

'As soon as the sacred pledge of our redemption came in sight . . . though before she was so exceedingly exhausted with her illness and oppressed with her pains, that she could not move at all out of her place, she sprang up

---

[1] Thus the first friar who had offered himself for her Reform ministered to her at the last, although he had not been as much to her in life as many others, St. John of the Cross, Gratian, &c.

without anyone's help . . . and with her face shining with an unusual beauty, darting forth rays of light, and looking after a far other manner, and much younger, than formerly it was wont, and with a venerable kind of majesty, closing her hands, she began, out of the abundance of her heart, to utter certain high, sweet, and amorous expressions ; . . . amongst the rest were these : " O my Lord and my Spouse, the desired hour I have so often wished for is now come. Now the time is come that we may see each other. It is now time, Lord, for me to depart. And happy and prosperous may the journey prove : Thy will be done. The hour is come, at last, wherein I shall pass out of this exile, and my soul shall enjoy, in Thy company, that which she hath so exceedingly longed for." '[1]

Surge, propera, amica mea, et veni. The call of the Bridegroom had come : already she ' hears the unexpressive mystical song.' His words, in life, she ' did use to gather for her food, and for antidotes against her faintings.' To her, as to the departing pilgrim in the great Dream, His name had been as a civet box ; yea, sweeter than all perfumes. His voice had been to her most sweet ; and His countenance she had more desired than they that have most desired the light of the sun. Wherever she had seen the print of His shoe in the earth, there she had coveted to set her foot too ; and now she was at the end of her journey, her toilsome days were ended, and the thought of being with Him in Whose company she delighted lay as a glowing coal at her heart.

But mingled with the joy was deepest self-abasement and penitence, and the aged saint went down to the river's bank with the *Miserere* on her lips. 'She said,' Ribera

[1] *Ribera,* l. iii. c. vii.

tells us, 'that she hoped for eternal salvation through the merits of Jesus Christ, and prayed her daughters to ask this for her from the Lord. From time to time she murmured those verses: *Sacrificium Deo spiritus contribulatus: cor contritum et humiliatum, Deus, non despicies. Ne projicias me a facie tua, et Spiritum Sanctum tuum ne auferas a me. Cor mundum crea in me, Deus.* And chiefly that hal.-verse, *Cor contritum et humiliatum, Deus, non despicies*, was continually on her lips until speech failed her.'[1]

Many times also she repeated the words, 'Still, O Lord, I am a daughter of the Church.' All that by God's grace she had *done* seems, in that supreme hour, to have passed from her vision. In words too beautiful to omit, 'farther and deeper still reaches the gaze of the dying Christian, till it rests on the font in the parish church at Avila, where her soul had been washed in the Blood of Jesus, that *Fountain of the Saviour*, whence had been drawn all the streams of the marvellous spiritual life by which she had made glad the city of God. "After all, O Lord, I am a child of the Church." She pleads for pardon and acceptance in words which belong equally to every baptized infant, who departs with his chrisom robe still wet from the life-giving font; to every returning penitent, for whom the Angel of " penitence " has descended once more, even at the eleventh hour, to stir its healing waters.'[2]

'At nine o'clock the same evening,' Ribera's narrative continues, 'she desired and received extreme unction, joining with the nuns in the penitential Psalms and the Litany ... and answering to the prayers. Then F. Antonio asked her whether she would have her body, after her death, be

[1] *Ribera*, l. iii. c. vii.
[2] *Life of St. Teresa*, Dublin, 1867

carried to Avila, or to continue at Alva. She seemed displeased with the question, and only answered, "Am I to have any property in anything? Will they deny me here a little earth for my body?" All that night she endured excessive pains, yet omitted not the often repeating the forementioned verses of the Psalm. The next day, at seven in the morning, she turned herself on one side, just in the posture and manner that the blessed Magdalene is commonly drawn by painters, and holding a crucifix in her hand, so fast that she let it not go till the nuns took it away when she was to be interred.'[1]

She lay thus for fourteen hours, in silence, 'perfectest herald of joy.' Two days before she died she had said to her devoted nurse, when they were alone, 'Daughter, the hour of my departure has now come.' From that time, Anna tells us, she would not leave her for a moment, but begged the other sisters to bring her whatever was needful to the cell. 'The day that she died, when speech had already failed her, I changed her coif and her sleeves. She smiled sweetly at me, to signify her thanks, being pleased at the fresh linen. And truly during her life she had always shown this care for cleanliness and grace in everything. . . . Towards evening, F. Antonio de Jesus, who was with her, bade me to go and take some food. While I was away, our mother looked restlessly about, and when F. Antonio asked her if she wished for me, she gave signs of assent, so I was called back. When she saw that I had returned, she put her arms round me with much love, and caressing me tenderly, laid her head in my arms, and thus I held her and was embraced by her until she expired. I seemed rather to die than she; for she so burned with love for her Lord, that

[1] *Ribera*, l. iii. c. vii.

she desired nothing but the hour in which, the chains of the body being broken, she might enjoy His Presence for ever.'[1]

'She surrendered her spirit into the hands of her Creator, in the sixty-eighth year of her life, on October 4, 1582, the next day, by the reformation of the calendar, which was made that year, being the 15th, the day now appointed for her festival. Her end was so quiet and calm that they who had seen her often in prayer would have thought her now also intent on the same heavenly exercise.'[2]

The nun who had the charge of the infirmary, one famed for sanctity, says Ribera, told him that, sitting at a low window of the room where Teresa lay, which looked into the monastery, at the time of her departure, 'she heard a confused kind of noise, as of a multitude exulting and rejoicing; and soon after saw a great number of persons, glittering with wonderful splendour, and clothed in white robes, who, passing through the monastery, and coming into the same room, full of joy, so filled it with their company that, though all the nuns were there present, none were visible; and, when they came near to the bed where the holy mother lay, she immediately rendered up her soul to her Creator, from whence it appeared that they had come, at that last moment, to accompany her departing spirit.'[3]

Whether the vision were real or not, we may not doubt of the conduct that waited for her, and followed her in at the Beautiful Gate of the City.

> 'Angels, thy old friends, there shall greet thee,
> Glad at their own home now to meet thee,
> All thy good workes which went before,
> And waited for thee at the door,

---

[1] *Acta Sanct.* § lii. 1016.   [2] *Ribera*, l. iii. c. vii.   [3] Ibid.

> Shall own thee there ; and all in one
>   Weave a constellation
> Of crowns, with which the King, thy Spouse,
> Shall build up thy triumphant brows.
>
> ' All thy old woes shall now smile on thee,
> And thy pains sit bright upon thee,
> . All thy sorrows here shall shine,
> All thy sufferings be divine :
> Tears shall take comfort, and turn gems,
> And wrongs repent to diadems.
>   .   .   .   .   and so
> Thou with the Lamb, thy Lord, shalt go,
> And wheresoe'er He sets His white
> Steps, walk with Him those wayes of light,
> Which who in death would live to see,
> Must learn in life to die like thee.' [1]

Her sisters watched by the earthly tabernacle, which had been the temple of the Holy Spirit, until ten o'clock next day. Ribera says that her face, which was lined and furrowed by age, became smooth and without wrinkles, and more beautiful than in life. All the clergy, nobles, and people of Alva thronged to her burial. She was laid in her habit on a bier covered with a pall of cloth of gold, and placed in a vault between the inner and outer chapel. Teresa Layz, foundress of the convent, wife to the Duke of Alva's steward, caused the grave to be filled up with a great quantity of stones, lime, and bricks, hoping to prevent the body from being removed. Nine months later, Gratian, on his arrival at Alva, opened the grave secretly, at the request of the nuns, who feared lest the lime should burn the body ; and having disinterred it, he placed it in a coffin, and laid it again at the same place. But in 1585, when Nicholas Doria, then Provincial of the Reformed Carmelites, held a general

---

[1] Richard Crashawe.

Chapter at Pastrana, Alvaro de Mendoza, Bishop of Palentia, produced an agreement between himself and Gratian, by which the latter promised to restore the remains of Teresa to Avila, in case she should die elsewhere, to be buried on the Gospel side of the altar at St. Joseph's; the Bishop having specially reserved to himself the right of sepulture on the Epistle side, when, as Bishop of Avila, he yielded to her wish to transfer the convent from his jurisdiction to that of the Order.

The whole city of Avila joined with the Bishop in claiming the right of giving her a resting-place; and the Chapter granted it, seeing that she had been on her way thither when brought to Alva, and that it was her native place and home. The body was therefore removed to Avila in November 1585, under the care of Juan de Carillo, sent by the Bishop, and of Julian of Avila, who during Teresa's life had been her companion in so many journeyings. It was received with immense pomp and rejoicing in her native city. Alvaro de Mendoza, Bishop of Palentia, died in the next year, and was laid, as he had desired, near his friend. But a perfect storm arose at Alva: the Duke, who had been absent when the remains of St. Teresa were removed, was very angry; and his influence with the Pope, Sixtus V., prevailed to procure an order that they should be restored to his city. Nicholas Doria was charged with this duty: he arrived at Alva on St. Bartholomew's day 1586, having brought the saint's body from Avila, and delivered it to the Prioress of the convent of Alva. It was laid out for identification in the chapel: the scene must have been strange and overwhelming for those who had known and loved her in life. Ribera, who was present, says that 'truly there was need to place the body behind railings, for the multitude so pressed in on each other, and such was the anxiety of all to see, and the violence of the thronging, that if the sacred relics had been exposed in the outer part of the church, the people would have cut the clothes to pieces, and not even have left the body untouched.'[1]

For three years the cities of Alva and Avila carried on a bitter strife with each other as to the right of possessing the saint's remains. The dispute was at last referred to the Pope, who in 1589 decreed that Alva should be their perpetual resting-place.

The family of the Duke of Alva and Philip II. of Spain took a principal part in promoting her canonization. Her beatification was decreed by Paul V. in 1614; and on March 12, 1622, she was canonized by Gregory XV., together with Isidore the Ploughman, Ignatius Loyola, Francis Xavier, and Philip Neri.

Her Order spread with extraordinary rapidity. She had lived to see fifteen convents of discalced friars and seventeen of nuns;[2] but when St. John of the Cross died, nine years later, the number had risen to seventy-eight in all; and more than seven hundred houses had been founded before the French Revolution. By far the larger proportion of these were established during the seventeenth century (only forty-nine after 1700), and were convents of friars, including thirty-six missions in different parts of the world—China, Persia, Malabar, Africa, America, &c.; so that Teresa's special desire was fulfilled, that houses of preaching friars should be multiplied, in order to carry the Gospel to the ignorant. Two hundred and sixty-six of these foundations belonged to the 'Spanish Congregation,' and were situated in

---

[1] *Ribera*, l. v. c. i.   [2] See Note B.

Spain, Portugal, and Mexico (where eighteen convents were founded).[1] The Reformed Order took no root in England, but in Ireland a 'Province of St. Patrick' was established, which was shortly after entirely destroyed by Cromwell.

The Discalced Carmelites had especially flourished in France. All are familiar with the story of the Carmelite nuns of Compeigne, who were condemned to death in 1794, and the whole community brought together to the scaffold on July 17, singing the *Miserere, Te Deum,* and *Veni Creator* on the way from prison to the guillotine; no voice failing until quenched in death; the Prioress, who had chosen to bear the sight of the sisters' deaths, at last continuing the song alone, until having seen her children go before her, she followed them to the land of rest.

The last foundation made before the Revolution was in 1773. The full list of houses, under the heads of the different provinces, is given at the end of the Bollandist volume containing St. Teresa's *Acta,* and concludes with these words, which are on the last page of the folio : 'Such was formerly the numerous religious offspring of that fertile parent Teresa. Alas! the dire tempests raised by impious men have dispersed the greater part of them. Yet if the branches have been torn away the trunk remains, and the root lives, from which every year we happily see new shoots spring forth, which the superiors of the Order cherish, careful to preserve thorough and entire discipline, and mindful of the spirit of Teresa.' The history of the Reformed Carmelites since her death—of their Missions, and influence on the spiritual life of the Church—would fill many volumes. Their foundress had bequeathed to them no easy task :—to observe, not

---

[1] See Note C.

only the outward letter, but the spirit of her Rule; to bear witness, before a world impatient of prayer and adoration, that they are no dreamy idleness, but, if real, the highest work; to keep the difficult heights which she had attained; and to bear worthily the great possession which she left to her Order—'the glory and the burden of her name.'

NOTES.

A.

THERE is a vivid description of Teresa's native city, and the cathedral which was her mother-church, in 'A Summer in Spain,' by Mrs. Ramsay. The writer, in a long account of her visit to 'lordly Avila,' does not once allude to St. Teresa; but a spot where earth seemed unfinished, and only air and heaven perfect, was for her a fit cradle and dwelling-place.

'After we passed Medina del Campo,' Mrs. Ramsay writes, 'the scenery improved. We came to refreshing clumps of stone-pines ; and presently to rugged broken ground, ending in a perfect wilderness of huge boulders of every form. We were in the midst of a high table-land, and the view was most extraordinary. We looked down on the Sierra, tinged by the varying sunbeams with every shade of pale yellow and vivid light green ; while the flitting clouds threw azure and purple shadows, changing every moment, and in the distance stretched away among an illimitable depth of blue ether. It was like some of Breughel's wondrous aerial pictures ; with the addition of that strange chaos of granite in the foreground. It seemed as if earth were unfinished, without inhabitants, or any life ; and only air and heaven perfect. Apparently we were hundreds of miles from any town, so utterly wild was it ; when all at once, almost close to us, against the sky, rose Avila, many-towered Avila. Never was there a grander position, the Apennine cities shrink into nothing in comparison. It is said to have eighty-six towers and ten gateways. I did not count them, but certainly they formed a "diadem of towers," much more perfect than that of Cortona. The granite walls are said to be forty feet high, and twelve feet thick ; and, indeed, they look massive enough for anything. . . .

'It had now begun to rain so heavily that we gave up thoughts of going round the town that day, and ran across the Plaza into the cathedral. Never shall I forget that sight! I held my breath for very awe. Grey and dim, with nothing distinctly visible but the glorious gem-like windows, all dark rich crimson, blue, and orange, giving an impression of colour, glowing colour, *without light*: it was to me far grander, because simpler, than Burgos. Of course, in saying this, I speak only of the interior; outside, there can be no comparison. Yet even the exterior of the cathedral of Avila is interesting, being half-fortress, half-church: it is plain, at least for a Spanish Cathedral, they being usually very richly and lavishly decorated; and its severe early character is striking. It was founded a hundred and thirty years before that of Burgos, and about a hundred and thirty-four before the present cathedral of Toledo. In fact, it is one of the oldest in Spain, coming, I think, next to Barcelona, Tarragona, and Santiago as to date. It is dedicated to the Saviour, whereas most of the Spanish Cathedrals are in honour of the Virgin Mary. It is not very large, but its great height, its twilight gloom, and the forest of columns round and behind the High Altar, give an idea of greater size than it really has. It is also much less blocked up by the choir than is usual in Spain. The walls are very dark grey, and those marvellous windows, reaching far up to the very roof, seem to give, rather than admit, what light there is. Even if we could have seen the details, I could not have examined them. We sat down, and vespers began; a few black-veiled, black-robed figures came in, and crouched low on the floor in prayer.'

B.

THE following list of convents founded during St. Teresa's life is taken from the Preface to Mr. Lewis's translation of her 'Fondaciones;' the original MS. of which is preserved in the Escurial.

MONASTERIES OF NUNS.

1. Avila . . . . . . 24 August, 1562.
2. Medina del Campo . . 15 August, 1567.
3. Malagon . . . . 11 April, 1568.
4. Valladolid . . . 15 August, 1568.
5. Toledo . . . . . 14 May, 1569.
6. Pastrana . . . . 9 July, 1569.
7. Salamanca . . . 1 November, 1570.

8. Alba de Tormes	.	25 January, 1571.
9. Segovia . .	.	19 March, 1574.
10. Veas . . .	.	25 February, 1575.
11. Seville	.	29 May, 1575.
12. Caravaca . . .	.	1 January, 1576.
13. Villanueva de la Jara	.	21 February, 1580.
14. Palencia . . .	.	29 December, 1580.
15. Soria	.	3 June, 1581.
16. Granada . . .	.	20 January, 1582.
17. Burgos	.	22 April, 1582.

MONASTERIES OF FRIARS.

1. Durvelo . .	.	28 November, 1568.
2. Pastrana . .	.	13 July, 1569.
3. Mancera . .	.	11 June, 1570.
4. Alcara de Henares	.	1 November, 1570.
5. Altomira . . .	.	24 November, 1571.
6. La Roda . . .	.	April, 1572.
7. Granada . . .	.	19 May, 1573.
8. Peñuela . . .	.	29 June, 1573.
9. Seville . . .	.	5 January, 1574.
10. Almodovar . . .	.	7 March, 1575.
11. Mount Calvary (Corençuela)		December, 1576.
12. Baelza	.	14 June, 1579.
13. Valladolid . . .	.	4 May, 1581.
14. Salamanca . . .	.	1 June, 1581.
15. Lisbon . . .	.	19 February, 1582.

C.

'THERE is one House or Convent of the Reformed or Discalced Carmelites—and only one—at present in Spain. It is situate at Marquina, in the north of Spain, and not very far from Bilbao. Its foundation dates only from the reign of the present ex-Queen Isabella, who permitted some Carmelite Fathers of the French Province to found a House in Spain, on the express understanding that the said House should train up Missionary Fathers of the Order to labour in the Spanish Colonies. The Fathers there, however, are full of the hope that "Spanish Carmel" will again flourish as of yore, and that the foundation at Marquina will prove to be the cradle of its second birth in Catholic Spain. There is not *now* an English Province of the Carmelite Order. When there was one, it was of the Calced Carmelites *only*. At this present (1875) there are but two Houses of Carmelites (men) in all Great Britain. One of these two is at London, and belongs to the Reformed · or Discalced Carmelites, the other is at Merthyr-Tydfil, Glamorgan, S. Wales, and belongs to the Calced Carmelites. The former foundation is connected with the Irish portion of the Discalced Order,—the latter is directly subject to the Father-General of the Calced Carmelites. In connection with this question, it may be stated that the "Province of St. Patrick" (as it was called) was solely of Discalced Carmelites, and that prior to the year 1638 it embraced nine Houses or Convents in Ireland. As a "Province," it has not yet been restored. The two Houses (of men) which the Discalced Brethren possess in Ireland, i.e. at Dublin and at Loughrea, together with the House at London previously mentioned, form what may be called a "Semi-province." Fr. A.' In 1844 there were nine convents of Carmelite nuns in Ireland, and two in England—one at Llanherne, Cornwall; the other near Darlington, Durham. Both of these had originally been established for Englishwomen in the Low Countries, and were removed to England at the time of the French Revolution.

LONDON : PRINTED BY
SPOTTISWOODE AND CO., NEW-STREET SQUARE
AND PARLIAMENT STREET

www.ingramcontent.com/pod-product-compliance
Lightning Source LLC
Chambersburg PA
CBHW020314240426
43673CB00039B/806